The Other Side of the Bar

"In today's fast-moving world, conflict parties cry out for transformative solutions that go beyond what courts can provide. This book provides lawyers with a useful overview of the many processes from which creative outcomes can be generated. Inspired by wisdom from diverse cultural inheritances, it shows how transformation occurs in many forms, including councils and ceremonies. It offers lawyers ways of addressing conflicts that are responsive to the people involved, to what the issues mean to them, and to the underlying structures that perpetuate particular kinds of conflicts. In this, the authors offer a great service to lawyers."

—Professor Michelle LeBaron, *Peter A. Allard School of Law, University of British Columbia*

Laura E. Reimer · Richard Jochelson
Editors

The Other Side of the Bar

Conflict Transformation in Legal Practice

palgrave
macmillan

Editors
Laura E. Reimer
Faculty of Law
University of Manitoba
Winnipeg, MB, Canada

Richard Jochelson
Faculty of Law
University of Manitoba
Winnipeg, MB, Canada

ISBN 978-981-96-9747-2 ISBN 978-981-96-9748-9 (eBook)
https://doi.org/10.1007/978-981-96-9748-9

Cover illustration: Cover art by Bruce Reimer

This Palgrave Macmillan imprint is published by the registered company Springer Nature Singapore Pte Ltd.
The registered company address is: 152 Beach Road, #21-01/04 Gateway East, Singapore 189721, Singapore

Foreword

It may seem somewhat incongruous for a Chief Justice of a superior trial court to be writing the foreword of a book focused on the resolution of disputes outside of the court and litigation context. But this incongruity hides an important truth. That truth is that the justice system, and indeed the courts who serve it, can only be enriched by a greater commitment to collaborative and constructive problem solving by the legal professionals who populate its ranks.

For many years now and from different corners of the civil justice system, we have heard earnest if not familiar calls for less adversarial approaches that may better settle and in some cases, pre-empt disputes and conflicts. What is often envisioned in these calls are approaches that might not require nor produce the zero-sum starkness of some typical judicial adjudications. The chapters in this concise and focused volume make a valuable contribution to the exploration of new and diverse ways to both actualize and realize the objectives of resolving disputes and conflict in ways that are both alternative and parallel to the court system.

Fostering public confidence in the justice system is foundational to the work undertaken by all legal professionals as protectors of the rule of law. In an era increasingly characterized by not only misinformation, but disinformation and distrust of public institutions, broadening and enhancing the tools available to the legal profession is a powerful and important mechanism to foster such confidence. Indeed, bolstering the ability of the profession to skilfully provide a range of conflict resolution services, can only serve to enhance public trust.

In my own annual remarks to those being called to the Bar of this Province, I consistently encourage new lawyers to adopt a mindset characterized by innovation, toleration, flexibility, and empathy. This important new book provides a road map to do just that. In the words of the editors, this volume "expands the role of the legal professional into that of a civic steward". It offers a timely and practical set of resources which highlight the power of knowledge sharing, the value of collaboration, and the reality of the pluralistic legal landscape in which Canadians live and work. In exploring the multifaceted nature of conflict and offering tools to address such conflict, these chapters also reflect a particularly Manitoban sensibility: a sensibility that is practical yet creative, and always alive to the diversity of our community.

In a modern Canada, whose very nature increasingly requires an appreciation for some of the potential solutions that may come from the insights associated with legal pluralism, the "legal system" or "justice system" may have to be more broadly defined and conceived. The chapters in this book provide important content to help facilitate reflection by citizens, judges and lawyers alike on how and why such a broader definition might well lead not only to a system which supports the enhanced resolution of disputes, but also, to one which promotes opportunities for transformation and change.

Winnipeg, Manitoba
May 2025

Glenn D. Joyal
Chief Justice, Manitoba Court
of King's Bench

Preface

In today's legal landscape, conflict is an inherent part of the profession. Whether in litigation, negotiation, mediation, or client counselling, lawyers are constantly navigating disputes—sometimes as advocates, other times as problem solvers. Yet, despite conflict being so central to legal work, most lawyers receive little formal training in the practical skills of conflict resolution beyond adversarial techniques taught in law school. This gap has significant consequences, not only for the effectiveness of legal representation but also for the broader justice system and the well-being of legal professionals themselves.

We live in a time marked by deep societal polarization, rapidly changing norms, and growing public dissatisfaction and mistrust with traditional legal processes. Access to justice is uneven. Courts are overburdened, cases drag on, and clients are often left frustrated by the cost and complexity of litigation. In this environment, the ability of lawyers to de-escalate conflict, foster productive dialogue, and facilitate fair outcomes outside of the courtroom is more vital than ever. The legal profession is being called to reimagine its role—not only as a guardian of legal rights but also as a bridge-builder and healer of societal divisions, from the family to the international context.

Moreover, lawyers themselves face unprecedented stress, burnout, moral injury, and trauma responses from constant exposure to high-conflict situations. Developing practical conflict resolution skills to transform conflict is not just a matter of professional competence; it is also a pathway to personal resilience and career sustainability. When lawyers can approach disputes with clarity, empathy, and creativity, they are better equipped to serve their clients, protect their own mental health, and contribute positively to their communities.

This book is written with the belief that practical conflict resolution is a core competency for every lawyer, regardless of practice area. It offers concrete tools, strategies, and interpersonal skills that empower lawyers to navigate conflict more skilfully and constructively. From active listening and interest-based negotiation to managing difficult personalities and resolving intra-organizational disputes, the chapters that follow are written by legal professionals and educators, and grounded in real-world experience, designed for immediate application.

The goal is not to turn every lawyer into a mediator, or to assume mediation offers resolution for every dispute, but rather to equip legal professionals with a broader, more nuanced toolkit for addressing the complexities of human conflict. By strengthening these skills, we can help reshape legal culture and extend access to justice—one conversation, one resolution, one client at a time.

Winnipeg, Canada

Laura E. Reimer
Richard Jochelson

Acknowledgements

The editors wish to thank Dr. Cathryne L. Schmitz, Dr. Natella Malazoniia, and Lily Deardorff for their acute and attentive editorial assistance in the production of the manuscript.

About This Book

This volume brings together a diverse range of scholars and practitioners to explore how conflict transformation can reshape legal practice. Rather than treating conflict solely as a problem to be managed, the contributors emphasize a deeper commitment: to see conflict as a relational and systemic reality that calls for transformation.

Chapters cover key tools of dispute resolution—mediation, arbitration, negotiation, restorative justice—and interrogate the values that must guide their use. Central to this collection is the principle of relational justice: the idea that legal processes must not only deliver outcomes but also honour the dignity and lived experience of all participants. Whether in interpersonal disputes or formal legal forums, how people are treated matters as much as the result.

Another core theme is epistemic repair—the ethical obligation to confront whose voices are privileged in law and whose are silenced. This is powerfully illustrated in the chapter on the Haudenosaunee Great Law of Peace, which reframes Indigenous legal orders as vital, living systems. Other chapters highlight how access to justice, legal research, and dispute resolution training often reflect entrenched norms that obscure alternative knowledges and practices.

The third binding commitment is the pursuit of transformative practice. Rather than viewing dispute resolution as a procedural skillset, this book presents it as an opportunity to reimagine legal relationships and institutions. From pedagogical insights in negotiation training to explorations of AI in ADR, the collection challenges readers to see legal education and practice as spaces for critical reflection, creativity, and connection.

In an era of institutional distrust and epistemic fragmentation, this book offers a vision of legal practice that is relational, inclusive, and transformative. It is a resource for law students, educators, and professionals committed to cultivating justice—not just as a legal outcome, but as an ongoing, participatory process of repair, recognition, and renewal.

A Bold Vision for Justice Beyond the Courtroom

The Other Side of the Bar brings together an inspiring range of voices to reimagine how lawyers, educators, and students approach conflict. Through chapters on mediation, negotiation, restorative justice, Indigenous legal orders, and more, this collection challenges the reader to center relationships, repair epistemic harms, and cultivate a legal culture rooted in dignity and inclusion.

At the heart of the book is a powerful call: to treat every dispute not merely as a case to close, but as a moment of possibility—for listening, healing, and systemic change. Whether exploring the Haudenosaunee Great Law of Peace, reflecting on legal pedagogy, or interrogating AI in dispute resolution, the authors reveal how legal practice can become a site of ethical engagement and civic renewal.

For legal professionals and academics alike, this is a timely and necessary invitation to step beyond the traditional bounds of the law—and into a more humane and transformative vision of justice.

Contents

Notes on Contributors

Ms. Natasha L. Brown is the director of Access to Justice & Community Engagement at the University of Manitoba, Faculty of Law. She received her Bachelor of Education from the University of Manitoba in 2001 and her Bachelor of Laws in 2005, also from the University of Manitoba. She was called to the Bar in Manitoba in 2006. Ms. Brown was awarded the National Lexpert Zenith Award in 2017, Robson Hall's Dean's Award for Teaching Excellence in 2020 and the Manitoba Bar Association's Access to Justice Award in 2024. She was designated a Jurist of Robson Hall in 2022.

Dr. Bruce J. Curran is an associate professor at the University of Manitoba Faculty of Law who is especially interested in experiential and multi-disciplinary approaches to teaching. He was the organizer of the inaugural Canadian National Negotiation Competition in Winnipeg, and has been on the organizing committee since then. His research and teaching interests include dispute resolution, negotiation, labour and employment law, and contracts. In his research, he is primarily focused on using empirical methods to study these topics. In addition to his research abilities, he is an outstanding teacher for which he has won numerous awards. Dr. Curran is a member of the Ontario Bar.

Dr. Martine Dennie is an assistant professor at the Faculty of Law, University of Manitoba. She is an interdisciplinary scholar who uses social research methods to empirically examine issues related to sports law.

Dennie earned a B.A. in law and justice from Laurentian University, a JD from the Université de Moncton, a Master of Arts in Sociology from Laurentian University, and a Ph.D. at the University of Calgary. Her doctoral research, funded by SSHRC and Sport Canada, examined participant liability and compensation for intentionally or negligently injured hockey players. She has published research on violence, hazing, abuse, and discrimination in sports.

Professor Daniel Diamond is a proud member of the Opaskwayak Cree Nation and an Assistant Professor at the Robson Hall Faculty of Law, University of Manitoba (Winnipeg). Professor Diamond's research areas include Indigenous legal traditions, Aboriginal law, legal theory, property law, and legal history. His research focuses on historic injustice and contemporary efforts at redress. His work synthesizes legal history, legal theory, and property law in analyses of Indigenous legal and political issues.

Ryan Hall articled with MLT Aikins LLP in 2024–2025, receiving his call to the bar in Manitoba in June of 2025 where he will continue his employment with MLT Aikins LLP as a litigation associate. Ryan has a passion for sports law and hopes to grow that passion through his future endeavours.

Dr. Richard Jochelson is the dean of the Faculty of Law at the University of Manitoba. He holds a Ph.D. in Law from Osgoode Hall, an LL.M. from the University of Toronto, an LL.B. (Gold Medal) from the University of Calgary, and a B.Sc. in Zoology (with Distinction). He began his legal career clerking for the Alberta Court of Appeal and Court of Queen's Bench, followed by practice at one of Canada's largest law firms. Before joining the University of Manitoba, he taught criminal law for a decade at the University of Winnipeg. A prolific scholar and dedicated educator, Dr. Jochelson brings a passion for justice, pedagogy, and interdisciplinary insight to his work—and picks up his guitar whenever he can.

Michaela Keet is a professor at the College of Law, University of Saskatchewan, where she has led the College's dispute resolution curriculum for the past twenty-five years. She has published extensively about negotiation and problem-solving models, and presents regularly to professional groups including judges, lawyers and mediators. Her most recent work focuses on the assessment of litigation risk as a tool for informed decision-making in negotiated resolutions. She has been involved with the Canadian National Negotiation Competition since its inception ten years ago. In 2011, Prof. Keet was awarded the Provost's College Award for Outstanding Teaching in Law.

John C. Kleefeld is a professor and former dean of Law at the University of New Brunswick. He previously taught at the University of Saskatchewan, where he received the 2012 Provost's Award for Outstanding Innovation in Learning and the 2015 Brightspace/STLHE Innovation Award in Teaching & Learning. Before that, he was at the University of British Columbia, where he taught for eight years and directed the Legal Research & Writing Program. He has a longstanding involvement in negotiation competitions, both nationally and internationally. His research and teaching interests include dispute resolution, legal research and writing, tort law, and private international law. He is a member of the Bar of British Columbia.

Dr. Natella Malazoniia is a family mediator at Mediation Services and former Desautels Postdoctoral Scholar at the Faculty of Law, University of Manitoba. She earned her Ph.D. in Law in 2021 from V. N. Karazin Kharkiv National University (Ukraine), specializing in mediation and restorative justice within the civil law tradition. Since 2015, she has been actively engaged in alternative dispute resolution through extensive training in both Ukraine and Canada, completing over 300 hours of certified mediation programs. Natella has taught, researched, and practiced ADR in academic and community-based contexts. Her work is grounded in empathy, accountability, and a deep belief in the transformative potential of dialogue.

Dr. Laura E. Reimer is a director of Program Development at the University of Manitoba Faculty of Law and Director of the Marcel A. Desautels Centre for Private Enterprise and the Law. She brings extensive experience in conflict transformation across public and private sectors, offering a distinct and practical lens on legal education. A recipient of the Clifford J. Robson Memorial Award for Teaching Excellence, she previously taught Public Administration and completed a post-doctoral fellowship at the University of North Carolina Greensboro, where she co-authored *Transformative Change*. Her scholarship focuses on innovation, reconciliation, and systems change. Dr. Reimer has served on the University of Manitoba Board of Governors, the Manitoba Law Reform

Commission, and as President of the Canadian Academy of Legal Studies in Business. She is an avid and licensed sailor.

Matthew Renaud is a law librarian at the University of Manitoba's E.K. Williams Law Library. He holds a B.A. (Hons.) and M.A. from the University of Manitoba and an MLIS from the University of Alberta. He currently co-teaches the Advanced Legal Research course at the U of M's Faculty of Law and instructs in their first-year legal research and writing program. Prior to starting at the University of Manitoba, Matthew worked at the County of Carleton Law Association Library in Ottawa, Ontario.

Dr. Illia Roskoshnyi held a Post Doctoral Fellowship under the Asper Chair for International Trade and Business Law at the Faculty of Law. He arrived in the summer of 2022 through the University of Manitoba's Scholars at Risk program as a visiting scholar, then as a research associate. Dr. Roskoshnyi completed his Ph.D. in Law at V.N. Karazin Kharkiv National University and represented clients as a lawyer in various judicial and administrative bodies, including the Supreme Court of Ukraine and the European Court of Human Rights. He has taught at the University of Manitoba and the University of Winnipeg.

Dr. Jennifer L. Schulz is a professor and former associate dean at the Faculty of Law, University of Manitoba, Canada. She is also a Fellow of the Winkler Institute for Dispute Resolution at Osgoode Hall Law School. She has been a visiting mediation scholar at the Universities of Cambridge, London, Harvard, Toronto and British Columbia. Dr. Schulz has won four teaching awards, a national ADR service award, and is a federal and international research grant recipient. She is certified as a Chartered Mediator by the ADR Institute of Canada and presents around the world on mediation.

Professor Gemma Smyth is an associate professor and externship director at the Faculty of Law, University of Windsor, on the territories of the Three Fires Confederacy. She runs the Judicial Internship and Externship Programs at Windsor Law. She is also the academic clinic director for the Class Action Clinic. Professor Smyth researches and writes in the areas of clinic law, dispute resolution, lawyering skills, and legal education.

Introduction: Transforming Legal Practice

Richard Jochelson and Laura E. Reimer

Abstract In an era defined by polarization, epistemic fragmentation, and institutional distrust, legal professionals are increasingly called upon not only to resolve disputes but to restore dialogue, foster recognition, and navigate the turbulent terrain of competing truths. The conflicts that present themselves in today's legal landscape rarely exist in isolation—they are deeply embedded in systemic inequities, historical legacies, cultural frameworks, and mediated realities. This collection, *The Other Side of the Bar: Conflict Transformation in Legal Practice*, responds to these challenges with urgency and care, offering a comprehensive, theory-informed, and practice-oriented resource for legal professionals, educators, and students.This book offers more than techniques—it proposes a reimagining of legal practice. In an age marked by climate crisis, democratic instability, and epistemic confusion, the principles of Alternative Dispute Resolution (ADR)—dialogue, relationship(s), accountability, transformation—are no longer peripheral. They are civic infrastructure. We posit

R. Jochelson · L. E. Reimer (✉)
University of Manitoba, Winnipeg, Canada
e-mail: Laura.Reimer@umanitoba.ca

R. Jochelson
e-mail: Richard.Jochelson@umanitoba.ca

L. E. Reimer and R. Jochelson (eds.), *The Other Side of the Bar*,
https://doi.org/10.1007/978-981-96-9748-9_1

that legal professionals can listen deeply, uncover denial, and build bridges through dialogue. The Other Side of the Bar is a call to action. It is an invitation to practice law not just as technical problem-solving, but as an ethical, cultural, and relational vocation. It equips readers with the skills to engage conflict(s) with humility, to navigate difference with care, and to pursue justice with clarity and competence.

Keywords Dispute resolution · Legal professionals · Conflict transformation · Legal practice · Distrust · Systemic inequities

Introduction

In an era defined by polarization, epistemic fragmentation, and institutional distrust, legal professionals are increasingly called upon not only to resolve disputes but to restore dialogue, foster recognition, and navigate the turbulent terrain of competing truths. The conflicts that present themselves in today's legal landscape rarely exist in isolation—they are deeply embedded in systemic inequities, historical legacies, cultural frameworks, and mediated realities. This collection, *The Other Side of the Bar: Conflict Transformation in Legal Practice*, responds to these challenges with urgency and care, offering a comprehensive, theory-informed, and practice-oriented resource for legal professionals, educators, and students.

Why This Collection?

Despite the demonstrable value of alternative dispute resolution (ADR)—including mediation, negotiation, restorative justice, and arbitration—legal education remains largely entrenched in adversarial models. Courts play a crucial role in ensuring accountability, but many conflicts, particularly those involving relational, community, or cross-cultural elements, may benefit more from collaborative and dialogic processes. Domestic and international arbitration are adversarial, but more flexible than the traditional court system, and provide parties with opportunities to tailor the process to their unique needs and expectations. The methods gathered in this collection reflect a rethinking of legal practice: one that centres human dignity, cultural competence, epistemic responsibility, and social justice. This rethinking is the other side of licensed practice; the "other side of the bar."

The contributors to this book come from a range of disciplines and traditions. What unites them is a commitment to equipping legal professionals with tools not only to settle disputes but to transform them—turning moments of dissonance into opportunities for insight, repair, and even structural change.

Transforming Conflict

At its core, conflict arises when individuals or groups perceive threats to their needs, interests, or values within a specific context. These disagreements may emerge from many sources—divergent goals, competing interests, communication styles, cultural norms, historical grievances, or differences in identity and positionality (Reimer et al., 2015, 3). In a legally plural and relationally complex world, conflict is rarely reducible to simple disagreement; it is embedded within broader socio-cultural, political, and historical frameworks.

Conflict can unfold across interpersonal, community, institutional, or even global levels. Lawyers and legal advocates often encounter conflict in its most structured form—through formal disputes or adversarial processes—but its roots often lie beneath the surface. Positional arguments may mask deeper, shared interests or unresolved values tensions. Recognizing this distinction is essential in a transformative practice: interests, which represent negotiable needs or desires, can open pathways to resolution; values, more deeply held and often non-negotiable, require acknowledgment and respect rather than mere settlement (Reimer et al., 2015, 4).

In relational justice frameworks, understanding the people behind the positions is paramount. This means engaging with the whole person—their cultural identity, social context, and lived experiences—and seeing law as one of many systems through which justice can be pursued. Cultural legal pluralism reminds us that multiple normative orders coexist, and lawyers must learn to navigate these layers with humility and cultural fluency. In this way, conflict is not simply something to be resolved, but a relational opportunity for transformation—of people, systems, and relationships.

Theoretical Foundations and Contemporary Imperatives

The conceptual framing of this volume draws from four intersecting frameworks: relational justice, cultural legal pluralism, transformative practice, and critical socio-legal theory. These themes are evident in the chapters throughout the collection.

Relational Justice posits that justice is not merely transactional but relational—it concerns the repair, restoration, and sustenance of human relationships. As Llewellyn (2011) writes, relational justice is grounded in mutual recognition and the conditions required to live together in just relations. This framework undergirds the volume's attention to emotional and psychological dimensions of conflict, as seen in chapters on mediation, restorative justice, and interpersonal communication.

Cultural Legal Pluralism affirms that Canadian law is not singular but coexists with diverse legal orders, particularly Indigenous ones. Scholars like Borrows (2002) and Napoleon (2013) argue that Indigenous legal traditions are not historical remnants but dynamic systems with principles and procedures capable of responding to modern legal problems. This view is exemplified in Daniel Diamond's chapter on the Great Law of Peace, which demonstrates how Haudenosaunee practices such as condolence and consensus offer sophisticated legal logics grounded in relationality and respect.

Transformative practice as articulated by Bush and Folger (1994), emphasizes empowerment and recognition over expediency. Transformative mediation seeks to shift how parties understand themselves, each other, and the conflict they inhabit. This lens supports pedagogical innovations described in the volume and informs many contributors' emphasis on process over outcome.

Conflict resolution can be understood as a response to epistemic injustice, systemic conflict can be understood as foregrounding the role of ignorance—coerced, curated, or normalized—as a mechanism of social control and injustice. Gacek and Jochelson (2024) argue that this type of injustice is due to more than simply a lack of knowledge, but a deliberate structuring of non-knowledge, often through institutional mechanisms, legal rationalities, and cultural narratives. From settler colonial denialism (Singh & Trask, 2024) to whitewashed ideals of motherhood (Bromwich, 2024), lack of knowledge shapes legal consciousness and policy. Within dispute resolution, confronting these gaps require tools that can unmask denial, facilitate truth-telling, and foster epistemic accountability. ADR practitioners must recognize when a conflict is rooted not in misunderstanding alone but in systematically produced ignorance.

Together, these frameworks challenge practitioners to go beyond procedural fairness toward substantive justice—centred in relationships, grounded in diverse legal traditions, open to transformation, and committed to dismantling epistemic injustice.

Dispute Resolution in the Age of Disinformation

This volume is especially timely given the crisis of disinformation and epistemic distrust. As Wardle and Derakhshan (2017) observe, falsehoods now spread faster than corrections, aided by social media algorithms and polarized media ecosystems. Disinformation is not simply a matter of factual inaccuracy; it is an assault on the very conditions under which people can reason together.

In this context, ADR processes emerge as essential sites of epistemic repair. Techniques such as active listening, narrative reframing, consensus-building, and trauma-informed engagement allow parties to slow down, listen deeply, and co-construct shared realities. Moreover, understanding the dynamics of misinformation allows legal professionals to recognize when power is obfuscated, accountability is deferred, or oppression is fostered. Legal professionals trained in dispute resolution are uniquely positioned to intervene in these dynamics—not as neutral arbiters, but as facilitators of critical dialogue and ethical accountability.

Whether working in community-based justice settings, institutional reforms, or high-conflict public forums, dispute resolution practitioners can act as mediators of truth, care, and relationships.

Epistemic Repair and the Role of Dispute Resolution in the Current Era

In the context of deepening societal polarization, contested truths, and an ongoing crisis of misinformation, alternative dispute resolution (ADR) emerges as a vital mechanism for what scholars have termed *epistemic repair*. While ADR is typically associated with conflict de-escalation and relational healing, its potential extends further into the realm of rebuilding trust in knowledge systems, especially where dialogue has been fractured or rendered dysfunctional. Dispute resolution practices, when thoughtfully applied, enable participants not only to resolve differences but to reconstruct the shared understandings that make peaceful coexistence and equitable outcomes possible.

Central to this function are a series of interrelated techniques widely employed in contemporary ADR processes. Active listening, for instance, is a foundational skill that encourages mediators and participants alike to listen without judgment, with the goal of deeply understanding the speaker's perspective. This approach validates the emotional and experiential truths of participants, creating space for healing and rehumanization—an especially important step in conflicts involving trauma or marginalization (Brown, 2020).

Equally significant is the practice of narrative reframing, in which participants are guided to reconsider their conflict narratives in ways that emphasize underlying interests, shared experiences, or relational interdependence. Drawing from the transformative mediation tradition (Bush & Folger, 1994), narrative reframing allows parties to move beyond rigid positions and explore more constructive interpretations of the events in question.

Consensus-building, another core feature of many ADR models, underscores the collaborative pursuit of solutions that honour the diverse values and interests of all stakeholders. Rather than relying on imposed outcomes, consensus-driven approaches foster a sense of ownership, dignity, and mutual recognition. These processes are increasingly essential in multi-party, cross-cultural, or community-based disputes where legitimacy depends on the participation and empowerment of all affected groups (Susskind & Cruikshank, 1987).

Further enriching these practices is the incorporation of trauma-informed engagement, which prioritizes emotional safety, transparency, and participant agency. This approach acknowledges the lasting impacts of trauma on cognition and participation and seeks to mitigate the risk of re-traumatization in dispute resolution contexts (Bloom, 2013; Herman, 1992). A trauma-informed lens encourages mediators and facilitators to adapt processes to the psychological needs of participants, thereby enhancing accessibility and fairness.

Taken together, these techniques contribute to what can be described as the epistemic dimension of justice work. They allow parties to slow the tempo of conflict, listen more deeply, and collaboratively reconstruct the frameworks through which they interpret their shared reality.

In light of these insights, the role of dispute resolution practitioners must be reconceptualized. Rather than acting merely as neutral arbiters who enforce procedural fairness, legal professionals trained in ADR are increasingly called upon to serve as *facilitators of epistemic justice*. This involves recognizing when a conflict is animated not simply by competing interests or miscommunication, but by systematically curated ignorance that obscures key truths or excludes marginalized perspectives. In such contexts, neutrality may function less as a safeguard and more as a shield for dominant power structures.

Drawing on Miranda Fricker's (2007) foundational work on *epistemic injustice*, this collection advocates for a practice of dispute resolution that consciously attends to the knowledge-related harms inflicted through testimonial silencing, hermeneutical gaps, and cultural erasure. Practitioners must develop the capacity to identify these harms and to foster spaces where alternative epistemologies—particularly those of Indigenous, racialized, or otherwise marginalized communities—can be heard, affirmed, and meaningfully engaged.

Ultimately, the promise of dispute resolution lies in its ability to create conditions where knowledge can be shared safely, disagreements can be explored ethically, and silences can be interrogated with care. The methods outlined throughout this volume are not merely procedural techniques; they are epistemological tools for truth-seeking in complex, contested environments.

This volume expands the role of the legal professional into that of a civic steward: one who cultivates the preconditions for trust, dialogue, and justice amid the fog of disinformation, denial, and systemic exclusion.

Roadmap of the Book

The book opens with *Interpersonal Conflict* by Laura E. Reimer, grounding the volume in the communicative roots of conflict. Reimer's chapter draws from psychology, peace and conflict studies, and communication studies to illustrate how interpersonal conflict often stems from misrecognition, unmet needs, and misaligned narratives. She introduces listening techniques and dialogue practices that set the stage for the restorative and facilitative approaches elaborated later in the book.

Natella Malazoniia's *Restorative Justice* follows with a comprehensive account of a paradigm rooted in healing, participation, and accountability. Drawing from Howard Zehr and contemporary scholarship, she maps restorative justice's historical evolution, key principles, and diverse forms—from victim-offender dialogue to community conferencing. Malazoniia's chapter explicitly addresses the limitations of restorative justice in systems marked by structural inequity, inviting readers to consider how restorative principles must be adapted in contexts of racialized or institutional harm.

Daniel Diamond's *Condolence Ceremonies, Council Meetings, and Conflict Resolution* is a contribution to legal pluralism and Indigenous resurgence. His chapter shows how condolence rituals and consensus-building within the Haudenosaunee Confederacy exemplify relational dispute resolution. Diamond also links these practices to treaty-based understandings of law and diplomacy, offering a vision of justice that decentres Eurocentric legalism.

Jennifer L. Schulz's *Mediation* presents both the theory and practice of mediation across various contexts. She walks readers through mediation stages, compares styles (evaluative, facilitative, transformative), and reflects on mediation's growing role in institutional and online contexts. Schulz emphasizes that mediation offers not just efficiency but justice—especially when practitioners attend to emotion, narrative, and power.

In *Negotiation,* Laura E. Reimer offers a principled negotiation model rooted in interest identification, collaborative problem-solving, and mutual gain. Drawing from Fisher and Ury (1981), the chapter explores how legal negotiation can resist adversarial escalation and foster durable, ethical agreements. Reimer also addresses the emotional and cultural dynamics often neglected in doctrinal treatments.

The Pedagogical Value of the Canadian National Negotiation Competition by Bruce J. Curran, Michaela Keet, John C. Kleefeld, and Gemma Smyth, argues that experiential learning in negotiation develops competencies that traditional case-based learning cannot. The authors make a compelling case for the integration of practice-based, reflective learning in legal education to develop empathy, strategic thinking, and professional identity.

Natella Malazoniia returns with *Arbitration*, an overview of the arbitration process and its increasing relevance in commercial, family, and international law. She addresses the strengths and risks of arbitration—including power asymmetry, limited appeals, and procedural opacity—while introducing hybrid models like Med-Arb. Her treatment of arbitration as both legal process and relational encounter is consistent with the book's broader themes.

Martine Dennie and Ryan Hall contribute *Dispute Resolution in Sports,* using the world of Canadian amateur and professional sport as a case study in regulatory conflict. With insight into recent controversies, safe sport initiatives, and collective bargaining, this chapter highlights the role of ADR in maintaining fairness and accountability in complex institutional ecosystems.

In *Access to Justice*, Natasha Brown connects ADR to systemic reform, arguing that accessible and culturally responsive dispute resolution processes are key to addressing legal deserts and underserved communities. Brown emphasizes the importance of reducing barriers not only to participation, but to meaningful justice outcomes.

Matthew Renaud's *Legal Research as ADR: The Three Keys Method* offers practical insight into an often-overlooked aspect of ADR: legal research. His accessible framework helps non-lawyers and lawyers alike gather, interpret, and apply legal information effectively in negotiation and mediation settings.

In the final chapter, Illia Roskoshnyi's *Intelligence Augmentation in Alternative Dispute Resolution* surveys emerging digital tools—from online dispute resolution (ODR) platforms to AI-assisted negotiation—and considers their implications for procedural fairness and access to justice. Roskoshnyi urges thoughtful integration of technology, grounded in ethical safeguards and relational justice.

Conclusion: Dispute Resolution as Civic Infrastructure

This book offers more than techniques—it proposes a reimagining of legal practice. In an age marked by climate crisis, democratic instability, and epistemic confusion, the principles of ADR—dialogue, relationship, accountability, transformation—are no longer peripheral. They are civic infrastructure. We posit that legal professionals can listen deeply, uncover denial, and build bridges through dialogue.

The Other Side of the Bar is a call to action. It is an invitation to practice law not just as technical problem-solving, but as an ethical, cultural, and relational vocation. It equips readers with the skills to engage conflict with humility, to navigate difference with care, and to pursue justice with clarity and competence.

Competing Interests The authors have no conflicts of interest to declare that are relevant to the content of this chapter.

References

Bloom, S. (2013). *Creating sanctuary: Toward the evolution of Sane societies*. 2nd Ed. Routledge.

Borrows, J. (2002). *Recovering Canada: The resurgence of indigenous law*. University of Toronto Press.

Bromwich, R. (2024). Whitewashed motherhood: Legal aesthetics and gendered violence. In J. Gacek & R. Jochelson (Eds.), *Justice in the age of agnosis: Socio-legal explorations of denial, deception, and doubt*. Palgrave Macmillan.

Brown, B. (2020). *Dare to lead: Brave work*. Random House.

Bush, R. B., & Folger, J. (1994). *The promise of mediation: The transformative approach to conflict*. Jossey-Bass.

Fisher, R., & Ury, W. (1981). *Getting to yes: Negotiating agreement without giving in* (3rd Ed.). Penguin Books.

Fricker, M. (2007). *Epistemic injustice: Power and the ethics of knowing*. Oxford.

Gacek, J., & Jochelson, R. (Eds.). (2024). *Justice in the age of agnosis: Socio-Legal explorations of denial, deception, and doubt*. Palgrave Macmillan.

Herman, J. (1992). *Trauma and recovery: The aftermath of violence—From domestic abuse to political terror*. Basic Books.

Llewellyn, J. (2011). Restorative justice: Thinking relationally about justice. In J. Downie & J. Llewellyn (Eds.), *Being relational: Reflections on relational theory and health law*. UBC Press.

Napoleon, V. (2013). *Thinking about indigenous legal orders*. Research Paper for the National Centre for First Nations Governance.

Reimer, L. E., Schmitz, C. L., Janke, E., Askerov, A., Strahl, B., & Matyok, T. (2015). *Transformative change: An introduction to peace and conflict studies*. Lexington.

Singh, S., & Trask, B. (2024). Faded by design: Manufacturing agnosis of settler-colonialism. In J. Gacek & R. Jochelson (Eds.), *Justice in the age of agnosis: Socio-Legal explorations of denial, deception, and doubt*. Palgrave Macmillan.

Susskind, L., & Cruikshank, J. (1987). *Breaking the impasse: Consensual approaches to resolving public disputes*. Basic Books.

Wardle, C., & Derakhshan, H. (2017). *Information disorder: Toward an interdisciplinary framework for research and policy making*. Council of Europe.

Interpersonal Communication

Laura E. Reimer

Abstract Several principles guide interpersonal communication and equip legal practitioners to implement appropriate interventions for transforming interpersonal conflict into resolutions in which all parties can be satisfied. The common techniques and strategies for improved communication and dispute resolution include active listening, the principles of communicating value and affirmation, recognition of trauma in evidence, and the ways the conversations we dread can be approached and navigated. While interpersonal communication is a direct tool for instigating conflict (often unwittingly), it is also the way to build relationships and transform conflict for better outcomes. The principles shared in this chapter provide a foundation for the dispute resolution methodologies outlined in the rest of the book.

Keywords Miscommunication · Conflict resolution · Interpersonal communication · Conflict style · Reactive responses · Trauma-informed practice · Identity · Affirmation · Crucial conversations · Difficult conversations

---

L. E. Reimer (✉)
Faculty of Law, University of Manitoba, Winnipeg, MB, Canada
e-mail: laura.reimer@umanitoba.ca

L. E. Reimer and R. Jochelson (eds.), *The Other Side of the Bar*,
https://doi.org/10.1007/978-981-96-9748-9_2

Introduction

In the beginning, there was conversation. In an ideal world, people talk to one another with the kindness, dignity, respect and understanding that make conflict resolution unnecessary. But history has demonstrated that conflict, while a normal part of life, is a difficult yet common experience with satisfactory resolution an apparent mystery. At one extreme, people simply stop communicating with the parties who share their conflict; at the other extreme is violence and war. For legal professionals, one of the most encouraging characteristics of interpersonal communication is its universality. Everyone wants to be clearly understood.

Communication skills are fundamental interpersonal competencies. Whether in personal relationships, professional environments, or high-stakes international diplomacy, legal conflicts can often be mitigated or entirely averted through deliberate, respectful, and strategic communication. By employing principles of affirmation, respect, and professionalism while alert to indicators of personal conflict styles and potential trauma, legal practitioners can facilitate conflict resolution, promote client advocacy, and uphold the principles of justice. Miscommunication, whether intentional or inadvertent, frequently underlies disputes, making the ability to convey and interpret messages accurately an essential skill in legal proceedings and sets the ground work for more satisfied clients. This chapter provides tools for effective communication and interpersonal understandings that when engaged, can complement legal training and equip lawyers to resolve disputes to the satisfaction of everyone involved.

Most people assume that they communicate effectively and are vexed when challenged. Assumptions also lead to conflict. At the initiation of a conflict, involved parties experience a substantial influx of negative emotions as they perceive their hopes and needs to be obstructed by the opposing party. Ignorance about the way communication takes place, and ignoring what is actually being communicated is a common habit that can be damaging to relationships—both personal and professional—and a primary source of interpersonal conflict. Hartwick and Barki (2004, 8) identified three key components of interpersonal conflict: negative emotions, interference, and disagreements, and defined it as "a dynamic process that occurs between interdependent parties as they experience negative emotional reactions to perceived disagreements and interference with the attainment of their goals." Although verbal communication is almost universal, people involved in legal work must also be mindful of the complexities and potential for ineffective interpersonal communication.

Dispute resolution requires a number of skills and strategies for effective interpersonal communication, many of which are subtle and not verbal. Implicit in the term communication is an assumption of understanding but herein lies the challenge. Although the idea of information transfer is common among most people, the mental representations, associations, and meanings attached to that information can be as numerous as the people sending and receiving information. Classic games like Charades and Telephone and social media on various platforms are examples of some of the many ways we now transfer information.

Although there can be much that is fun or uplifting in communication, carelessness is fairly prevalent. Insensitive or inappropriate communication can be hurtful; for some people it triggers trauma or other forms of pain. Communication is affected by what is heard by a listener, regardless of what sender intended to communicate. Culture and identity can also alter communication. The influences on effective and ineffective communication are important for legal practitioners working in the complexities of dispute resolution.

There is a true story that ends well, but demonstrates how innocent communication across identity and culture, complicated with insensitivity, can lead to miscommunication (Reimer et al., 2015). There was a young Irish woman who moved to the Eastern United States (US) to attend University. The young woman was placed with a family in the US that was kind, loving, and fun. The young woman, who was homesick for her family and home in Northern Ireland was grateful to the family. She especially appreciated the décor of the home, which resembled her home among the mountains of Donegal County. One day, wanting to express her joy to her host family, the young woman spread her arms out to encompass the house symbolically, and said seriously to the family, "Your whole house is homely." The faces around her were crestfallen; they did not understand that this was a fine Irish compliment. Fortunately, one of the family members asked the young woman how the word 'homely' was defined in Ireland (in North America, it is another word for unattractive and undesirable).

While the word 'homely' communicated something less than complimentary to the family, the message from their Irish guest is summed in the North American understanding of 'homey.' The home, like the family, was welcoming, attractive, and pleasing; it produced a sense of belonging in the young Irish woman. She said 'homely,' meaning lovely; they heard 'homely,' meaning 'ugly.' The communication had to cross cultural lines and was not received as it was intended! Although it was brief and unintended, the communication produced interpersonal conflict.

Conflict Styles and the Thomas Kilmann Instrument

Everyone has a conflict style. That is, each person responds to conflict in a way that is an effort to meet their own needs, even if they are oblivious to that need. Conflict styles vary among people, and sometimes within the same person. The variated emphasis across the balance importance of an issue and the emphasis and important of relationship is recognized in literature as a conflict style (Thomas & Kilmann, 2025). For legal practitioners, the recognition of how each conflict style manifests in associated behaviors and interests is important in the satisfactory resolution of most disputes.

In 1974, Kenneth Thomas and Ralph Kilmann developed the Thomas-Kilmann Conflict Mode Instrument (TKI) which categories the common styles people manifest when they are in conflict. This instrument identifies five primary conflict styles: Competing, Accommodating, Avoiding, Compromising, and Collaborating (Thomas & Kilmann, 2025). Each of the conflict styles falls on a continuum of importance of relationship from low to high, and on a continuum of importance of an issue, from low to high. While most people tend to manifest one of these styles more than the others, conflict styles can be changed through education, and a sometimes change in response to the conflict style one is confronting across the table.

That is, if someone dreads conflict (likely they are a Conflict Avoider), they can learn how to collaborate through a conflict, so that both parties are truly satisfied with the outcome. Similarly, someone who is Competitive and feels they must "win" every conflict, can also learn how to change the competitive behavior and truly resolve conflict. This is a simple but extremely useful tool that can be applied to a range of legal situations, from negotiation to litigation, mediation, and dispute resolution, merely through careful observation of the parties involved. Legal professionals often recognize that different types of conflict require different responses, so that recognizing and understanding these response styles allows practitioners to navigate disputes in a way that is tailored to the situation at hand. At play in all responses to conflict are two factors: the value one places on "winning" an issue, and the value one places on protecting the relationship in conflict.

The Thomas Kilmann model is widely recognized and is especially popular in organizational and workplace conflict literature and practice. The Thomas Kilmann Instrument (TKI) identifies five common strategies people use for dealing with and managing conflict: competing, accommodating, avoiding, compromising, and collaborating. These are not difficult to recognize and can be useful when legal practitioners are looking for appropriate strategies for dispute resolution.

Competing is an aggressive style of communication in which people take a firm stand or position and express with certainty what they want. The competitive response to conflict places high priority on winning and low priority on relationship, so that they seek control over a discussion, in both substance and ground rules. They tend to manipulate power, and draw upon authority, expertise, or their own persuasive abilities to "win." Individuals engaged in a competitive conflict style assert their own interests at the expense of others and are often unaware of potential damage to relationship. In legal disputes, this style is often seen in highly contentious situations, such as courtroom litigation, where the focus is on winning the case, regardless of the impact on the future relationship. Lawyers may be pleased to see a competing style when quick decisions are necessary, however it can alienate the other party and result in feelings of resentment that hinder the potential for future collaboration.

The Accommodating style focuses on preserving relationships by yielding to the other party's interests. It is the opposite of the competing style. People who are accommodators tend to be diplomatic and highly cooperative but not necessarily assertive because the relationship is the most important element in the conflict, and preserving that relationship is paramount. Accommodators are willing to meet the needs of others at the expense of their own needs. In legal practice, this style may be recognized in cases where maintaining a working relationship is more important than winning the dispute. When the accommodating style is recognized, it can be useful in mediation or negotiation when it is important that preserving the relationship is more important than the outcome of the issue. However, this style usually results in agreements that do not address the core issue or that leave the accommodating party feeling unfulfilled. This is because accommodators do not actually address the conflict, so that it can be difficult to guide parties toward satisfactory conflict resolution if both are accommodators.

Avoiding is a common conflict response from people who will do almost anything to avoid conflict. They will agree to virtually anything because the relationship they are striving to preserve is themselves. An additional dimension to conflict avoidance is called the chilling effect (Roloff & Cloven, 1990, 53). They appear to place little to no value on their own positions or interests, because they just want the conflict to be avoided, or over as quickly as possible. Individuals who use the avoiding style typically hope the conflict will resolve itself and often sidestep conflict, either by withdrawing from discussions or delaying resolution. The style is typified by delegating controversial decisions, accepting default decisions, and not wanting to hurt anyone's feelings.

The Avoidance style is weak and ineffective and usually causes internal distress to the point that the distress can no longer be ignored. Sadly, this style often accepts the termination of a relationship rather than confronting conflict. Those involved do not understand what went wrong, but when one party is a conflict avoider, no views are expressed or interests revealed that are the building blocks for resolution. In legal settings, this could manifest as parties refusing to engage in settlement discussions or avoiding necessary confrontations. While avoiding may seem like a way to preserve peace, it often leads to unresolved issues, contributing to long-term frustration and potentially escalating the dispute. When recognized, this style can be beneficial when the issue at hand is trivial or when other parties are in a better position to resolve the issue.

The Compromising conflict style seeks a middle ground between Competing style and Accommodating style in which the solution partially satisfies everyone but also means that no one gets what they really want. When the compromising style is evident each party gives up something in order to reach a partial resolution and usually happens in some kind of near balance between winning and preserving relationship. In legal contexts, compromise is often employed in negotiations where both sides must make concessions. While compromise can lead to timely resolutions, it often results in an outcome that does not fully satisfy either party. When the cost of the conflict is higher than the cost of losing ground, or when opponents are deadlocked, or if there is a deadline looming, the compromising style can be useful, but the resolution often leaves lingering dissatisfaction.

The Collaborative style is widely recognized as an ideal approach to conflict because it is characterized by an effort to meet the needs of all the people involved in a dispute. Collaboration offers a chance for consensus and the integration of needs in a settlement. In this way, the best possible outcome for everyone offers an ideal balance between winning and relationship preservation through a high level of cooperation and communication, and an acknowledgement that everyone involved is important. In legal practice, this approach is seen in dispute resolution processes where all parties work together to find a solution that benefits everyone. Importantly, the final decision is delayed until all parties are truly satisfied. Often the most effective approach when the issue is complex and the relationship between parties is critical, the collaborative style is ideal for situations where long-term relationships and creative solutions are key.

The Thomas- Kilmann model provides a visual model to indicate that in a conflict, the importance of relationship to each party, or the importance of the issue to each party, can be recognized to identify direct indicators of conflict styles. Consider that the horizontal axis indicates the willingness of the conflict style to cooperate with others to satisfy their needs. The further one moves to the right along the axis, the greater the level of cooperation, meaning there is a greater focus on maintaining the relationship by focusing increasingly on the needs of the other party. The avoiding style tends to be uncooperative, not focused on the relationship or the needs of the other party, only desperate to avoid conflict. In contrast, the compromising and the accommodating styles are increasingly cooperative, focused on relationship and on the other's needs. That is, the avoiding conflict style, closest to the vertical access, is less focused on relationship and more focused on self-preservation, while the compromising conflict style, furthest from the vertical access, is focused on maintaining relationship, and is not as concerned with winning the issue, or with self-preservation.

If one observes the vertical axis, conflict styles are increasingly assertive in terms of selfish needs and desires, and on achieving their own outcomes and agenda. The avoiding style is least like this, but the compromising style and then the competing style are increasingly focused on self, on their own outcomes, and on their own agenda, with decreasing concern for relationship. The collaborating style is the style most balanced between agenda or outcomes, and preservation of relationship. It is important to know that although conflict styles are habitual they are not permanent, and people can change their conflict style and develop a collaborative conflict style into habit.

In the context of legal practice, where adversarial relationships prevail, understanding and managing conflict is simplified with a knowledge and recognition of conflict styles. Recognizing the five styles in oneself, one's client and in opposing counsel provides knowledge and guidance for approaching conflicts.

Reactive Responses

A common issue in legal disputes, particularly in negotiations or mediation, is reactive responses. These occur when individuals, rather than listening attentively to the other party, focus on crafting their next response. The response, then, is a reaction to emotion, rather than a carefully crafted advance toward resolution. In the legal context, reactive responses can derail negotiations and hinder progress toward resolution, in addition to escalating emotions. When legal professionals respond prematurely with judgments, solutions, or advice without fully understanding the issue, they risk exacerbating the conflict. In this way, it is very important that lawyers are able to diffuse conflict.

Reactive listening manifests in several ways: offering unsolicited solutions, sarcasm, accusations, making hasty judgments, or showing disinterest. These responses can cause significant harm, including alienating clients, reducing the likelihood of a resolution, and fostering further mistrust between parties. Legal professionals must be mindful of these behaviors and focus on truly listening to the words and unspoken messaging of the other party before responding.

Active and Reflective Listening

Active listening is one of the most powerful conflict transformation techniques in legal practice. It requires practitioners to engage fully with the speaker, verbally reflecting back not only the content of their words but also the emotions and concerns underlying them. This skill is particularly important in legal negotiations, mediations, and client interactions, and requires little more than discipline and practice. Active or reflective listening encompases the behaviors and attitudes that communicate that one is attentive to (or reflecting upon) the thoughts and feelings of another person. This, in turn, conveys an understanding of what the other person or party is saying, and meaning is conveyed according to the speaker's point of view or frame of reference (Katz et al., 2011, 5). Active listening helps ensure that all parties feel heard and understood, which is a critical step in building trust and finding mutually acceptable solutions.

Many people find active listening to be a difficult practice, as our society seems to encourage us to pause speaking and prepare our next verbiage while someone else is speaking. This is not listening. A strong example of active listening is evident in the *Great Law of Peace* (Wallace, 1990), protected within the Haudenosaunee (or Iroquois) Confederacy, which is further explained in the chapter by Daniel Diamond.

The Haudenosaunee Confederacy is a peace pact established by The Peacemaker between six traditionally warring Haudenosaunee nations before recorded time. These nations, the Oneida, the Cayuga, the Mohawk, the Onondaga, the Seneca and later, the Tuscarora were identified in English history as the Six Nations. The Great Law is a living constitution that guides this very old confederacy and is outlined in this chapter as a long-standing practice of active listening.

When the nations were to attend to governance matters, they would gather in a building called the Longhouse. There was one talking piece, which would be passed from one speaker to the next, and only the holder of the talking piece could speak. The process required that before anyone could express their views or respond to another person, they had to accurately summarize the views of all of those people who had spoken previously in the meeting. Active listening requires both attending and responding skills. In this way, all listeners had to be active listeners, reflecting on the words of the others while pondering their own responses. If a speaker was inattentive, they were not allowed to hold the talking piece. The process was monitored by someone holding a large stick which was used on those who did not follow the agreed and collective rules of communication of the group. Since no decisions would be made until a decision could be made unanimously, active listening was critical to the process.

Attending skills are important to effective communication and are useful in a number of settings outside legal practice including trauma, workplace conflict, and meetings among international dignitaries. Attending skills describe the way the listener communicates verbally and non-verbally with a speaker. There are five common behaviors that describe attending skills: comfortable eye contact, relaxed posture leaning slightly toward the speaker, non-distracting gestures, and refraining from fidgeting (Reimer et al., 2015). In contemporary times, positive attending behaviors also include concealing or silencing mobile phones or other forms of electronic media so that the speaker will not be interrupted.

Another related responsibility for attentive listening includes ensuring that the setting is an environment conducive to communication and that there is enough time for listening so the speaker can take as long as is needed to speak. Attending skills keep the focus on the person who is communicating their concerns, affirming their value and indicating that their communications are being received. Attending skills also assist the listener in refraining from thoughts or behaviors that might distract them from their goal of dispute resolution.

Responding skills are an additional and a critical part of active or reflective listening. Responding skills are the listener's demonstrated behaviors of respect and attention that reflect the meaning and content of the speaker's experience back to the speaker. Reflection can include repeating content, feelings, meaning, or a summarization of what has been said by paraphrasing. For the speaker, these practices provide assurance that the message they are communicating is accurately understood.

Expressions of Affirmation and Appreciation

It seems that everyone needs compassion, the kindness of a stranger, a sense of belonging and the dignity of feeling valued. In a world of great diversity, many characteristics are shared across and within cultures, and across geographies, and these shared human traits contain many of the keys for meaningful interpersonal communication. For example, research has indicated a universal sense of connectedness about the quality of interpersonal relationships shared with other people at home, work, and in the marketplace (Chapman, 2009, 225). People are more productive and less conflictual when they feel their value is affirmed by others (Chapman & White, 2011). And when people feel unacknowledged, undervalued and belittled in any of these contexts, conflicts are generated. Strain within relationships are indicators of escalating conflict. When people want peace and harmony in their interpersonal relationships, an awareness of how they and others express affirmation and appreciation constructively can transform difficult relationships at home, at work, and within other places.

The affirmation of human dignity preserves and maintains strong relationships; recognizing and exercising the languages that express appreciation to others in ways that are meaningful to those people is a tool legal professionals may engage to improve relationships with and between their clients. Psychologists Chapman and White (2011) have identified that people communicate appreciation in one of five ways, which they have identified as languages of appreciation. These 'languages' are easy to recognize and to 'speak:' tangible gifts, words of affirmation, quality time, acts of service, and physical touch. Although individuals tend to express one more than they do the others, the expressions can change with circumstances and over time.

According to Chapman and White, people tend to express the language that affirms them in the circumstances they are in. This might mean that a person who is most affirmed by words of appreciation may shift to feeling most appreciated by acts of service if their workload at the office becomes intense and demanding. If that same lawyer finds themselves carrying the load when tasks are intended to be shared among colleagues, they will begin to feel undervalued or underappreciated. Similarly, a work-worn lawyer may appreciate receiving a gift-card or having a report copied for them more than they would normally appreciate a kind word. To those who are astutely watching the languages of appreciation, they will observe people 'speaking' their language of appreciation. There is someone at the office who always washes the dishes (acts of service) while another brings donuts once a week (gifts), and yet another writes "You are the best!" on the bulletin board (words of affirmation). The colleague who is affirmed by quality time will linger at your door, and the one who affirms and is affirmed by physical touch may shake your hand, pat you on the back, or lay the back of their hand across your arm as they speak. It is important to watch for the indicators of personal value and affirmation that are communicated by people with whom we work, live, serve, and socialize. In some legal settings, simply reading the language of affirmation of one's clients and acting on those observations can diffuse conflict and build trust.

Similarly, people can be discouraged, devalued and sometimes devastated when these same languages of appreciation are employed to intentionally (and sometimes unintentionally) harm them. Often this is done unwittingly, but as legal practitioners, it is important to look for indications of another person's language of appreciation and affirm them whenever possible. This simple kindness transcends culture, language, and other potential barriers or discriminations. While name-calling is usually intended to be cruel, it is particularly cruel to someone for whom words of affirmation are their language of value. Striking a person for whom physical touch conveys value and affirmation is particularly devastating for them, as are the withholding of simple acts of service like clearing the dishes from the table when someone is hurting or refusing to meet with an individual when a quality time person asks for a walk or company for coffee. They are speaking their language of affirmation clearly; one has only to 'hear' what they are communicating.

Observing people to understand how they express appreciation and affirmation to others is a highly effective way to repair harm, diffuse conflict, and improve interpersonal relationships in all contexts, especially in legal practice. It is a simple yet highly dignifying form of communication. Understanding the concept of languages of appreciation and specifically learning to recognize each of the five expressions, assists in the transformation of interpersonal conflict so that communications are received and interpreted with more accuracy (Chapman, 2009, 225).

Dreaded Conversations

We are all familiar with the physiological and psychological indicators of anxiety and apprehension when confronted with the necessity of discussing something difficult. As legal professionals, it is helpful to have a strategy to guide the dreaded, yet necessary conversations encountered in the practice of law. Recognizing the real challenges inherent in confrontation, in the early 2000s the Harvard Negotiation Project published a practical guide entitled *Difficult Conversations: How to Discuss What Matters Most* (Stone et al., 2000). Since then, and in recognition of the very real challenges to authentic communication, the Harvard Project released *Crucial Conversations: Tools for Talking When Stakes are High* (Grenny et al., 2022). And then in 2016 and 2017, the Harvard Project released *Negotiating the Nonnegotiable: How to Resolve Your Most Emotionally Charged Conflicts* (Shapiro, 2016, 2017). Each of these books offer a strategy in the form of a common structure so that difficult, crucial, and emotionally charged conflicts may be discussed and can be resolved satisfactorily. This is conflict transformation in action and there is much literature beyond the scope of this chapter to facilitate conflict transformation. The purpose here is to provide a brief outline of each of these strategic frameworks for approaching and potentially working through dreaded conversations and seemingly unresolvable conflicts. Readers are strongly encouraged to seek qualified education in each of the areas below. Unskilled or arrogant efforts toward conflict transformation without proper conflict analysis and methodologies can exacerbate rather than diffuse conflict.

Difficult Conversations

Difficult conversations are different perceptions of the same reality, and in those differences is the conflict. Difficult conversations happen because better conversations did not. The challenge is to hear what people are *really* thinking and feeling but not saying to one another. Difficult conversations contain three distinct conversations, or stories, each with a common structure (Stone et al., 2011). There are three layers, or stories, within a difficult conversation (Landry, 2022). These are what happened; how the speaker feels about what happened; and how the incident intersects with or threatens each person's identity. The Harvard Project categorizes these as The Story Conversation (the stories people tell themselves and tell others), The Feelings Conversation (the difference between the intent of the story and its effect), and The Identity Conversation (the way one's identity needs to be restored after important conflict).

Recognizing this framework in a conversation allows one to navigate through conflict toward resolution by shifting the internal stance of the listener. This shift diffuses some of the emotion and facilitates improved conversation by assisting in the discernment of the root of the conflict. While they are conversing, or telling their story, people engaged in what can be categorized as a 'difficult conversation' will provide the listener with clues to move the conversation toward a shared perception of what happened (Stone et al., 2011; Wilmot & Hocker, 2014, 241–242). As a legal practitioner confronting a difficult conversation, it is critical to create a space in which people feel accepted and affirmed, because they will be feeling threatened and overly criticized—mostly because they have not been able to express their perception in a way that is understood by the other party. There is tendency to lead with one's own perception, but in fact it is less threatening if one leads as though there is a third neutral person leading the conversation, describing the problem as the difference between the stories. Ask questions and paraphrase, and invent options that meet the most important concerns and needs of each party.

Crucial Conversations

Crucial conversations are discussions between two or more people from which the outcome could have a great impact on either relationships or have a great impact that may forever alter one's life (Grenny et al., 2022, 2). Three elements are readily recognized in a crucial conversation: there are opposing opinions, there is a high-stakes issues, and emotions run strong. Typically, we avoid crucial conversations or we handle them poorly. One's conflict style can be a key component in finding the shortest path to effective communication. Skilled communicators look for ways to be both honest and respectful in order to create dialogue, which is a condition where meaning flows freely between parties so that there is a larger pool of information upon which to move toward resolution (Grenny et al., 2022, 33). One of the greatest challenges in a crucial conversation is to have the correct conversation: what is the real topic that needs discussing? As and lawyer and the facilitator in a crucial conversation, it is critical to keep the conversation on the right topic. Indicators that one is not on the right topic is the presence of escalating emotions, one party walking away literally or disengaging, and a sense of a circular conversation (Grenny et al., 2022, 55). The problem is usually not that there are problems between people, it is that they do not have the time to engage in a crucial conversation. Because the stakes are high and the outcome of not conversing can be life-changing, it is very important that people, and legal practitioners in particular, try to keep the conversation on the right topic, respect and affirm the parties involved, and let them take the time they need to effectively communicate and ultimately resolve the issue before them.

Non-Negotiable Impasses

One of the greatest challenges to dispute resolution are those adversarial situations in which tensions rise in individuals, within their group and between larger groups. It seems to be no road back to peaceful relationships. These are recognized in literature as identity conflicts and require great expertise and time to identify, transform, and resolve. It is critical to know that identity conflicts are not identity crises. Identity conflicts are a prevalent yet most difficult form of conflict and because they are complex, deeply rooted, and extend beyond the intrapersonal into the realm of interstate; they are very difficult to resolve (Northrup, 1989; Taras &

Ganguly, 2010). Sometimes, a legal practitioner may find themselves in an unresolvable conflict. When this happens, it may be that one has encountered an identity conflict. There is hope for resolution, but it takes a lot of time, skill, and experience. Identity conflicts are at the roots of conflicts like Gaza, Northern Ireland, the US Civil War, and the ongoing struggle between the Canadian governments and Indigenous people. It is important for legal practitioners to recognize the extreme complexity of this type of conflict as it will manifest in individuals, yet be part of a much larger group identity.

Research has shown that there are five hidden emotional forces at work in such situations, all related to identity, and when these are recognized and acknowledged, seemingly intractable conflicts can be reconciled through careful address (Shapiro, 2017, 4). The five pillars of identity define a part of someone, and they define the group they belong to. The five pillars are beliefs, rituals, allegiances and loyalties, guiding principles and ideals, and emotionally meaningful experiences (Shapiro, 2017). Usually, in an intense and emotionally charged conflict, one of these elements of identity feels threatened at the individual level, and typically is actually threatened at the group level.

For those people on each side of the conflict, they feel their very core self, that part of identity that they derive from the larger group to which they belong, is at risk. The deep pain and sense of threat experienced by those submerged in an identity conflict causes desperation and so the group reaches for terminology like genocide in an effort to be heard. Identity conflict is best learned from the field of peace and conflict studies but is included here because lawyers will encounter it at times, and it is crucial to recognize that this is not a conflict that may be litigated, mediated or resolved through traditional legal channels.

It is important to know that there is now literature and research to guide groups and individuals through the identity conflict journey with effective communication, respect, and a willingness to not demonize 'the other side,' and to remember that they, too, are desperate, hurting people experiencing a similar threat to their deeply held values and identity. Dr. Jay Rothman has designed the ARIA method (2008; 2012), Dr. Dan-Baron developed positive encounter dialogue which has been useful in the middle east and in Ireland (2008), and Dr. Jean-Paul Lederach has created a number of conflict transformation analytical models (2003). These scholar practitioners focus on issues of intergroup identity conflict and have demonstrated success transforming conflicts that would otherwise be considered intractable. They have developed sophisticated yet approachable tools for navigating identity conflict (Reimer, 2020). Many conflict transformation skills are applicable to international conflict settings (Reimer & Schmitz, 2022). Accessing and familiarizing oneself with the work of practicing scholars is important knowledge for legal practitioners working in international arbitration and other peace-building efforts.

Identity is defined as an abiding sense of the self and of the relationship of the self to the world (Kriesberg & Dayton, 2017). It is a system of beliefs or a way of construing the world that makes life predictable rather than random and is deeply rooted in a person's or a group's sense of how that person or group is in relationship with others (Taras & Ganguly, 2010, 3). In order to function, human beings must have a reasonable level of ability to predict how their behavior will affect what happens to them. When defined this way, identity is extended to encompass a sense of self-in-relation-to-the-world (Northrup, 1989, 55). Therefore, identity conflicts are triggered and inflamed by identity concerns; at the same time, identities are created and transformed in the waging of conflicts (Cook-Huffman, 2009, 25). In this way, identity is very much relational, and understanding identity conflict requires the context of relationships.

Research has taught that at the deepest level, identity is lodged in the narratives of how people see themselves, and so the kernels of identity conflict may be discerned in the conversations people have. Identity is about who people are, where they have come from, and what they fear they will become or lose. In this way, identity is deeply rooted in a person's or a group's sense of how that person or group is in relationship with others (Byrne et al., 2022). Identity conflict poses the potential for great help from legal practitioners who are listening closely to determine what conflict they are witnessing within or among their clients (Lederach, 2003, p. 55).

Identity conflicts are difficult to recognize because they are well established before the indicators are evident. In many ways, this suggests they are intractable. Intractability means that some conflicts seem never to get resolved and just go on and on and on.

Although identity conflicts are among groups, the individuals within identity conflicts carry the pain of the conflict. This type of conflict is protracted and difficult to mitigate because there are many causes, and the role of history, especially in struggles over land and resources and history that is painful to one of the parties, plays a much larger and important role than it does in other forms of conflict (Reimer, 2014). Identity conflict threatens culture, beliefs, and values, and it affects people's dignity, safety, and purpose. When the goals of at least one party are defined in identity terms, history plays a much larger role in the conflict than it may in other types of conflict (Wolff, 2006, p. 64). At the collective level, minority and majority groups often struggle over land, resources and power (Wolff, 2006, p. 2). Within the struggle, identity conflict is not based on the competition around economics and power issues, but, instead, 'revolves around questions of communal identity'" (Korostelina, 2009, p. 100). In this way, the symbols of identity contribute to the intractability of the conflict because some parties insist that their identities are primordial, or biological, and so those identities must not be ignored or altered. This makes resolution even more challenging, and is an indication that the confronting conflict is intractible.

Conflict is difficult and resolution spans everything from the ceasefire in an armed conflict to the apologetic hug to a friend. When seeking to resolve or diffuse emotionally charged conflicts, whether they may be recognized as difficult conversations, crucial conversations, or intractable identity conflicts, the three core dimensions of conflict transformation must be addressed: rationality, emotions, and identity (Shapiro, 2017, 9). Reconciliation, which is the goal after conflict resolution is achieved, requires a dialogue among people. At work against reconciliation are what have been identified as competing "relational dialectics" (Shapiro, 2017, 220). These are the contradictory impulses within all of us that pull us both toward and away from relationship: the desire to forgive but also to punish, to be accepted but not be expected to change, to forgive and not seek revenge. It is difficult to monitor, challenge, and resist the very real forces of relational dialectics, but when we do, there can be reconciliation—even within international identity conflicts. And conversation is the first step.

Trauma-Informed Legal Practice

A critical consideration in legal practice, especially when handling sensitive or high-conflict cases, is an awareness of the manifestations of trauma, and then how to engage in trauma-informed practices. There has been a growing awareness of the wide-spread presence of trauma across societies and that has flowed from the field of conflict or dispute resolution because responses to trauma can be misunderstood as inter or intrapersonal conflict. Trauma is—the body's response to traumatic events (Maté, 2022). There is much evidence that people can experience traumatic events but not become traumatized. How the body responds to a traumatic event is what can become trauma.

Individuals involved in legal disputes may have experienced significant trauma, which can influence their conflict style and responses to legal proceedings. A trauma-informed approach is respectful and affirming. It emphasizes understanding, recognizing, and responding to the effects of trauma on a person's behavior, which is also dignifying for the person who is evidencing trauma (Hetherington, 2008). Within the rapidly growing literature about trauma and trauma-informed practices, there is a generally accepted recognition of four responses to trauma. For legal practitioners, it is important to recognize that the person embodying them is not being difficult or unreasonable, but rather are responding to something that traumatized them. It is critical that legal practitioners recognize that they are not trained to heal trauma, but when they recognize it, they can engage in trauma-informed practices that can be helpful to their clients. There are four responses to trauma that manifest with behaviors that can alert an observer to the presence and interference of trauma. Briefly, the four responses to trauma most recognized in the literature are Fight, Flight, Fawn, and Freeze (Maté, 2022). These are survival mechanisms triggered in response to a perceived threat to safety in its many meanings.

Legal professionals who adopt a trauma-informed approach are aware that trauma can affect individuals in ways that impact their ability to engage in conflict resolution constructively. For example, a person with a history of trauma may be more likely to adopt an avoiding style, withdrawing from conflict to protect themselves. On the other hand, someone who has experienced power dynamics rooted in past trauma may gravitate toward a competing style as a means of regaining control. Understanding these dynamics is critical in ensuring that all parties are treated with respect and that solutions are crafted in a way that considers their emotional and psychological well-being.

Trauma is defined as an emotional response to a terrible event, deemed terrible by the person who experienced it (Maté, 2022). Immediately after the event, shock and even denial are typical. Sometimes people cannot remember the event. If left unaddressed, trauma can become chronic and complex, and left unattended, will never heal (Matsakis, 1996). There is a growing global consensus that "everyone is traumatized." This is not a widely held opinion in the trauma literature. The truth is closer to the fact that everyone may have experienced traumatic events, but not everyone develops trauma in response to those events. Some people heal quickly, some do not, and others develop behaviors that allow them to appear to be functioning while the trauma lurks beneath.

There are three main classifications of trauma: acute, chronic and complex. Acute trauma is the result of exposure to a single, overwhelming event, and most often manifests as detailed memories, hyper-vigilance, exaggerated startled responses, overreactions, and misperceptions (Maté, 2022). Chronic trauma is the result of extended exposure to traumatic situations, and is recognized through the following behaviors: denial, psychological numbing, disassociation, rage, social withdrawal, and a sense of shortened future. Complex trauma is the result of a single traumatic event that is devastating enough to have long term effects on a person (Wolynn, 2016).

People that are experiencing long-term traumatic disorders develop triggers that may appear in a legal context and so it is helpful for legal practitioners to be trauma informed. Traumatized people feel unsafe, often cannot manage their emotions, and have difficulty building relationships. Triggers are associated with the traumatic event are signals to that person that there is possible danger to their safety (Matsakis, 1996). Panic attacks are not unusual manifestations of a trigger. Triggers can become numerous and appear to be unrelated to the traumatic event to an outsider, and sometimes to the individual experiencing them. A triggered individual experiences fear, panic, upset and agitation in settings where this may seem to be an unusual response. To heal triggers, a person must seek professional assistance; this is not the work of a lawyer. Trauma does not heal over time and individuals must seek professional assistance to overcome it (Matsakis, 1996). When working with a traumatized person, legal practitioners are wise to recognize that what they are seeing is more than an antagonistic or agitated client and seek guidance from trauma-trained professionals.

A trauma-informed legal practice involves creating an environment that fosters safety, trust, and respect. It also means providing clients with clear and accessible information about their legal rights and options while being sensitive to their emotional needs. In conflict resolution, it is essential to provide space for clients to feel heard and validated, while avoiding re-traumatizing them through aggressive or dismissive behavior.

Conclusion

Interpersonal communication is not ancillary to the practice of law—it is fundamental. People tend to be quite clear when they are communicating, especially in conflict. Sometimes, they use words. As outlined in this chapter, the ability to listen actively, respond reflectively, and recognize the emotional and psychological landscapes in which clients and colleagues operate is not merely a matter of courtesy; it is a matter of professional competence. Communication underpins every client interview, negotiation, courtroom interaction, and interoffice exchange. It is, in essence, the lawyer's first tool—sharpened not by rhetoric alone but by self-awareness, empathy, and intentional listening.

This chapter introduced foundational elements of effective communication and applied them to the legal context, where interpersonal dynamics often determine the success or failure of legal processes. The inclusion of the Thomas-Kilmann Conflict Mode Instrument provides law students with a valuable framework to understand how individuals approach conflict based on differing priorities regarding relationships and outcomes. Recognizing whether a client, opposing counsel, or even a colleague is engaging from a competitive, avoidant, accommodative, collaborative, or compromising stance allows the legal professional to adapt strategy accordingly. Conflict style recognition, in this way, becomes both a diagnostic and strategic tool in navigating interpersonal friction in legal settings.

Furthermore, the distinctions made between reactive, active, and reflective listening are not merely academic—they are practical competencies. Reflective listening is a skill that can profoundly influence a client's sense of being heard and understood. In a legal environment where emotions often run high, reflective listening can de-escalate tension, reveal underlying interests, and build the trust necessary for effective advocacy and conflict resolution.

The section on the languages of appreciation adds a nuanced layer to the understanding of interpersonal interaction. Lawyers are often trained to focus on facts, precedents, and logic, yet they operate in a world where clients are governed as much by feeling as by reason. By attending to how clients express and receive appreciation—whether through words, time, service, touch, or gifts—legal professionals can build rapport and foster relational trust. These modes of appreciation are not just soft skills; they are gateways to emotional safety in communication, which is essential for honest dialogue and meaningful resolution.

The exploration of difficult, crucial, and identity-based conversations positions future legal professionals to anticipate and manage some of the most challenging interactions in their careers. Difficult conversations—whether around fees, case outcomes, or personal disclosure—require not only tact but emotional intelligence. Identity-based conflicts, in particular, challenge lawyers to recognize when disagreements transcend the surface level of legal issues and tap into deeply held beliefs and values. These require a trauma-informed, culturally sensitive approach—one that aligns with the evolving expectations of the profession and the public it serves.

Trauma-informed communication, as introduced in the final section of the chapter, is particularly relevant in today's legal landscape. Many clients have histories of psychological, social, or systemic trauma. Legal practitioners who are mindful of this—who communicate in ways that minimize retraumatization and foster empowerment—are not only more effective advocates they are also agents of justice in a fuller sense. Trauma informed practice is not a niche competency; it is increasingly a standard of care.

Taken together, the insights in this chapter emphasize that conflict and its resolution are communicative phenomena. While the legal profession has traditionally outsourced interpersonal conflict management to other disciplines—such as psychology, political science, or social work—today's lawyer must be fluent in the language of interpersonal conflict and resolution. Communication is both the site of breakdown and the medium of repair. As such, developing communication skills is not just about improving client satisfaction or enhancing workplace harmony. It is about equipping future lawyers with the tools to lead, to mediate, to advocate, and to resolve—skills that are essential in a profession charged with the pursuit of justice.

Legal education must recognize that communication is not simply an ancillary skill but a foundational element of competent and ethical legal practice. Whether in courtrooms, negotiation spaces, or correctional facilities, the nature and quality of communication can shape trust, outcomes, and the experience of justice itself. Each legal interaction holds the potential to either foster understanding or entrench harm. Legal work, at its core, is not only about applying rules—it is also deeply rooted in relationships, recognition, and the capacity to engage others meaningfully.

This perspective also demands attention to whose voices and knowledge are centered in legal processes. Systems that present themselves as neutral often carry forward long-standing exclusions, sidelining the experiences and wisdom of those most affected by injustice. A commitment to epistemic repair highlights the need to confront these patterns and to create space for diverse, often marginalized, forms of knowledge within legal reasoning and practice.

Finally, a shift toward transformative practice calls for more than procedural improvements. It challenges legal systems to support processes that do more than resolve disputes—they must help reshape how individuals relate to one another and to institutions of law. True transformation involves designing practices that not only deliver outcomes but also build dignity, inclusion, and deeper trust. Legal education, therefore, carries the responsibility of preparing future practitioners to engage in this deeper, more relational vision of justice.

In conclusion, legal education must embrace the reality that interpersonal communication is integral to competent, ethical, and humane legal practice. Each conversation—no matter how mundane or momentous—can either build bridges or deepen divides. Whether in a courtroom, a negotiation room, or a prison visitation space, the quality of communication will shape the outcomes achieved and the lives touched. The insights from this chapter can inform legal practice, underscoring that law is not only a system of rules, but a human endeavor—one deeply grounded in speech, listening, and relationship.

Questions

1. Observe the communication behaviors of colleagues in your legal workplace, members of your legal study group, and two professionals you regularly network with (maybe professors). Based on their interactions, what are their preferred forms of professional appreciation (e.g., verbal recognition, task delegation, mentorship)? What led you to these conclusions? What are your own primary, secondary, and tertiary modes of receiving appreciation in a professional legal environment, and how might this impact your collaborative effectiveness?
2. Using the five conflict management styles—competing, collaborating, compromising, avoiding, and accommodating—create a realistic scenario in which members of a legal team must negotiate responsibilities for preparing a complex case (e.g., a class-action suit

or appellate brief). Illustrate how each style might approach the division of labor, deadlines, and leadership in the project.
3. Discuss the visualization of conflict styles using both the conflict resolution "cube" (multidimensional approach) and the "circle" (relationship-focused model). Which model do you find more applicable to legal practice, particularly in client advocacy or negotiation strategy, and why?
4. Select a current legal issue (e.g., data privacy, labour disputes, or environmental regulation) and identify three distinct conflicts embedded within it—these could be between stakeholders, legal frameworks, or social perspectives. Drawing on conflict resolution interventions discussed in this chapter (e.g., mediation, principled negotiation, arbitration), suggest plausible legal or quasi-legal strategies to achieve constructive resolutions.

Glossary

Active Listening / Reflective Listening:	A conflict transformation technique in legal practice that requires full engagement with the speaker. It involves verbally reflecting back not only the content of their words but also the emotions and concerns underlying them. Active or reflective listening encompasses behaviors and attitudes that communicate that one is attentive to (or reflecting upon) the thoughts and feelings of another person. This conveys an understanding of what the other person or party is saying. It helps ensure that all parties feel heard and understood, which is critical for building trust and finding mutually acceptable solutions. It includes attending and responding skills.
Attending Skills:	Describe the way the listener communicates verbally and non-verbally with a speaker. Five common behaviors

include comfortable eye contact, relaxed posture leaning slightly toward the speaker, non-distracting gestures, and refraining from fidgeting. In contemporary times, positive attending behaviors also include concealing or silencing mobile phones or other electronic media. These skills keep the focus on the person communicating their concerns, affirming their value.

Responding Skills: An additional and critical part of active or reflective listening. They are the listener's demonstrated behaviors of respect and attention that reflect the meaning and content of the speaker's experience back to the speaker. Reflection can include repeating content, feelings, meaning, or a summarization by paraphrasing. For the speaker, these practices assure that the message they are communicating is more accurately understood.

Affirmation and Appreciation (Languages of Appreciation): People are more productive and less conflictual when they feel their value is affirmed by others. When people feel unacknowledged, undervalued, and belittled, conflicts are generated. Recognizing and exercising the languages that express appreciation to others in ways that are meaningful to those people is a tool legal professionals can use to improve relationships. Psychologists Chapman and White identified five ways people communicate appreciation, identified as languages of appreciation: tangible gifts, words of affirmation, quality time, acts of service, and physical touch. These can be recognized and "spoken." Observing how people express appreciation and affirmation to others is a highly effective way to repair harm, diffuse conflict, and improve interpersonal relationships.

Conflict Style: Everyone has a conflict style, which is a way a person responds to conflict in an effort to meet their own needs. Conflict styles vary among people and sometimes within the same person. They represent a varied emphasis across the balance of the importance of an issue and the importance of the relationship.

Thomas-Kilmann Conflict Mode Instrument (TKI): Developed in 1974 by Kenneth Thomas and Ralph Kilmann, this instrument categorizes the common styles people manifest when they are in conflict. It identifies five primary conflict styles: Competing, Accommodating, Avoiding, Compromising, and Collaborating. Each style falls on continuums of importance of relationship (low to high) and importance of an issue (low to high).

Competing Style: An aggressive style of communication where people take a firm stand or position and express with certainty what they want. This style places high priority on winning and low priority on relationship. They seek control over a discussion, manipulate power, and use authority, expertise, or persuasive abilities to "win". Individuals assert their own interests at the expense of others and are often unaware of potential damage to the relationship. In legal disputes, this is often seen in highly contentious situations like courtroom litigation.

Accommodating Style: Focuses on preserving relationships by yielding to the other party's interests. It is the opposite of the competing style. People using this style tend to be diplomatic and highly cooperative but not necessarily assertive, as preserving the relationship is paramount. They are willing to meet the needs of others at the expense of their own needs. This style usually results in agreements that do not address the core issue or leave the accommodating party feeling unfulfilled.

Avoiding Style: A common conflict response from people who will do almost anything to avoid conflict. They appear to place little to no value on their own positions or interests. Individuals using this style typically hope the conflict will resolve itself and often sidestep conflict by withdrawing or delaying resolution. This style is typified by delegating controversial decisions, accepting default decisions, and not wanting to hurt anyone's feelings. It is described as weak and ineffective and usually causes internal distress.

Compromising Style: Seeks a middle ground between the Competing style and the Accommodating style, resulting in a solution that partially satisfies everyone but means no one gets what they really want. Each party gives up something to reach a partial resolution, usually in a near balance between winning and preserving relationships. In legal contexts, it is often employed in negotiations where both sides must make concessions. It often results in an outcome that does not fully satisfy either party.

Collaborative Style: Widely recognized as an ideal approach to conflict because it is characterized by an effort to meet the needs of all people involved. Collaboration offers a chance for consensus and the integration of needs. It offers an ideal balance between winning and relationship preservation through a high level of cooperation and communication. The final decision is delayed until all parties are truly satisfied. It is often the most effective approach when the issue is complex and the relationship is critical.

Reactive Responses: Occur when individuals, rather than listening attentively, focus on crafting their next response. The response is a reaction to emotion rather than a carefully crafted advance toward resolution. In the legal context, they can derail negotiations, hinder progress, and escalate emotions. Examples include offering unsolicited solutions, sarcasm, accusations, making hasty judgments, or showing disinterest.

Difficult Conversations: Developed and described by the Harvard Project as different perceptions of the same reality, where conflict lies. They happen because better conversations did not. The challenge is hearing what people are really thinking and feeling but not saying. Difficult conversations contain three distinct layers or "stories": what happened, how the speaker feels, and how the incident intersects with or threatens each person's identity. These are categorized as The Story Conversation, The Feelings Conversation, and The Identity Conversation.

Crucial Conversations: Developed and described by the Harvard Project, these are discussions between two or more people where the outcome could have a great impact on relationships or significantly alter one's life. Three elements are readily recognized: opposing opinions, high-stakes issues, and strong emotions. Skilled communicators aim for dialogue where meaning flows freely between parties to build a larger pool of information for resolution. A challenge is ensuring the conversation stays on the right topic.

Identity Conflict/ Non-Negotiable Impasses: Adversarial situations within groups but also within individuals who are members of the group, where tensions rise, and there seems to be no road back. Research shows five hidden emotional forces related to identity are at work in identity conflicts. These are complex, deeply rooted, and very difficult to resolve. They are lodged in the narratives of how people see themselves. Identity is about who people are, where they have come from, and what they fear they will become or lose. Identity conflicts are not based on competition around economics and power issues but revolve around questions of communal identity. They are difficult to recognize because they are well established before indicators are evident. Identity conflicts are not the identity crises identified in psychology.

Trauma The body's response to traumatic events. People can experience traumatic events but not become traumatized; how the body responds is what can become trauma. It is defined as an emotional response to a terrible event, deemed terrible by the person who experienced it. If left unaddressed, trauma can become chronic and complex and will not heal on its own.

Trauma-Informed Practice: An approach that emphasizes understanding, recognizing, and responding to the effects of trauma on a person's behavior. It is respectful and affirming. Legal professionals adopting this approach are aware that trauma can affect individuals in ways that impact their ability to engage in conflict resolution constructively. It involves creating an environment that fosters safety, trust, and respect.

Trauma Responses (Fight, Flight, Fawn, Freeze): These are survival mechanisms triggered in response to a perceived threat to safety. They manifest with behaviors that can alert an observer to the presence and interference of trauma. Fight, Flight, Fawn, and Freeze are the four responses most recognized in the literature.

Triggers: Developed by people experiencing long-term traumatic disorders. Triggers associated with the traumatic event are signals to that person that there is possible danger to their safety. They can become numerous and appear unrelated to the traumatic event. A triggered individual experiences fear, panic, upset, and agitation in settings where this may seem to be an unusual response. To heal triggers, a person must seek professional assistance.

Competing Interests The author has no conflicts of interest to declare that are relevant to the content of this chapter.

References

Barki, H., & Hartwick, J. (2004). Conceptualizing the construct of interpersonal conflict. *International Journal of Conflict Management, 15*(3), 216–244. https://doi.org/10.1108/eb022913

Byrne, S., Levasseur, K., & Reimer, L. (2022). Building peace in Northern Ireland: Hopes for the future. *Humanity & Society*. https://doi.org/10.1177/01605976221107093

Chapman, G. (2009). *The five love languages: Singles edition chicago*. Northfield Publishing.

Chapman, G., & White, P. (2011). *The 5 languages of appreciation in the workplace: Empowering organizations by encouraging people*. Northfield Publishing.

Deutsch, M., Kriesberg, L., Northrup, T., & Thorson, S. J. (1991). Intractable conflicts and their transformation. *Contemporary Sociology, 20*(2), 246. https://doi.org/10.2307/2072947

Grenny, J., Patterson, K., McMillan, R., Switzler, A., Gregory, E. (2022). *Crucial conversations: Tools for talking when stakes are high* (3rd ed.). McGraw Hill.

Hetherington, M. (2008). The role of towards understanding and healing. In *Stories in conflict: Towards understanding and healing*. Yes! Publications.

Katz, N., Lawyer, J. W., & Koppelman Sweedler, M. (2011). *Communication and conflict resolution skills* (2nd ed.). Kendall/Hunt Publishing Company.

Kilmann Diagnostics. (2025). *An overview of the Thomas-Kilmann conflict mode instrument (TKI)*. Kilmann Diagnostics. https://kilmanndiagnostics.com/overview-thomas-kilmann-conflict-mode-instrument-tki/. Accessed April 8, 2025.

Korostelina, K. (2009). Identity conflicts: Models of dynamics and early warning. In *The Handbook of Conflict Analysis and Resolution* (pp. 100–115). Routledge.

Kriesberg, L., & Dayton, B. W. (2017). *Constructive conflicts: From escalation to resolution*. Rowman & Littlefield.

Landry, L. (2022, August 30). *How to have difficult conversations with employees.* Business Insights Blog. https://online.hbs.edu/blog/post/how-to-have-difficult-conversations-with-employees
Lawyer, N. H. (2021). *Communication and conflict resolution skills.* Kendall Hunt.
Lederach, J. P. (2003). *The little book of conflict transformation.* Good Books, an Imprint of Skyhorse Publishing, Inc.
Maté, G. (2022). *Trauma.* Dr. Gabor Maté. https://drgabormate.com/trauma/
Matsakis, A. (1996). *I can't get over it: A handbook for trauma survivors.* New Harbinger Publications.
Patterson, K., Grenny, J., Switzler, A., & Mcmillan, R. (2012). *Crucial conversations: Tools for talking when the stakes are high.* Mcgraw-Hill.
Reimer, L. (2014). Conflict transformation: Canadian democracy and aboriginal relations. *Global Journal of Peace Research and Praxis, 1*(1), 32–45.
Reimer, L. (2015). *Transformative change: An introduction to peace and conflict studies.* Lexington Books.
Reimer, L. (2020). Storytelling research for and as conflict transformation: Indigenous Canadians explain dropping out of school. In *Expanding the edges of narrative enquiry: Research from the Mauro institute* (207–234). Lexington.
Reimer, L., & Schmitz, C. L. (2022). International conflict transformation: The pursuit of positive peace. In *The Palgrave Handbook of Positive Peace* (pp. 329–346). Palgrave MacMillan.
Roloff, M., & Cloven, D. (1990). The chilling effect in interpersonal relationships: The reluctance to speak one's mind. In *Inmates in conflict: a Communication Perspective.* Lawrence Erlbaum Associates.
Shapiro, D. (2016, 2017). *Negotiating the nonnegotiable how to resolve your most emotionally charged conflicts.* Penguin Books. Viking.
Stone, D., Patton, B., & Heen, S. (2000, 2011). *Difficult conversations: How to discuss what matters most.* Penguin.
Taras, R., & Ganguly, R. (2010). *Understanding ethnic conflict* (4th ed.). Longman.
Thomas & Kilmann. (2025). Thomas-Kilmann conflict mode instrument. *TKI.* https://kilmanndiagnostics.com/overview-thomas-kilmann-conflict-mode-instrument-tki/
Wilmot, W. & Hocker, J. (2014). *Interpersonal conflict.* McGraw-Hill Companies.
Wolff, S. (2006). *Ethnic conflict: A global perspective.* Oxford University Press.
Wolynn, M. (2016). *It didn't start with you: How inherited family trauma shapes who we are and how to end the cycle.* Penguin Books.

Restorative Justice

Natella Malazoniia

Abstract This chapter explores the restorative justice paradigm as a distinct alternative to traditional retributive justice, providing a detailed examination of its philosophical foundations. It starts with a review of the complexity of defining restorative justice and then contrasts it with conventional punitive approaches, highlighting key differences in objectives and practices. The chapter also outlines the historical context and evolution of restorative justice, emphasizing the necessity of understanding its limitations and the potential for coexistence with traditional justice systems. By addressing these critical aspects, the chapter aims to present a comprehensive view of restorative justice as a viable response to wrongdoing. It underscores the benefits of this approach, which includes promoting healing for victims, fostering accountability among offenders, and restoring harmony within communities. The discussion emphasizes that restorative justice is not merely an alternative but can offer significant advantages in achieving more inclusive and meaningful resolutions to conflicts while also addressing the emotional and social needs that arise from criminal behaviour. Overall, the chapter seeks to enrich the dialogue surrounding justice and its multifaceted dimensions.

N. Malazoniia (✉)
University of Manitoba, Winnipeg, MB, Canada
e-mail: natella@mswpg.ca

L. E. Reimer and R. Jochelson (eds.), *The Other Side of the Bar*,
https://doi.org/10.1007/978-981-96-9748-9_3

Keywords Restorative justice · Accountability · Healing · Conflict · Community · Victim participation · Trust

Introduction

When someone's rights are violated, the resulting harm is never insignificant. Such violations undermine feelings of safety and trust and often have far-reaching consequences that require an appropriate response. There is a compelling need for justice and a fair process. This raises the question: what constitutes a proper response to wrongdoing?

Our current traditional justice system serves as the default means of addressing crimes, supported by a sophisticated set of norms tailored to each type of offence. It imposes punishments that are proportionate to the severity of the crime committed and guarantees the right to a fair trial. This system forms the fundamental foundation of public order, and it is difficult to imagine a justice system without courts and punishments. However, it is crucial to recognize that this form of justice is not as universal or inherent as it may seem. The foundations of the contemporary traditional justice system, characterized by an emphasis on formal court proceedings and state-administered penalties, began to take shape in Europe during the Medieval period. This historical development, while significant, occupies a relatively brief span within the broader context of human existence. What we today view as a fair process for resolving criminal conflicts arose from complex societal changes, including the decline of kinship-based connections and the rise of private property and individualism (Weitekamp, 2015). When affiliation with a tribe or a close-knit community shifted from being essential to optional, the process of conflict resolution evolved to address offences in a different manner. The influence of the community diminished, leading to scenarios where the individual who commits an offence may no longer be critical to the tribe's survival. Consequently, for the offender, the pursuit of forgiveness may lose its significance, particularly if the relationship lacks value. The state emerged as the primary guarantor of law and order, taking on a central role in upholding legal compliance and enforcing public norms. However, beneath this rationale, other factors may still hold importance for those directly involved in the conflict, which we will explore further in this chapter.

Approaches to justice have changed due to social system transformations. While the traditional justice system remains necessary, it does not impede the natural evolution of alternative conflict resolution methods or the ongoing search for better options. The overload of courts, the lengthy processes that leave victims sidelined, the overrepresentation of minorities in prisons, and the substantial costs associated with the administration of legal cases all highlight the need for alternatives.

The emergence of the restorative justice movement in the 1970s was inevitable as a response to the shortcomings of the conventional punitive justice system. It started as a movement to enhance victims' voices and humanize the justice system. In contrast to punitive justice, restorative justice prioritizes repairing damaged relationships and restoring peace. It offers a way to address conflicts involving the main stakeholders - the offender, victim, and community. Restorative justice represents a distinct paradigm not only in responding to crime but also in understanding the nature of crime and determining the necessary steps to address it. While it encompasses different values, principles, methods, and results, the current literature does not provide a comprehensive understanding of what restorative justice truly is, as it can be interpreted differently by different individuals (Miller & Blackler, 2016, pp. 77–91). It is better perceived as a philosophical concept with a set of pillars and principles that guide actions based on certain values, which can be employed in various methods and procedures.

This chapter explores what constitutes a restorative justice philosophical approach to resolving criminal conflicts. The chapter delves into the nature of conflict and crime, restorative justice principles, and its definition, then examines what represents the paradigm shift from traditional criminal justice system values. The roles of victims, offenders, and the community within the restorative justice process are discussed. To foster a deeper understanding of the concept, the history of restorative justice and an overview of the diversity of its forms are presented, and the key points of each process are discussed and the differences between them highlighted. Finally, the chapter assesses how this transformative approach can be further integrated into contemporary justice systems to create a more inclusive and humane response to crime.

Understanding Restorative Justice

Restorative justice expands upon the conventional understanding of crime, harm, and the resulting obligations. It goes beyond the structured court procedures centred on factual evidence. However, grasping the true essence of restorative justice presents a challenge due to its multifaceted nature without strict boundaries. Essentially, restorative justice embodies a paradigm and philosophical approach rooted in specific principles and concepts that can be employed in diverse conflict situations.

Psychologist Albert Eglash coined the term "restorative justice" in the late 1950s and outlined three types of criminal justice: retributive, distributive, and restorative (Gavrielides & Campbell, 2015). Retributive justice focuses on punishment with limited opportunities for the offender to participate in the process, leaving the victim sidelined. Distributive justice aims to apply therapeutic treatments to offenders. Restorative justice, however, is focused on repairing the harm caused by wrongful actions and encourages all parties to participate actively in the process.

Restorative justice is often associated with addressing criminal conflicts, but it extends beyond criminal conflict resolution methods. Its scope is not limited to criminal conflicts. Harm can take different forms and relate to various fields of law, such as labour law and torts. The applicability of restorative justice principles and methods can vary widely, from conflicts between private citizens to broader practices like the Truth and Reconciliation Commission in South Africa (Asmal, 2017, pp. 431–454). Because the concept of restorative justice lacks a rigid definition and scope, it is important to understand its key principles.

Dr. Howard Zehr, now the Director of the Zehr Institute for Restorative Justice, is widely regarded as "the grandfather of restorative justice" (Zehr Institute, 2018). Zehr began as a practitioner and theorist in restorative justice in the late 1970s at the foundational stage of the field. His work laid the groundwork for comprehending the fundamental principles of this concept. At the core of restorative justice lies the notion of repairing the harm that has been caused. It is a justice approach that seeks to address harm by engaging the primary stakeholders in meaningful dialogue. The objective is to attain a deeper understanding of the conflict and formulate suitable solutions that cater to the interests and needs of all involved parties. According to the philosophy of restorative justice, crime is not simply a violation of the law, it is, first and foremost, a violation of relationships (Zehr, 1990). Central to this approach is the repair of relationships that have been damaged by wrongdoing, accountability and the pursuit of amicable solutions to address the harm.

The principles of restorative justice can be summarized as follows: encouraging participation and striving to reach mutually acceptable agreements, working to repair the harm that has been done, encouraging accountability, reintegrating where there has been separation, and empowering the community and individuals to prevent future harm.

Thus, restorative justice is not merely a method or process of conflict resolution. The paradigm is a different perception of what crime or wrongful action is and what constitutes a proper response to it. Howard Zehr compares the restorative justice approach to conflict as a lens (Zehr, 1990) because the lens through which one perceives crime influences one's reaction to it. That is why it is important to ask the right questions and have certain perspectives in mind when approaching conflict. To make the conflict-resolution process truly restorative, those who have been involved in that conflict must be engaged with its resolution.

Understanding the impact of the incident on the parties involved and the wider community is crucial in identifying their needs and developing solutions to prevent similar situations in the future. Therefore, active participation of the individuals in the conflict resolution process is essential, as the primary harm caused is to their relationship, rights and liberties rather than solely to public order (Morris & Young, 2016, pp. 11–31).

In contrast to traditional justice, where the main role in the penal process is played by authorities, restorative justice emphasizes the importance of bringing affected individuals together to share their perspectives and work towards making amends. This significantly changes the role of the victim in the pursuit of justice. Victims finally have the opportunity to speak their voices, ask questions, influence the decision on what needs to be done to achieve justice and advocate for their interests and needs in the process. Importantly, through restorative justice processes, they can regain a sense of control over the justice process and find closure if they seek it.

The offender or accused is given the opportunity to meet their victims, express their perspective on the situation, and seek forgiveness. While some skeptics question the authenticity of such interactions, this process possesses significant power and can profoundly impact everyone involved. Engaging with the victim often fosters a strong sense of accountability for the offence committed. Numerous surveys on restorative justice highlight the challenges offenders face when confronting their victims, including the common fears they experience beforehand.

The community is a crucial stakeholder in the restorative justice process. Defining the community may not be straightforward, but it typically consists of individuals who are connected to the lives of the victim or offender and have been indirectly affected by the crime (Morris & Young, 2016, pp. 11–31). At the same time, volunteers who facilitate restorative justice processes sometimes can also represent the community and speak on their behalf. More commonly, family members are involved in resolving conflicts. The presence of the community is vital as it provides a broader perspective on the impact of wrongful actions and supports both the victim and the offender through the dispute-resolution process. It's important to acknowledge that when a violation occurs, it affects not only the immediate victim but also the broader community, creating a ripple effect of harm.

Therefore, restorative justice transforms the very core of the justice process. It does not presume what should be done when criminal conflict occurs and how to achieve justice. Instead, it provides an opportunity for the main stakeholders to be actively involved in the search for a suitable solution that could potentially satisfy all of them. Justice shifts from being an abstract category to something tangible and achievable because it brings satisfaction, from being state-oriented to people-oriented and from being about punishment to being about restoration.

The restorative process demonstrates its transformative power not only by allowing offenders to avoid the traditional criminal process and associated penalties but also by providing victims with the opportunity to engage in conflict resolution. Its true impact lies in the core belief of restorative justice that individuals are not solely defined by their actions. This approach recognizes that good people can make mistakes and poor decisions, and it takes into account the complexities of human nature and the circumstances surrounding an offence (Zehr, 1990). Emphasizing the importance of relationships, emotions, and community support, restorative justice empowers victims to have a voice, encourages offenders to seek forgiveness and accountability, and involves the community in the resolution process. This transformative approach shifts the focus from punishment to restoration, providing a platform for all stakeholders to actively participate in the pursuit of a just and fair outcome. By giving individuals a sense of control over the justice process and fostering a deeper understanding of the impact of wrongful actions, restorative justice offers a tangible and people-oriented path toward healing and resolution.

Paradigm Shift from Traditional Justice

To better comprehend restorative justice, it is crucial to compare it with the traditional punitive system. In his seminal work, "Conflict as Property" (Christie, 1977), Nils Christie argued that conflicts are often treated as the property of the state, which holds the authority to resolve them. This perspective may overlook the transformative potential inherent in conflicts, as they can provide valuable insights and different perspectives to those involved. He contended that when conflict resolution is left solely to professionals, the genuine value of conflicts as a tool for transformation is lost. Reflecting on this issue reveals that allowing the involved parties to resolve their conflicts can help them understand the real causes, identify their needs, recognize any obligations created, and develop solutions to prevent similar situations in the future (Christie, 1977). This approach not only aids in truly resolving the conflict but also enhances one's ability to navigate broader life challenges and improve connections.

In criminal disputes, it is often considered appropriate to transfer the responsibility of resolving the conflict to law enforcement, prosecutors, and judges. Criminal law is deemed a matter of public interest due to its inherent violation of state laws and perhaps the severity of actions. As the state is committed to respecting, protecting, and fulfilling human rights, it's natural for state authority to be involved in the traditional criminal process and to view any failure to protect someone's rights as its own. However, proponents of restorative justice argue that conflicts primarily affect individuals, and those individuals own the conflict and have the authority to engage in a process that will address their interests and needs first (Ashworth, 2017, pp. 179–196).

Both of these approaches have their merits and can be effective. The crucial question is not which approach is superior but rather which one is most suitable for a given situation. The two perspectives on understanding and responding to crime are not necessarily in opposition. Instead, they provide different tools for addressing wrongdoing.

To further explore these two paradigms of criminal conflict resolution, comparing the questions of each paradigm reflect the values and principles of each approach. According to Howard Zehr (1990), the pertinent questions to consider when harm has occurred within the framework of restorative justice include:

- Who has been affected?
- What are their needs?
- Whose obligations are involved?
- Who has a stake in this situation?
- What is the appropriate process to involve stakeholders in addressing the underlying causes and making amends?

Conversely, Zehr (1990) notes that a traditional retributive system of justice focuses on questions such as:

- What laws have been violated?
- Who is responsible?
- What punishment do the offender(s) deserve?

These questions illustrate that the two approaches to addressing crime differ not only in terms of who participates in conflict resolution and decision-making but also in their fundamental objectives.

Restorative justice strives to repair what has been damaged and heal emotional wounds. It promotes accountability without focusing on punishment. Instead, it aims to create opportunities for offenders to make amends and rectify their actions. The restorative justice process typically concludes with the establishment of an agreement among those involved, outlining the measures to address the harm and potentially prevent similar situations from occurring in the future. Often, this may involve paying restitution, completing community service hours, attending counselling, or engaging in anger management, among other options. A notable feature of these agreements is their potential for creativity as long as they reflect the offender's acknowledgment of responsibility for the harm caused and their commitment to pursuing restoration. This leads to a pertinent question: who determines whether the agreement is truly restorative and if the proposed actions are sufficient? A mediator or facilitator acts as a neutral party but cannot function as a judge to decide for the participants. Leaving this decision to the victim could disrupt the power dynamics inherent in the process. Thus, a valid question arises regarding who holds this authority.

There is no definitive answer to this, but since the power dynamics are relatively balanced among all participants, the responsibility for the restorative nature of the agreement lies with everyone involved. Furthermore, this agreement is typically submitted to a judge or crown, depending on the stage of the process, who will then approve or deny the written outcome.

In contrast, traditional punitive justice emphasizes determining guilt, collecting sufficient evidence to support that conclusion, and imposing punishment for the crime. This approach does not actively involve the victim and can be perceived as less human-centred, often leaning more toward retribution. It tends to lack opportunities for direct dialogue between the primary stakeholders of the conflict, overlooks the significance of relationships and healing, and is typically formal, strict and rigid. Traditional criminal justice operates on principles of fear and power, which come into play when compliance is not observed. The ultimate decision-makers in such cases are judges and juries, with juries responsible for determining guilt or innocence based on the evidence presented, while judges impose sentences according to legal guidelines. In this framework, public order is generally considered the main victim. Viewed as a violation of the law and a challenge to established authority, crime will inevitably lead to negative life-long consequences for the offender, including a criminal record and various difficulties in addition to the punishment imposed by the court.

Although the restorative justice approach is often employed in cases involving youth offenders or those who have committed less severe crimes, traditional justice continues to be the predominant method for resolving criminal conflicts. Some jurisdictions have demonstrated the effectiveness of applying restorative justice in more serious cases, including homicide; however, such applications remain relatively uncommon and are often viewed as radical examples, albeit indicative of the potential for broader implementation.

The comparison between these two paradigms reveals their fundamentally opposing approaches to addressing wrongdoing, yet they currently coexist, supplementing each other and indicating a gradual shift in the understanding of criminal justice and fair processes. Restoration and retribution, though leading to different outcomes, both represent forms of justice or methods for resolving criminal conflict. Further exploration of the historical context will provide deeper insights into the dynamics between these two concepts and highlight the values of restorative justice, as well as the preconditions for its emergence.

Historical Context and Evolution

Navigating the historical context of restorative justice presents considerable challenges, primarily due to its inherently flexible and adaptable nature. Broadening the conceptual framework beyond the specific terminology of "Restorative Justice" reveals that the roots of such ideas can be traced back to pre-state societies. The concepts of restitution, reparation, compensation, reconciliation, atonement, redress, community service, mediation and indemnification all can reflect restorative justice principles before the term restorative justice was invented and popularized.

Some scholars advocate for recognizing the existence of restorative justice paradigms prior to the advent of formal state structures, with particular emphasis on acephalous (non-state) societies (Weitekamp, 2015). In these societies, characterized by their lack of hierarchical authority, members often resolved conflicts through means such as blood revenge, retribution, ritual satisfaction, or restitution.

While blood revenge is included as a method of conflict resolution, it functioned as a last resort in instances of homicide and did not dominate the landscape of dispute resolution at that time. Retribution, reminiscent of contemporary, traditional criminal justice systems, served as an effective mechanism for dispute resolution wherein offenders were expected to undergo a form of punishment in relation to the harm inflicted upon the victim. In some cases, this could entail the victim or their kin retaliating against the offender, thereby failing to achieve a genuine resolution to the conflict.

Other dispute-resolution methods, such as ritual satisfaction and restitution, embody more peaceful dimensions and closely align with contemporary restorative justice practices. This approach seeks to hold marginal deviants accountable while preserving social cohesion and community bonds. In contexts of conflict, resolution methods that reflect restorative justice principles were predominantly used. Practices like restitution and ritual satisfaction emphasized the accountability of the offender and their responsibility to make amends. In the absence of formal legal frameworks, resolving disputes depended on the satisfaction of the victim or their family. This early model of societal functioning was fundamentally based on recognizing the intrinsic value of each tribe or clan member, their designated roles, and the interconnectedness of their lives. The small size of clan groups and the relational dynamics within such social structures significantly influenced the dispute-resolution mechanisms of the time, highlighting the critical importance of maintaining social cohesion within these groups.

Restitution for harm inflicted on victims was a key aspect of restorative justice practices before reforms led to a more centralized justice system. As Weitekamp (Weitekamp, 2015) insightfully noted, the emergence of a clear central authority representing state power resulted in victims being sidelined in the resolution of criminal conflicts, with the interests of the state taking precedence over those of the individuals who were harmed. This shift marked a transition from focusing on the needs of victims and affected individuals to prioritizing the interests of the ruler and public order. As a result, restitution became viewed not as a means of rectifying the wrongs done to victims but rather as a form of punishment imposed by the state on behalf of the ruler, with payments directed to the state's treasury. By the end of the twelfth century, the state had taken control of criminal law (Weitekamp, 2015).

While the restorative justice practises in pre-state societies may not fully encompass the contemporary understanding of the concept, the payment of restitution to victims, alongside a focus on their satisfaction and needs related to the harm endured, can indeed be viewed as a fundamental foundation and historical precursor to the restorative justice movement. A thorough analysis of restorative justice practices across the globe and over different time periods is beyond the scope of this chapter. However, it is important to note that restorative justice approaches and principles are frequently utilized in tribes and communities where interpersonal ties are strong, and relationships within the group are highly valued.

The evolution of societal structures and the increasing involvement of state entities in resolving criminal disputes have led to a significant shift in how these conflicts are addressed. This transition has resulted in a reduced emphasis on restorative justice principles and the establishment of a more rigid traditional justice system. The recent rise of what is now known as "restorative justice" can be seen as a byproduct of social movements advocating for civil rights and women's rights that emerged in the 1970s (Ptacek, 2015). This movement sought to promote antiracist practices within the United States justice system, amplifying the voices of victims who had been overlooked and addressing the broader crisis within the court system.

One of the first instances of using the restorative justice concept in a modern era was a 1974 case of vandalism in Kitchener, Ontario. Yantzi was a probation officer working with the Mennonite Central Committee, a Christian organization with a tradition of working on peace and justice issues. Confronted with two teenagers who had vandalized a number of homes, two churches, and a business during a night of drinking, Yantzi had a suggestion: "Wouldn't it be neat for these offenders to meet the victims?" (Ptacek, 2015, p.144). The young offenders met with the victims of their crimes and took responsibility for their actions. They were fined, placed on probation, and ordered to make restitution to all they had harmed. The Mennonite Central Committee, encouraged by this case, created victim-offender reconciliation programs in Canada and the United States (Ptacek, 2015, p.144).

This notable case, coinciding with the work of Zehr and Christie, marked the beginning of the restorative justice movement in Canada and the US, igniting the creation of programs and research focused on exploring restorative justice as a viable approach to resolving criminal conflicts.

Forms of Restorative Justice Practices

The philosophy of restorative justice offers a distinct perspective on the nature of wrongdoing, its implications, and appropriate responses. This theoretical foundation is reflected in various well-established practices, the most prominent of which include Victim-Offender Mediation, Family Group Conferences, and Peacemaking Circles. Among these, Victim-Offender Mediation stands out as the most widely used and recognized form of restorative justice.

Victim-offender mediation (VOM), also referred to as the Victim Offender Reconciliation Program (VORP), is a structured process in which trained mediators facilitate discussions between victims and offenders of a certain crime. The primary objective is to promote a deeper understanding of the incident, including the events or circumstances that led to it, its impact on the parties involved, and the wider community. Additionally, the process aims to explore possible ways to address the harm that occurred.

Participants are encouraged to discuss steps that can be taken to restore the situation as closely as possible to its state before the harm. If the mediation is successful, the mediators will draft an agreement outlining the steps the offender must take to rectify the consequences of their wrongdoing. Typically, once these steps are completed, the charges will be stayed, allowing the offender to avoid a criminal record. However, some Victim-Offender Mediations (VOMs) occur after sentencing and do not offer the possibility of avoiding a criminal record. In cases of pre-charge or post-charge diversion, should the offender fail to fulfill the agreed-upon actions, the traditional criminal process will resume, and the case will proceed to court. This same outcome will occur if an agreement cannot be reached or if the process does not adhere to the principles of restorative justice.

The individual responsible for facilitating the process in alignment with restorative justice principles is the mediator. Often trained volunteers from the community, mediators do not engage in judgment or fact-finding. Their role is not to determine who is right or wrong but to foster a safe environment that encourages open dialogue regarding the incident and its resolution. The confidentiality of the process ensures the safety of all participants involved, meaning that nothing said during the proceedings can be used against them.

Mediators are dedicated to upholding neutrality and impartiality throughout the process. They utilize active listening techniques and strategic questioning to encourage progress. Victim-offender mediation is a more informal process than a court hearing, involving a conversation between mediators, the victim and the offender. In certain instances, both the victim and the offender may also bring a support person, which is generally permitted in the proceedings. This is also often a requirement in cases involving youth offenders.

The stages of the process usually follow the next logic:

- Pre-session considerations;
- Stage 1 Introduction;
- Stage 2 The narrative (storytelling);
- Stage 3 Exploration of the impact;
- Stage 4 Agreement.

Pre-session considerations for mediators typically involve familiarizing themselves with the specifics of the case, consulting with the caseworker overseeing the file, and facilitating discussions among co-mediators if they are working together. During the introduction stage, mediators provide an overview of the restorative justice process, establish ground rules, and set a positive tone for the meeting. This is followed by the storytelling stage, in which the victim generally begins by recounting the events of the incident in question. This allows both the mediators and the offender to gain valuable insight into the victim's perspective. The offender then shares their understanding of the incident and the factors that contributed to it. With the mediators' assistance, they work together to develop a comprehensive understanding of each other's viewpoints. The process then transitions to exploring the impact of the incident on the victim, the offender, and potentially others involved. This exploration aims to identify their needs and develop a suitable solution to address the consequences of the harm caused, which is the primary focus of the Agreement stage. Once a solution is reached and the agreement is signed, it is submitted to the relevant authority for approval, followed by a period of waiting to see if the offender fulfills all the steps outlined in the agreement.

The main distinction between Victim-Offender Mediation and other forms of restorative justice is the number of people involved in the process. The credit for the popularity of Victim-Offender Mediation can be taken by the convenience of not involving a large number of people in the process. Unlike Family Group Conferences or Peacemaking Circles, it usually involves just a victim, an offender and one or two mediators. It makes the process easier to organize and administer.

The Family Group Conference is a form of restorative justice that originated from traditions in New Zealand. This practice is rooted in the conflict resolution methods of the Māori people, which inspired New Zealand's legal system to adopt a different approach to addressing criminal conflicts involving youth (Maxwell et al., 2006). Over time, these practices have expanded beyond New Zealand to countries such as Australia, England and Wales, Canada, Ireland, Singapore, and others. The Family Group Conference bears some resemblance to the Victim-Offender Mediation process but typically focuses on cases involving youth offenders, with significant involvement from family members. In this process, the Facilitator acts as a manager, guiding the proceedings without participating in the substantive discussions.

The Conference usually follows a similar logical structure, beginning with the offender explaining the event that led to the meeting, followed by the victim's account and then contributions from other attendees. As the discussion progresses, it shifts towards examining how the harm has impacted everyone involved, ultimately leading to the development of appropriate solutions that are documented in an agreement. In certain instances, the process may also include participation from police officers, lawyers, probation officers, and social workers (Maxwell et al., 2006).

Peacemaking Circles represent restorative justice practices inspired by Indigenous traditions worldwide. These circles embody restorative justice principles by engaging the broader community in discussions that extend beyond the immediate parties to the conflict and their family members. Often, Peacemaking Circles include a community representative with strong ties to those affected, along with support workers, lawyers, police officers, and colleagues and friends (Stuart & Pranis, 2005). A distinctive feature of Peacemaking Circles is their emphasis on community involvement. It aimed at addressing the harm while fostering healing and creating robust support for both the victim and the offender. This approach encourages open dialogue and helps achieve restorative outcomes through a transformative and meaningful process led by the keeper – a person who manages the process.

All of these practices share common elements and are anchored in the same principles, all guided by a central idea: addressing harm, healing, and restoring balance with a strong emphasis on needs and emotions—an inherent aspect of the human experience. Inspired by Indigenous cultures, these processes focus on the primary stakeholders in conflict: the victim, the offender, and the community. The underlying belief of this concept is that open dialogue among these individuals can spark transformation, ultimately leading to peace and the restoration of damaged relationships.

Legal Framework and Limitations

Criminal conflicts represent a sensitive issue that often evokes fear when discussing alternative approaches to handling them. The traditional retributive system operates on a foundation of punishment and fear, neglecting to delve into individuals' feelings and needs and providing little opportunity for sharing personal narratives. The system primarily seeks answers to three key questions (Zehr, 1990):

- What laws have been violated?
- Who is responsible?
- What punishment should the offender(s) receive?

This traditional system is rigid, straightforward, and clear-cut. Criminal codes outline specific offences; once a person is convicted of a crime, punishment is swiftly administered, thus achieving the goals of the conventional criminal justice framework.

In contrast, discussions about restorative justice are inherently more complex, especially when considering the limitations of this model. The limitations of restorative justice can be examined from various perspectives. One key question that arises when discussing these limitations is: which cases are suitable for resolution through restorative justice programs?

Globally, restorative justice practices exhibit many similarities, albeit with some minor variations. For instance, in Canada, there are no specific limits on the types of cases eligible for referral to restorative justice programs, nor is there a time restriction on when such referrals can be made. Alternative measures can be pursued at any stage of the criminal process, provided they do not conflict with societal protection and the individual does not deny their participation or involvement in the offence. This approach allows for decisions to be made on a case-by-case basis regarding which matters are suitable for referral to particular programs while also helping to manage the case flow according to the capabilities of organizations involved in court diversion programs. In Canada (CRCVC, 2022), restorative justice can only take place when:

- An offender admits guilt, accepts responsibility for their actions and agrees to participate in the program;
- The victim of the crime freely agrees to participate in the program without feeling pressured to do so; and
- Trained facilitators are available in the community and a restorative program is in place.

Norway and Belgium adopt a similar methodology, permitting victim-offender mediation (VOM) and other restorative justice practices at any stage of the criminal process, irrespective of the nature of the offence (Scottish Government, 2019). Historically, in Belgium, there was a limit that only victims could initiate the restorative justice process, but this restriction has since changed, and now offenders initiate the restorative process. In contrast, some countries, like Ukraine, impose limitations on restorative justice practices, such as VOM, allowing their use only in cases where the offence carries a maximum prison sentence of five years.

This examination of the restrictions on restorative justice practices highlights its promising potential in resolving criminal conflicts. Legislators, in most cases, appear reluctant to impose limitations on the types of offences eligible for mediation or the stages at which the restorative process can occur. However, the frequency of using restorative justice processes in more severe cases proves that the restorative justice approach can not be universally applied, and cases that involve attempts at homicide, sexual assaults, or murder are rarely referred to restorative justice programs.

There are several concerns regarding the implementation of restorative justice, including the potential for revictimization, whether offenders will truly take accountability for their actions, the level of preparation required, and the overall effectiveness of the process in promoting restoration. However, it is important to acknowledge the existence of programs in Canada that utilize restorative justice approaches for such crimes. For instance, the Region Community Justice Initiatives Association in Langley, British Columbia (CJIBC), fosters peacemaking and conflict resolution within the community through mediation and conciliation techniques. Similarly, the Collaborative Justice Program in Ottawa (CJP) employs restorative justice methods to demonstrate how a comprehensive approach to addressing serious crimes can offer a more satisfying form of justice for victims, offenders, and the community as a whole.

Research shows that despite the restorative justice movement amplifying victims' voices in the criminal process, quite commonly, victims do not want to take part (Reeves, 1989). This brings another question about the limits of restorative justice and the feasibility of implementing these practices in cases where victims are unwilling to participate. The question poses a philosophical consideration of the opportunity for restorative justice to happen without one party's desire to be involved. Should justice depend on the willingness of the victim to participate in the process? Does this make the dynamic surrounding restorative justice practices unevenly imbalanced or should restorative justice happen no matter what the victim decides? Recent practices demonstrate that restorative justice can occur between offenders and mediators without the victim's presence or participation. This approach is commonly known as Restorative Action. Another way restorative justice can be implemented is through the involvement of surrogate victims. These are individuals who have experienced similar crimes and share attributes with the actual victim of the crime, and they are willing to take part in the process.

When considering the benefits of restorative justice practices, it is essential to acknowledge the limitations regarding their application in certain criminal cases, as well as the potential negative consequences, such as victims' revictimization or a lack of accountability from offenders. The application of restorative justice in Canada and around the world illustrates its potential as an alternative method for resolving particular criminal conflicts. While there are ongoing discussions about the limitations of restorative justice, it continues to evolve as a movement, practice, and philosophical approach.

Conclusion

Conflicts are an inevitable aspect of human existence, often accompanied by harm. It is essential to recognize that there are alternative approaches to resolving conflicts beyond traditional justice, even in sensitive areas such as criminal matters. Restorative justice presents a distinct perspective on crime and what is required to address it. Rather than offering a definitive solution, it provides a conceptual framework that unites various methods and practices to explore and respond to these complex questions.

The roots of restorative justice practices can be traced back to early human societies and kin-based tribes, where each member was deemed important and valuable. This understanding greatly influenced the conflict resolution process, fostering a supportive and humane environment and providing opportunities for individuals to reintegrate into the community after accepting accountability. The modern restorative justice movement emerged in the 1970s and has since evolved globally, facilitating opportunities for victims and offenders to meet and engage in conflict resolution with the help of trained volunteers or professionals.

There is a wide array of restorative justice forms, with the most common being Victim-Offender Mediation, Family Group Conferences, and Peacemaking Circles. While these forms typically share similar procedural logic, goals, and principles, they vary in terms of the number of participants involved and the techniques employed.

These practices do more than resolve individual disputes—they embody relational justice, where the process itself becomes a site of dignity, mutual recognition, and respect. Rather than treating procedures as mere tools for efficiency, restorative justice views them as relationships in action, encouraging participants to see and hear one another fully. This orientation ensures that those affected by harm are not reduced to legal categories but are instead invited into meaningful processes that affirm their humanity and interdependence. In this way, the law becomes a medium for recognition, not erasure.

Moreover, restorative approaches compel us to engage in epistemic repair by challenging dominant narratives about justice and harm. These processes create space for marginalized voices, often excluded or undervalued in conventional legal systems, to contribute their lived knowledge. This not only exposes how structural exclusion persists under the guise of neutrality but also opens the door to transformative practice—an invitation to reshape legal and communal norms. By fostering participation, accountability, and trust, restorative justice expands our understanding of law from a system of rules to a dynamic field of relationships capable of healing and transformation.

Restorative justice has demonstrated its effectiveness as a method for resolving criminal conflicts, although limitations remain. The appropriateness of applying restorative justice processes to serious crimes, such as murder or sexual assault, continues to be a subject of debate. Nonetheless, some programs have shown that restorative justice can hold significant potential in these challenging contexts. In this way, restorative justice enhances our understanding of conflict and justice, rendering the process humane, realistic, and effective.

Questions

1. Critically examine the core principles that define a restorative justice approach. How do these principles challenge traditional notions of justice?
2. In what fundamental ways does restorative justice diverge from retributive justice models, and what are the broader social implications of embracing one approach over the other?
3. Explore the various forms that restorative justice processes can take. How do different cultural, legal, or institutional contexts shape these practices?
4. Analyze the limitations and critiques of restorative justice. Under what circumstances might restorative practices fall short of delivering meaningful justice for all parties involved?

Glossary

Accountability: A core principle of restorative justice involving the offender taking responsibility for their actions and their impact. Engagement with the victim often fosters a strong sense of accountability. In pre-state societies, practices like restitution and ritual satisfaction emphasized the accountability of the offender and their responsibility to make amends.

Community: A crucial stakeholder in the restorative justice process, typically consisting of individuals connected to the lives of the victim or offender who have been indirectly affected by the crime. It provides a broader perspective on the impact of wrongful actions and supports both the victim and the offender. It is also empowered to prevent future harm.

Conflict: Resulting from violations of rights, conflict causes harm and undermines feelings of safety and trust. In traditional justice, conflict is often treated as the property of the state. Restorative justice proponents argue that conflicts primarily affect individuals, who own the conflict and have the authority to address their interests and needs.

Distributive Justice: One type of criminal justice that aims to apply therapeutic treatments to offenders.

Family Group Conferences: A form of restorative justice inspired by Māori traditions in New Zealand, typically focusing on cases involving youth offenders with significant involvement from family members. It includes contributions from the offender, victim, and other attendees, explores the impact of the harm, and develops solutions documented in an agreement.

Harm: The negative consequences resulting from wrongful actions or violations of rights, which undermines feelings of safety and trust. Restorative justice views crime primarily as a violation of relationships that causes harm. Repairing harm is a core notion and principle of restorative justice.

Healing: A key objective and benefit of restorative justice, aiming to address the emotional and social needs that arise from criminal behaviour. Restorative justice strives to heal emotional wounds and provides a path toward healing for victims.

Mediator: An individual, often a trained volunteer from the community, who facilitates the Victim-Offender Mediation process. Mediators do not engage in judgment or fact-finding but foster a safe environment for dialogue, upholding neutrality and impartiality.

Paradigm Shift: Restorative justice represents a distinct way of perceiving crime and determining the necessary steps to address it, offering a different perspective compared to the traditional criminal justice system.

Peacemaking Circles: Restorative justice practices inspired by Indigenous traditions, engaging the broader community beyond the immediate parties and their families. They emphasize community involvement to address harm, foster healing, and create support for both the victim and the offender.

Repairing Harm: A central tenet of restorative justice, focusing on taking action to address the negative consequences caused by wrongdoing and restoring the situation as closely as possible to its state before the harm occurred.

Restitution: A practice involving compensation or payment to victims for the harm inflicted. It was a key aspect of conflict resolution in pre-state societies and is often included as part of agreements in modern restorative justice processes.

Restorative Action: A method of implementing restorative justice that involves offenders meeting with mediators when the victim is unwilling to participate.

Restorative Justice: A paradigm and philosophical approach that serves as a distinct alternative to traditional justice. It focuses on repairing the harm caused by wrongful actions by engaging the primary stakeholders—victim, offender, and community—in meaningful dialogue to understand the conflict, identify needs, and formulate suitable solutions. It is rooted in principles such as repairing harm, accountability, participation, reintegration, and community empowerment.

Retributive Justice: One type of criminal justice that focuses on punishment for the offense committed. It operates with limited opportunities for offender participation and typically leaves the victim sidelined. It is characteristic of contemporary traditional criminal justice systems.

Stakeholders: The main individuals or groups involved in a conflict and affected by it. In restorative justice, the primary stakeholders are the victim, the offender, and the community. Active participation of stakeholders is essential for resolving the conflict.

Surrogate victims: Individuals who have experienced crimes similar to the one in question and share attributes with the actual victim. They are willing to participate in a restorative process when the actual victim is unwilling or unable to do so.

Traditional Justice (or Conventional Punitive Justice): The default justice system that addresses crimes primarily by focusing on violations of law, determining responsibility (guilt), and imposing punishment. It emphasizes formal court proceedings and state-administered penalties, with less active involvement of the victim compared to restorative justice. Public order is generally considered the main victim.

Trust: A feeling undermined by the violation of rights that requires an appropriate justice response.

Victim-Offender Mediation (VOM) / Victim Offender Reconciliation Program (VORP): The most widely used form of restorative justice, a structured process where trained mediators facilitate discussions between victims and offenders to promote understanding of the incident and explore ways to address the harm.

Competing Interests The author has no conflicts of interest to declare that are relevant to the content of this chapter.

References

Asmal, K. (2017). Truth, reconciliation and justice: The South African experience in perspective. In D. Roche (Ed.), *Restorative justice* (pp. 431–454). Taylor & Francis.

Ashworth, A. (2017). Responsibilities, rights and restorative justice. In D. Roche (Ed.), *Restorative justice* (pp. 179–196). Taylor & Francis.

Canadian Resource Centre for Victims of Crime. (2022). *Restorative justice*. https://crcvc.ca/wp-content/uploads/2021/09/Restorative-Justice_DISCLAIMER_Revised-July-2022_FINAL.pdf

Christie, N. (1977). Conflict as property. *The British Journal of Criminology, 17*(1), 1–15.

Collaborative Justice Program. (n.d.). *About*. https://www.collaborativejustice.ca/en/about

Community Justice Initiatives. (n.d.). *Home*. https://cjibc.org

Gavrielides, T., & Campbell, T. (2015). Restorative justice: Ideals and realities. *Routledge*. https://doi.org/10.4324/9781315264868

Maxwell, G., Morris, A., & Hennessey, H. (2006). *Restorative justice and practices in New Zealand: Towards a restorative society*.

Miller, S., & Blackler, J. (2016). Restorative justice: Retribution, confession and shame. In H. Strang & J. Braithwaite (Eds.), *Restorative justice: Philosophy to practice* (pp. 77–91). Routledge.

Morris, A., & Young, W. (2016). Reforming criminal justice: The potential of restorative justice. In H. Strang & J. Braithwaite (Eds.), *Restorative justice: Philosophy to practice* (pp. 11–31). Routledge.

Ptacek, J. (2015). Resisting co-optation: Social movements and restorative justice. In D. Sullivan & L. Tifft (Eds.), *Handbook of restorative justice: A global perspective*. Routledge.

Reeves, H. (1989). The victim support perspective. In M. Wright & B. Galaway (Eds.), *Mediation and criminal justice: Victims, offenders and community* (pp. 44–56). Sage.

Scottish Government. (2019, May 3). Rapid evidence review: The uses of restorative justice. https://www.gov.scot/publications/rapid-evidence-review-uses-restorative-justice/pages/3/

Stuart, B., & Pranis, K. (2005). *Peacemaking circles: From crime to community* (1st Ed.). Routledge.

Weitekamp, E. G. M. (2015). The history of restorative justice. In D. Sullivan & L. Tifft (Eds.), *Handbook of restorative justice: A global perspective*. Routledge.

Zehr, H. (1990). *Changing lenses: A new focus for crime and justice.* Herald Press.

Zehr Institute for Restorative Justice. (2018). https://zehr-institute.org/what-is-rj/

Condolence Ceremonies, Council Meetings, and Conflict Resolution

Daniel Diamond

Abstract The Haudenosaunee Great Law of Peace is a peace treaty, a constitutional agreement, an expression of reconciliation, and a model for distinct nations to live in peace and cooperation. Under the Great Law, the Haudenosaunee utilize Condolence ceremonies and council meetings to resolve conflicts at the individual, societal, and international levels. This chapter explores the use of Condolence ceremonies and council meetings in interactions with the British Crown and Canadian state. First, the form and function of Condolence Ceremonies and council meetings are outlined. Second, the centrality of Condolence Ceremonies and council meetings to the the Silver Covenant Chain relationship between the British Crown and the Haudenosaunee is established. Finally, through an examination of the *R. c. Montour* (2023) decision, the force of the Silver Covenant Chain relationship in contemporary Canadian Common law is contextualized before reflecting on the wider implications of the decision to Canadian lawyers.

Keywords Indigenous Law · Conflict resolution · Legal history · Treaties

D. Diamond (✉)
University of Manitoba, Winnipeg, Canada
e-mail: daniel.diamond@umanitoba.ca

L. E. Reimer and R. Jochelson (eds.), *The Other Side of the Bar*,
https://doi.org/10.1007/978-981-96-9748-9_4

Introduction

The Haudenosaunee Great Law of Peace is a peace treaty, a constitutional agreement, an expression of reconciliation, and a model for distinct nations to live in peace and cooperation. This chapter will explore two conflict resolution mechanisms associated with the Great Law of Peace—the Condolence ceremony and council meetings.[1] These practices are not merely historical artifacts. Indeed, Condolence ceremonies and council meetings continue to animate Haudenosaunee conflict resolution practices. Examination of Council meetings and Condolence Ceremonies is relevant to law students for two reasons. First, understanding the significance and processes of council meetings and Condolence ceremonies provides important insight into the Haudenosaunee legal system. Knowledge of Indigenous legal systems and cultural competency are essential skills for Canadian lawyers. Second, and more specifically, consideration of Condolence ceremonies and council meetings provides insight into the broader principles that guide Haudenosaunee peacemaking, negotiation, and conflict resolution.

Section two briefly outlines the creation of the Great Law of Peace, and the function of Condolence ceremonies and council meetings in the Haudenosaunee Confederacy. Section three traces the international extension of Condolence ceremonies and council meetings to settlers through the Silver Covenant Chain relationship. Section four contextualizes the significance of the Silver Covenant Chain relationship and its associated conflict resolution mechanisms in contemporary Canadian Common law through an examination of the *R. c.* Montour (2023) decision, before reflecting on the wider implications of the decision to Canadian law and Canadian lawyers.

The Great Law of Peace, Condolence Ceremonies, and Council Meetings

It is difficult to pinpoint the exact date of the creation of the Great Law of Peace and the Haudenosaunee Confederacy. It is estimated that the Confederacy was established between 1400 and 1600 (Williams, 2018,

[1] Haudenosaunee translates to "People of the Longhouse". The Haudenosaunee sometimes refer to themselves as "The Six Nations".

p. 79–80).[2] While many non-Indigenous scholars “have been fascinated with the question of the date of the creation of the Great Law and the League it brought together [,] [t] he Haudenosaunee do not share that concern. For them, it has been enough that it existed long ago, before the arrival of the Europeans, and has continued to exist ever since” (p. 78). The creation of the confederacy, in highly simplified terms, is as follows.[3]

A man who became known as The Peacemaker was born in a time characterized by “cycles of war, bloodshed, and revenge so dark and deep that nobody could remember how, when or why they had begun” (Williams, 2018, p. 167). Katheryn Muller describes this as a period of “death and disorder [that] raged through the forests and along the rivers of what we now know as New York State and Ontario. Warriors wreaked havoc by burning villages and massacring the young and old alike, and the people feared they would never experience peace again” (Muller, 2008, p. 21). In an attempt to end the cycles of violence, the Peacemaker set out to unite the five “warring nations Mohawk, Oneida, Onondaga, Cayuga, and Seneca peoples together in a Confederacy founded upon the principles of peace, power, and good minds” (p. 21). In pursuit of this mission, the Peacemaker encountered many individuals stricken by anger, grief, and a desire for revenge and retribution. In each of his interactions with these individuals, the Peacemaker spread a message of peace, power and righteousness, and emphasized the importance of respect, alliance, and consensus building (Williams, 2018).

Ultimately, the Peacemaker was successful in uniting the five (now six) nations together under the Haudenosaunee confederacy and the Great Law of Peace. Two conflict resolution mechanisms associated with the Great Law of Peace and the Haudenosaunee Confederacy are discussed

[2] The Five nations of the Confederacy at the time of establishment were the Mohawk, Oneida, Onondaga, Cayuga, and Seneca. Later, the Tuscarora were incorporated into the confederacy in 1722. This is why the Confederacy is now often referred to as the ‘Six Nations’. See Hatton, H. (2019). Narrating Sovereignty: the covenant chain in intercultural diplomacy. *Journal of Early American History*, *9*(2–3), 118–144, p. 4.

[3] It is not within the scope of this chapter to provide a fulsome description of the creation of the Great Law of Peace. For a more fulsome account, see generally: Williams, K. P. (2018). *Kayanerenkó: wa: The Great Law of peace*. University of Manitoba Press. pp. 145–270; Muller, K. V. (2008) *Holding Hands with Wampum: Haudenosaunee Council Fires from the Great Law of Peace to Contemporary Relationships with the Canadian State* [Doctoral dissertation, Queens University] pp. 21–59; Lemlin. R. H. (1996) *Social Movements and the Great Law of Peace in Askwesasne* [Doctoral dissertation, University of Ottawa] pp. 20–52.

here: Condolence ceremonies, and council meetings. While Condolence ceremonies and council meetings can be conceptualized as distinct, the two are inextricably linked and interrelated. Council meetings often begin with a Condolence ceremony.

The Condolence Ceremony

The Condolence ceremony has been utilized since the creation of the Haudenosaunee Confederacy and is still in use today. The first Condolence ceremony was conducted by the Peacemaker and Hiawatha. Hiawatha was a man who had lived among the Onondagas and had moved to live amongst the Mohawks. Hiawatha underwent a series of personal hardships and was stricken with grief (Williams, 2018, p. 191). When the Peacemaker encountered Hiawatha, he quickly realized that Hiawatha "could not condole himself" (p. 201). He required assistance, and "[t]he path to restoring the rational mind was a deliberate, structured, deeply caring and compassionate ceremony, a ritual of both a spiritual and legal character" (p. 201). Here, the Peacemaker used "white deerskin to wipe the tears from the eyes, the white eagle feather to remove the dust from the ears, [and] the white or clear water to remove the obstruction from the throat" (p. 205). Afterwards, Hiawatha could see, listen, and speak clearly. Each subsequent Condolence ceremony is a symbolic re-enactment of the first Condolence performed by the Peacemaker and Hiawatha (p. 202).

The Condolence ceremony is designed to recognize the humanity and acknowledge the losses of the recipient (Williams, 2018, p. 205).[4] For individuals, the Condolence ceremony is designed to heal the pain, grief, and suffering of a person after they have experienced a loss, no matter

[4] For more on the condolence ceremony see generally, Pomedli, M. M. (1995). Eitheenth-Century Treaties: Amended Iroquois Condolence Rituals. *American Indian Quarterly* 19(3), 319–339; Foley, D. (2010). Iroquois Mourning and Condolence Installation Rituals: A Pattern of Social Integration and Continuity", in, Patrick, C. S. (Ed.), *Preserving Tradition and Understanding the Past: Papers from the Conference on Iroquois Research, 2001–2005* (pp. 25–34). The New York State Education Department; Johnson, L. (2004). *The Covenant Chain of Peace: Metaphor and Religious Thought in Seventeenth Century Haudenosaunee Council Oratory* [Doctoral dissertation, McGill University] pp. 47–53; Tahsuda, J. (1997). Twenty-First Century Wampum: The Use of Iroquois Diplomatic Protocols in Aboriginal Land Claim Negotiations. *Thomas L. Rev.*, *10*, pp. 154–155.

how great—and restore them to a good mind. On a national level, the condolence is used to heal a nation from the grief and suffering experienced after the death of a leader. This is accomplished by "peacefully raising up a new leader in his or her place" (Dragone, 2021, p. 154). The commonality between both uses of the Condolence ceremony is the conscious use of a compassionate act, designed to "raise up the minds of the people" (Williams, 2018, p. 7). Ultimately, this is because an individual's "mind must be working properly and rationally" (p. 7), in order accept peace.

The most important point for our purposes, is that the Condolence ceremony is a long-established conflict resolution practice utilized by the Haudenosaunee. The ceremonies are designed to promote peace and cooperation amongst groups of people who previously, may have experienced periods of mutual violence. The goal, is to raise up the minds of those who are grieving, recognize their humanity, and acknowledge the losses they have experienced, so that all the parties can think and behave rationally.

As I have shown, the Condolence ceremony is an important mechanism for conflict resolution under Haudenosaunee law. Moreover, as I will demonstrate in section III, the Condolence ceremony is not an insular practice, but rather, an essential element of Haudenosaunee international diplomacy. These diplomatic protocols were taken up and utilized by the English in their attempts to secure and maintain military and trade alliances with the Six Nations during the early and middle encounter periods.

Council Meetings

Council meetings are important for the functioning of the Haudenosaunee Confederacy because peaceful and positive relationships "[need] to be frequently revisited and renewed" (Hatton 2019, p. 4). Council meetings support the maintenance of these relationships by providing a formal venue for negotiation and consensus building (p. 4).[5] Ultimately, this is because within the Haudenosaunee confederacy, each nation remains distinct and independent whilst simultaneously forming a

[5] It is important to note that Council meetings were not merely diplomatic forums. They are also a form of renewal and affirmation of kinship ties amongst and across the nations.

part of the larger interdependent confederacy. In simple terms, council meetings facilitate collective decision-making and conflict resolution amongst and between the member nations.

Council-meetings are not mere gatherings, but rather, meetings that follow a well-defined, structured format that facilitates collective decision-making and peaceful resolution of conflicts (*R. c. Montour*, 2023, p. 10). As explained by Williams,

> The process of a Haudenosaunee council [is] carefully designed to promote consensus and avoid confrontation … Council opens with everyone giving thanks together. The opening words of thanksgiving are delivered by an Onondaga chief. As the speaker completes each part of the speech, ending it with 'and so our minds are one', all the men present indicate their agreement with 'yoh!' or 'tho!'" (p. 281).

The Haudenosaunee constitutional system is grounded in a spirit of "contribution and accommodation. Opinions, when they are spoken openly, are not to be individual opinions but to reflect the thinking of groups of people, this prevents council from descending into personal attacks, and it prevents individuals from domineering by the force of their personalities" (pp. 283–285). Relatedly, the goal in a Haudenosaunee council meeting is always to create agreement, unity and consensus. Of course, consensus is not always possible. Parties will inevitably disagree, and when there is disagreement this will often be indicated "by making positive statements about an alternative" (p. 289, footnote 42). Final decisions, nevertheless, must be made unanimously.

With respect to procedure, following the completion of a condolence ceremony, speeches are made which might bring forward a proposition—and there is an exchange of gifts to support that proposition. The council is then suspended to allow all the participants to reflect on the proposition and the answer they will give in response. Speeches are then given to present respective answers to the proposition, and more gifts are exchanged to support these answers. This procedure is then repeated until a mutually acceptable agreement or solution can be reached (*R. c. Montour*, 2023, p. 8).

The International Extension of the Condolence Ceremony and Council Meetings

It is important to note that the Condolence Ceremony, and Haudenosaunee peacemaking, conflict resolution, and treaty-making processes were not insular political, cultural, and spiritual mechanisms used exclusively by and for members of the Haudenosaunee confederacy. On the contrary, the Condolence ceremony was an important element of Haudenosaunee interactions with European settlers in the first few hundred years of contact. Indeed, as shown by Dragone, "[d]uring the first few centuries of contact, a modified version of the condolence ceremony was used by Haudenosaunee and colonial officials to open all political discussions and treaty negotiations" (2021, p. 154). The Condolence Ceremony ensured that all participants would enter the discussions or negotiations with healthy and rational minds, leading to peaceful and positive resolutions.

One reason why the Condolence ceremony was extended to relations with European officials was the highly flexible nature of the Great Law of Peace. Indeed, as noted by Williams, the Great law of Peace is designed to facilitate the inclusion and introduction of newcomers into the constitutional system. Indeed, the Peacemaker "recognized that a society with internal peace and with war around its edges would still be a society at war. His plan ... was for universal peace, and that would mean that all the peoples of the world would eventually accept both the peace and the family relationships that would make it possible" (2018, p. 275). Of course, there were significant cultural differences between the Haudenosaunee and their European counterparts.

As such, "the French, Dutch, and English could not be incorporated within the Extended Lodge because [these] differences abounded[6]; [and] therefore, a cooperative relationship developed where diversity thrived and similarities united distinct Longhouse and Christian peoples" (Muller, 2008, p. 60). This cooperative relationship was rooted in the ***kaswentha*** ethic, an "overarching worldview held by the ... Haudenosaunee Confederacy, [that] captures the crucial principles of Haudenosaunee morality: autonomy, peaceful alliance, and cooperation with friends and

[6] Inclusion into the Extended Lodge meant inclusion into the Confederacy itself. Rather than incorporate European allies into the Confederacy as members, Europeans were brought into a close and cooperative alliance with the confederacy.

allies" (p. 3). The *kaswentha* ethic embodies the core values of the Haudenosaunee and honors the expression of those values "in wampum belts mnemonic texts of ceremony, history, and diplomacy (p. 3). More precisely, the "underlying concept of the *Kaswentha* is the idea of a separate-but-equal relationship between two entities based on mutual benefit and mutual respect', depicted visually on wampum belts by two parallel lines of purple wampum against a background of white shells" (Hatton, 2019, p. 8). The two parallel lines represent the Haudenosaunee and their European counterparts joined in peace, friendship, and allyship. The lines run parallel to each other, because neither side is supposed to interfere with the independence of the other. Perhaps the most significant of these relationships was the Silver Covenant Chain.

The Silver Covenant Chain Relationship

The creation of the silver covenant chain relationship began in 1667. This process extended the *kaswentha* ethic from the Haudenosaunee confederacy to their English counterparts (Johnston, 1997, p. 81). As explained by Richter, these councils "were modeled upon the rites of the Great League of Peace and, for the [Haudenosaunee], helped to make the Covenant Chain a partnership much like that among the Five Nations" (1992 p. 141). The Silver Covenant Chain was created at councils modelled on the Longhouse councils of the Haudenosaunee (Johnston, 1997, p. 81). Put simply, the Haudenosaunee brought their diplomatic protocols under the Great Law of Peace to these international meetings, and settlers learned to respectfully engage with them.

Importantly, the Haudenosaunee, "saw their relationship with the Dutch and the English in terms of the "rope" and "chain" metaphors ... The bond thus created with the Europeans was not identical to that of the Circle Wampum, but the rope suggests a certain "entwining: and the chain a kind of "linking" (Johnston, 1997, p. 84). At councils with the English, wampum was exchanged, and expressions of condolence were given. Both of these actions represented a mutual 'polishing' of the Silver Covenant Chain which bonded the two interconnected, yet distinct and independent communities (Johnson, p. 84).

An iron chain is stronger than rope and symbolically represented the strength of the bond between the Haudenosaunee and the English. Nevertheless, iron can rust. The symbol of a silver covenant chain is significant, because silver will tarnish, but not rust, weaken, or break.

The potential for silver to tarnish is also symbolically important. Silver must be continually polished to avoid tarnishing. As explained by Louis Johnson "polishing the Silver Covenant Chain became integral to the [relationship] ... with each exchange of wampum, with each expression of condolence and with each step toward peace, the Silver Covenant Chain was ""brightened"". The mutual ""polishing"" of the Silver Covenant Chain helped deepen the bonds" (1997, p. 84) between the Haudenosaunee and the English. Polishing the Silver Covenant chain was also done through regularly holding council meetings, where both sides could discuss issues of mutual importance (*R. c. Montour*, 2023, p. 8).

The creation of the Covenant Chain relationship is as follows. In 1677, following the conclusion of King Philips War a treaty conference was held "at the insistence of New England's Puritan colonies so that they could ""deal with the tribes themselves face to face"" (Williams Jr., 1999, p. 117–118). The rationale for the Haudenosaunee and the English to enter into a treaty was largely pragmatic (Johnston 1997, p. 81). Both parties desired peace and stability in order to support positive and ongoing economic trading relationships (p. 81). Unfortunately, most of the primary source material which recorded this conference has been lost (Morito, 2012, p. 15). Nevertheless, the creation of the Covenant chain "told as a story of law and peace achieved between the Iroquois and English over time through their treaty relationship appears throughout the treaty literature of the next century" (Williams Jr., 1999, p. 118). For example, in 1689 Mohawk Sachem chief Tahaidoris referenced the Covenant Chain the following terms:

> Brethren: You are come here to this prefixed place [Albany] which is by the Christians appointed to be the house of Treaty for all public business with us the Five Nations, and do Return *you* many thanks for your Renovation of the Covenant chain which is not of iron now as it was formerly, but of Pure Silver, in which Chain are included all their Majesty's Subjects from the Sinnekes [Senecas'] Country quite to the Eastward as far as any Christian Subjects of our great king lives and from thence Southward all along New England quite to Virginia (Williams Jr., 1999 p. 118).

Here, we see that the iron chain had evolved into a silver covenant chain. Similarly, in 1744 at the Treaty of Lancaster, an Iroquois speaker recounted the creation of the chain one hundred years prior (p. 118).

The use of condolence ceremonies, and the imagery of the Silver Covenant chain was not a one-sided endeavour. The English learned to actively participate in council meetings with the Haudenosaunee in order to ensure that issues of mutual importance were resolved peacefully and effectively. In simpler terms, the English understood, respected, and learned to participate in the treaty-making and diplomatic protocols of the Haudenosaunee.[7]

English Adoption of Condolence Ceremonies and Council Meetings

In the late 1750's and early 1760's the Mohawk communities of Khanawake and Kanesatake, located in New France, were considered by the English to be allied with the French. In 1762, "as [the] defeat of New France appeared imminent, the English looked to secure an alliance" with the two communities (Johnston 1997, p. 86). At the time, William Johnson served as Superintendent of Indian Affairs and lead the negotiations on behalf of the English.

William Johnson was familiar with and acculturated into Mohawk society. Johnson had learned the language, culture, traditions, and legal protocols. Accordingly, Johnson was intimately familiar with the Silver Covenant Chain and even used an official seal that "depicts an endless chain held by six indigenous and one white figure" (Hatton, 2019, p. 11). Johnson's understanding of Mohawk legal and political protocol proved particularly useful in the ensuing negotiations.

Specifically, Johnson began his address of the communities by engaging in a condolence ceremony (Johnston 1997, p. 87). Documentary evidence indicates that both communities had suffered outbreaks of disease, likely smallpox that had killed many people (p. 87). Accordingly,

[7] Learning to participate in Haudenosaunee legal, political and diplomatic protocols was strategcally important for the English. The Haudenosaunee were vital allies to the English along the Eastern Seaboard, and their military strength was needed in conflicts with both the French and the United States. See generally, Morito, B. (2012). *Ethic of mutual respect the Covenant Chain and aboriginal-crown relations*. UBC Press, pp. 46–47.

There is insufficient space in this chapter to provide an extensive historical overview of all the treaties and interactions between the Haudenosaunee and the Crown which eschew the ongoing use of Haudenosaunee diplomatic protocols in the form of Condolence Ceremonies and Council meetings. Other examples include the councils and treaties taking place in 1701, 1702, 1725, 1735, 1742, 1754, and 1760. See *R. c. Mountour* at p. 141–156.

Johnson began by stating "… you have … lost a great many of your people to sickness, for which I am sorry, I now take this opportunity … of condoling your loss, & wiping the Tears from your Eyes so that you may look up to the Divine … [and] With this … threw three ""Very long Strings"" of wampum" (p. 87). With one belt of wampum, Johnson reiterated promises he had made earlier, with another he

> thank[ed] the [communities] for "gathering together and burying the bones" of dead English soldiers … with another belt, he ""strengthened"" and "brightened" the Covenant Chain so all would be "one people with us". [Finally], [h]e presented two more belts praising the Warriors for ""maintaining peace and friendship …"" (p. 87).

This encounter is significant, because it demonstrates the use of both Condolence ceremonies and council meetings by the English in order to maintain and strengthen their relationship with the Haudenosaunee.

English engagement in Condolence ceremonies and council meetings continued well into the late eighteenth century. As an example, the Treaty of Niagara, created in 1764 represents an extension of the Silver Covenant Chain relationship. More precisely, the Treaty of Niagara is an essential part of a larger agreement between First Nations and the Crown that includes the Royal Proclamation of 1763 (Borrows, 1997 p. 155).

The impetus for the creation of the Treaty of Niagara is as follows. As a result of

> rapid European settlement on the eastern seaboard of the North American continent, First Nation peoples in the southern Great Lakes region began to feel pressures to leave their traditional homelands and resettle west of the Mississippi River … The discontent created by this conflict necessitated the formulation of principles to mediate First Nation/Settler contention … [t]o alleviate the conflict, the Royal Proclamation was declared to delineate boundaries and define jurisdictions between First Nations and the Crown" (Borrows, 1997, p. 159)

Indigenous communities were aware of the Proclamation and were eager to discuss its precise legal effects with the English at a council where the Silver Covenant Chain relationship would be polished and renewed (Borrows, 1997, p. 161).

Accordingly, a meeting was convened in Niagara in 1764 (Borrows, 1997, p. 161). Importantly, at the "gathering a nation-to-nation relationship between settler and First Nation peoples was renewed and extended, and the Covenant Chain of Friendship, a multination alliance in which no member gave up their sovereignty, was affirmed" (p. 161). William Johnson described the purpose of the meeting as the creation of a "Treaty of Offensive and Defensive Alliance'" (p. 162), wherein the British Crown promised to protect their Indigenous counterparts from enemies, ensure free and open trade, unrestrained passage through the country, and safeguard Indigenous territories from settlement or encroachment in the absence of permission. (p. 162). William Johnson further stated, "at this treaty … we should tie them down (in the Peace) according to their own forms of which they take the most notice, for example by exchanging a very large belt with some remarkable & intelligible figures thereon". (p. 162). Here, Johnson is referring to the creation and exchange of Wampum belts which would record the promises made by both sides. The treaty was officially entered into in July and August of 1764. The significance of the agreement was considerable. Indeed, the meeting was "the most widely representative gathering of American Indians ever assembled, as approximately 2 thousand chiefs attended the negotiations" (p. 163), representing at least 25 different nations.

Of equal importance for our purposes is the way in which William Johnson, acting as a representative of the English, utilized Haudenosaunee conflict resolution tools in order to convene this treaty discussion. Following the issue of the Royal Proclamation, Johnson met with the Algonquin and Nipissing nations at Oswegatchie and persuaded them to act as messengers inviting other Indigenous nations to the treaty discussions at Niagara in the summer 1764 (p. 162). Having agreed to serve as messengers, the representatives of the Algonquin and Nipissing nations "travelled throughout the winter of 1763-4 with a printed copy of the Royal Proclamation, and with various strings of wampum, in order to summons the various First Nations to a council with the British" (p. 162). Here, we see English use of Haudenosaunee diplomatic protocols including council meetings in their relationships with Indigenous nations.

It is clear that English use of condolence ceremonies and council meetings continued well into the eighteenth century. Thus, it is essential to recognize Condolence ceremonies and council meetings as effective tools for relationship building and conflict resolution which are not insular, and idiosyncratic, but rather, essential to Haudenosaunee relationships with the Crown and by extension, the Canadian state.

Canadian Law and the Silver Covenant Chain

In order to contextualize the significance of the Silver Covenant Chain relationship to Canadian law, it is instructive to discuss *R. c. Montour*,[8] a recent decision handed down by the Superior Court of Quebec (*R. c. Montour*, 2023). Here, Mr. White, and Mr. Montour, both members of the Mohawk Nation of Kahnawà:ke, were charged under the *Excise Act* for failing to pay taxes on a large amount of tobacco that had been imported from the United States. The accused argued that the charges were an unjustified infringement of their constitutional rights, inherent rights, and international rights.

Relatedly, and most importantly for our purposes, the accused argued that 10 treaties between the Haudenosaunee and the British Crown in the 1664–1760 period formed a binding and overarching meta-treaty, known as the Silver Covenant Chain. The Silver Covenant Chain guaranteed a right to trade tobacco, and to "discuss any related issue with the Crown" (p. 2). Ultimately, Justice Bourque found in favour of the accused, on the basis of both Aboriginal rights, and rights derived from treaties between the Haudenosaunee and the Crown. In particular, Justice Bourque determined that Silver Covenant Chain constitutes an active and binding treaty "that contains a conflict resolution procedure guaranteed by sec. 35(1) of the Constitution Act 1982." (p. 240). Under the Silver Covenant Chain, it is the responsibility of both parties to discuss issues of trade at council sessions in order to work through disagreements (p. 238–239).

[8] *R. c. Montour*, 2023, QCCS 4154. This case is a superior court decision, and an appeal has been filed by Canada—a trial and decision at the appeal level are still forthcoming. As a superior court decision, this judgement does not bind other courts to its findings or approach. Nevertheless, the decision, and its approach to the 'Indigenous perspective', as well as the approach to the substantive questions of law—and in particular, the test for Aboriginal rights—has received significant praise from the academic and practicing legal community. See Nerland, K. (2023, February 3). Quebec Superior Court releases ground-breaking decision in s. 35 tobacco trade case. https://www.oktlaw.com/quebec-superior-court-releases-ground-breaking-decision-in-s-35-tobacco-trade-case/; Gunn, K. & ONeil, C. (2004, January 18). Reframing Aboriginal Rights: *R.c. Montour* https://www.firstpeopleslaw.com/public-education/blog/reframing-aboriginal-rights-r-c-montour

To begin the decision, Justice Bourque conducted an extensive review of the Haudenosaunee perspective. That section of the decision totals more than sixty-five pages and is central to Justice Bourque's reasoning and analysis. Indeed, Justice Bourque emphasized that "[t]his judgment and its conclusions cannot be understood without first reading the part on the Indigenous perspective" (p. 4). With respect to the Silver Covenant Chain, Justice Bourque found that the relationship was a peace and friendship alliance (p. 9). The pivotal element of this alliance was the "utilization of councils as a conflict-resolution procedure" (p. 9). Holding councils as a means of conflict resolution was grounded in the Great Law of Peace and included ceremonies such as the Condolence Ceremony (pp. 9–10). Moreover, in the context of the Silver Covenant Chain relationship, these council meetings "served as a means to polish and keep the chain clean and bright" (p. 10) and the necessity of consistently polishing the chain to maintain its brightness was regularly and consistently referenced and acknowledged by all parties (p. 10).

Accordingly, Justice Bourque finds that the "British were not only aware [of], but also agreed, that holding councils was the designated process for resolving conflicts and governing their relationship with the Haudenosaunee" (p. 10). Ultimately, this is because the historical record makes clear that conflicts were consistently addressed through council meetings (p. 10).

In addition, Justice Bourque dedicated a significant portion of the decision to describing the significance of Condolence ceremonies to the Haudenosaunee and their relationship with the British Crown. Indeed, Justice Bourque takes care to note that the procedure of a council "involved a Condolence ceremony at the opening, which could sometimes last a few days" (p. 8). Condolence Ceremonies were an essential component of Council Meetings. Condolence ceremonies were essential, because they ensured that the participants could enter the negotiations with a good mind—or in the words of Justice Bourque—to "foster a favourable disposition for discussions" (p. 82). Ultimately, the *R. c. Montour* decision (2023) suggests that Canadian law can and should recognize the significance and legal force of the Silver Covenant Chain relationship, and the conflict resolution mechanisms which support the health and continuation of that relationship.

Implications for Canadian Law

In order to situate this discussion in the context of contemporary Canadian common law, it is instructive to recall some of the relevant Calls to Action (CTA) issued by the Truth and Reconciliation Commission of Canada (TRC). Specifically, CTA #27 calls upon law societies and law schools to "ensure that lawyers receive appropriate cultural competency training ... [t]his will require skills-based training in cultural competency, conflict resolution, human rights, and anti-racism". (Truth and Reconciliation Commission of Canada, 2015. CTA, 27). An important element of cultural competency, in the context of working with Indigenous clients in Canada, is knowledge of, and respect for, Indigenous culture, political institutions, and law. Lawyers and future lawyers alike, working in Canada have a high chance of interacting with Indigenous clients. This chapter is an attempt to give law students, articling students and lawyers an introduction to Haudenosaunee, law, conflict resolution and its relationship to the Canadian common law.

In addition, CTA #45 IV calls upon the

> Government of Canada on, behalf of all Canadians, to ... [r]econcile Aboriginal and Crown constitutional and legal orders to ensure that Aboriginal peoples are full partners in Confederation, including the recognition and integration of Indigenous laws and legal traditions in negotiation and implementation processes involving Treaties, land claims, and other constructive agreements" (TRC, CTA, 45 IV).

While often overlooked, the significance of this Call to Action should not be underestimated. If we are to take this Call to Action seriously, then it is essential that Canadian lawyers strive—at a minimum, to become familiar with Indigenous cultures, political systems, and laws.

Across the country, provincial law societies are beginning to require ongoing cultural competency training for lawyers specifically aimed at lawyer interactions with Indigenous people and Indigenous clients. In Alberta, lawyers are required to complete The Path. The Path was designed to "increase Indigenous cultural understanding" (Law Society of Alberta, n.d.) through a focus on Canadian history in relation to Indigenous peoples. The Northwest Territories have a similar requirement, but lawyers can choose from either The Path, or two other educational alternatives. Similarly, in Manitoba, lawyers can now complete The Path, for a total of seven Continuing Professional Development (CPD) hours (Manitoba Law Society, 2023). Likewise, in British Columbia, all lawyers are required to complete a course in Indigenous cultural competency which qualifies for CPD hours (Law Society of British Columbia, 2021).

This chapter is an attempt to facilitate increased cultural competency for Canadian law students and lawyers. While the focus has been on Haudenosaunee Condolence ceremonies, and council meetings, it is essential to recognize that all Indigenous communities in Canada have their own unique laws, legal and political culture, and methods of dispute resolution. The focus in this chapter, on a single community, is borne out of necessity. It would be inappropriate to speak of a pan-Indigenous approach to dispute resolution in Canada. At the same time, there is insufficient space, in this chapter, to meaningfully discuss every Canadian Indigenous communities' approach to dispute resolution in a substantive manner.

Accordingly, this chapter, provides law students, articling students, and young lawyers, with an introduction to two dispute resolution practices utilized by the Haudenosaunee. The emphasis on the Haudenosaunee, is particularly useful for law students and lawyers, because, as I have demonstrated, condolence ceremonies, and the dispute resolution practices of the Haudenosaunee are not insular, secretive, and reserved only for members of the Confederacy itself, but rather, essential to Haudenosaunee interactions with individuals and groups outside of the Confederacy—including the Crown and the Canadian state. This fact has now been recognized in the Canadian Common law through the *R. c. Montour* decision (2023). Additionally, while a significant portion of this chapter is dedicated to legal history, Condolence ceremonies and council meetings are not historical artifacts. These ideas, principles, and practices continue to animate Haudenosaunee interactions with members of the confederacy, and those outside of it.

Admittedly, this chapter is not a panacea for Canadian lawyers working with Haudenosaunee clients, or conflicts involving members of the Confederacy. Canadian lawyers are bound to act as zealous advocates for their clients, and their actions and behaviours must uphold the codes of conduct required by the relevant law societies. The goal of this project is considerably more modest. My aim here, is to introduce law students and Canadian lawyers to Haudenosaunee dispute resolution practices and their relationship to the Canadian common law.

Conclusion

This chapter has discussed the force and significance of Council meetings and Condolence ceremonies to the relationship between the Haudenosaunee and the Crown. Within I have shown that the Great Law of Peace has structured Haudenosaunee legal and political institutions for centuries. In addition, I have demonstrated that Condolence ceremonies and council meetings promote peaceful and positive relations and serve as mechanisms for the resolution of conflicts amongst and between Haudenosaunee individuals, families, clans, or nations. In addition, I have shown that council meetings and condolence ceremonies were central features of the Silver Covenant chain relationship established between the Haudenosaunee and their English counterparts. Indeed, the English were not passive recipients, but rather active participants in the use of these conflict resolution mechanisms. More precisely, the English learned to engage with the Haudenosaunee through use of Condolence ceremonies and council meetings in order to create, strengthen, and maintain strong diplomatic, legal, and political ties with their Indigenous counterparts.

In particular, through examination of the historical record, I have demonstrated that Condolence Ceremonies and Council meetings were of central significance to both the English and the Haudenosaunee in the creation and maintenance of the Silver Covenant Chain relationship. The Silver Covenant Chain relationship structured the relationship between the English and the Haudenosaunee for centuries. The Canadian common law has recently recognized the force and significance of Silver Covenant Chain relationship in the *R. c. Montour Decision* (2023). This case ultimately suggests that the Canadian Common law can and should recognize the force and significance of the Silver Covenant Chain relationship, and the Condolence ceremonies and council meetings that support the health and continuation of that relationship. The TRC CTA #45 IV calls upon the government of Canada on behalf of all Canadians to reconcile Aboriginal and Crown constitutional orders. Such a feat is by no means a simple task to accomplish. Nevertheless, understanding Indigenous law, conflict resolution practices, and intercultural diplomatic protocols is a small but important step to realizing this goal.

Questions

1. In what ways does the *R. C. Montour decision* enhance or alter your understanding of the relationship between the Haudenosaunee and Canadian democracy?
2. What practical steps can be taken by Canadian lawyers and law students to meet and uphold the Truth and Reconciliation Commision's Call To Action #45 IV?
3. What steps can Canada take to better uphold their responsibilities under the Silver Covenant Chain?
4. How does the Treaty of Niagara alter or enhance your understanding of the Royal Proclamation?

Glossary

Haudenosaunee Confederacy:	Also known as the Iroquois Confederacy or Six Nations, it is a union of Indigenous nations (originally the Mohawk, Oneida, Onondaga, Cayuga, and Seneca; later joined by the Tuscarora).
Good Mind:	A Haudenosaunee legal and moral concept referring to clarity, compassion, rationality, and collective concern. A person or community must have a "Good Mind" to participate meaningfully in conflict resolution or governance processes.
Consensus Decision-Making:	Decisions are made only when all parties reach mutual agreement
Thanksgiving Address:	An opening ceremony in council meetings expressing gratitude to natural elements and the Creator. It sets a respectful tone and aligns the minds of all participants before legal deliberations begin.
Restorative Justice:	Although not named as such in Haudenosaunee law, restorative justice principles are deeply embedded in practices like condolence ceremonies.

	Justice is achieved by healing relation ships, restoring rational thought, and reintegrating individuals into the community.
Conflict Transformation:	An approach that goes beyond resolving immediate disputes to address the underlying structures and relation ships that produce conflict.
Diplomatic Protocols:	Structured ceremonial and political practices— like condolence ceremonies and council meetings—used to negotiate and maintain alliances, including with European colonial powers. These protocols highlight the intersection of Indigenous law and international relations

Competing Interests The author has no conflicts of interest to declare that are relevant to the content of this chapter.

References

Borrows, J. (1997). Wampum at Niagara, the Royal Proclamation, Canadian legal history, and self-government. In M. Asch (Ed.), *Aboriginal and treaty rights in Canada: Essays on law*. Equality and respect for difference UBC Press.

Canada. (1982). Constitution Act, 1982, being schedule B to the Canada Act 1982 (UK), 1982, c. 11.

Dragone, N. (2021). Kissed by lightning: Mediating haudenosaunee traditional teachings through film. In N. Van Styvendale, J. D. McDougall, R. Henry & R. A. Innes (Eds.), *The arts of indigenous health and well-being* (pp. 147–166). University of Manitoba Press.

Foley, D. (2010). Iroquois mourning and condolence installation rituals: A pattern of social integration and continuity. In C. S. Patrick (Ed.), *Preserving tradition and understanding the past: Papers from the conference on Iroquois research, 2001–2005* (pp. 25–34). The New York State Education Department.

Gunn, K., & ONeil, C. (2004, January 18). Reframing aboriginal rights: R. C. *Montour*. https://www.firstpeopleslaw.com/public-education/blog/reframing-aboriginal-rights-r-c-montour

Hatton, H. (2019). Narrating sovereignty: The covenant chain in intercultural diplomacy. *Journal of Early American History*, *9*(2–3), 118–144. https://doi.org/10.1163/18770703-00902015

Johnson, L. (2004). *The covenant chain of peace: Metaphor and religious thought in seventeenth century Haudenosaunee council oratory* [doctoral dissertation, McGill University] pp. 47-53.

Johnston, L. (1997). Polishing the silver covenant chain: An address by sir William Johnson to the people of Kahnawake and Kanesatake, 1762. *Historical Papers*. https://doi.org/10.25071/0848-1563.39414

Law Society of Alberta. (n.d.). *Indigenous Cultural Competency Education*. Retrieved September 22, 2025, https://www.lawsociety.ab.ca/about-us/key-initiatives/indigenous-initiatives/indigenous-cultural-competency-education/

Law Society of British Columbia. (2021). Indigenous intercultural course. https://www.lawsociety.bc.ca/about-us/priorities/truth-and-reconciliation/indigenous-intercultural-course/.

Law Society of Manitoba. (2023). The path. https://lawsociety.mb.ca/regulation/education-requirements/the-path/.

Lemlin, H., & V. (1996). *Social movements and the great law of peace in Askwesasne*. (PhD thesis. University of Ottawa.

Morito, B. (2012). *Ethic of mutual respect the covenant chain and aboriginal-crown relations*. UBC Press.

Muller, V. K. (2008). *Holding hands with wampum: Haudenosaunee council fires from the great law of peace to contemporary relationships with the Canadian state* (pp. 21–59). [Doctoral dissertation, Queens University Kingston].

Nerland, K. (2023, February 3). Quebec superior court releases ground-breaking decision in s. 35 tobacco trade case. https://www.oktlaw.com/quebec-superior-court-releases-ground-breaking-decision-in-s-35-tobacco-trade-case/.

Pomedli, M. M. (1995). Eitheenth-century treaties: Amended Iroquois condolence rituals. *American Indian Quarterly, 19*(3), 319–339.

R. c. Montour, 2023 QCCS 4154. (2023).

Richter, D. K. (1992). *The ordeal of the longhouse: The peoples of the Iroquois league in the era of European colonization*. University of North Carolina Press.

Tahsuda, J. (1997). Twenty-first century wampum: The use of Iroquois diplomatic protocols in aboriginal land claim negotiations. *Thomas Law Review, 10*, 149–157.

Williams, K. P. (2018). *Kayanerenkó:Wa: The great law of peace*. University of Manitoba Press.

Williams, R. A., Jr. (1999). *Linking arms together: American Indian treaty visions of law and peace 1600–1800*. Routledge.

Legislation

Excise Act (1985) (R.S.C., 1985, c. E-14).

Reports

Truth and Reconciliation Commission of Canada. (2015). Honouring the Truth, Reconciling for the Future: Summary of the Final Report of the Truth and Reconciliation Commission of Canada. Ottawa, ON: Truth and Reconciliation Commission of Canada. https://www2.gov.bc.ca/assets/gov/british-columbians-our-governments/indigenous-people/aboriginal-people sdocuments/calls_to_action_english2.pdf

Mediation

Jennifer L. Schulz

Abstract This chapter explains the benefits of mediation as a dispute resolution process for legal disputes. Mediation can be used in virtually all areas of law. The pre-mediation process is described, as well as the four stages of the mediation process: introduction, issue identification, discussion, and closure. Disputants who use mediation are usually satisfied with the process and mediation has important access to justice benefits. Mandatory mediation, credentialing, mediator liability and the future of the field are also briefly canvassed.

Keywords Mediation · Dispute resolution · Self-determination · Mediator liability · Legal education

---

J. L. Schulz (✉)
Faculty of Law, University of Manitoba, Winnipeg, Canada
e-mail: j.schulz@umanitoba.ca

L. E. Reimer and R. Jochelson (eds.), *The Other Side of the Bar*,
https://doi.org/10.1007/978-981-96-9748-9_5

Introduction

Mediation is the intervention into a dispute or negotiation by an acceptable, impartial, neutral third party who has no authoritative decision-making power. The mediator controls and guides the process and assists the disputants in voluntarily reaching their own mutually acceptable settlement of the dispute. While the mediator controls the process, the disputants control the outcome. Unlike a judge or an arbitrator, a mediator does not render a decision. Therefore, mediators do not see disputes as competitive or win/lose. They often see disputes as opportunities for change, growth, transformation, or win/win resolutions.

Many mediators see themselves as facilitators who help others solve or transform their problems. Mediators are usually able to get disputants to speak more productively with one another than they could alone. Think about your last fight with a sibling or a friend and imagine if another person was present, merely watching. The tone of your argument would change just by being watched. Now imagine if the person was a trained mediator, whose job was to facilitate your negotiations. The quality of your conflict interaction would change dramatically, as would the likelihood that you would resolve your conflict.

The goal in mediation is to facilitate resolution, while the goal in litigation is besting one's opponent and winning; the processes are quite different. Mediated resolutions do not depend on what's right, "the truth," or evidence. Rather, the result is what the parties can live with and agree to. Therefore, creative resolutions are possible; the disputants and mediator can work together to reach resolutions that might be unattainable in a courtroom. The mediator does this by attempting to channel positive attitudes and behaviours. Mediators give disputants voice, agency, and problem-solving techniques. Mediators try to counteract the parties' adversarial impulses and keep them focused on cooperative, creative problem solving, because most disputants know what they want and what would work best for the resolution of their own disputes.

Quite simply, mediators attempt to satisfy disputing parties in a way that is different from traditional legal satisfaction. This is because their approach to conflict is very different than lawyers' approaches to conflict. Lawyers typically ask themselves: "how should I frame this case in law?" or "how does the law apply to these facts?" Mediators ask: "why are these people stuck?", "what needs to happen to make a difference?", and "will they be able to work together again?" Mediators try to reconcile the parties' underlying interests, not just their legal positions. When disputing parties' legal and non-legal interests are addressed, the chances of resolution increase and disputants' satisfaction with the settlement process also increases.

Approaches to Mediation

Mediation has been conducted for millennia. The earliest peoples would have gone to a third party to help them resolve conflicts they could not resolve themselves. In Canada and the United States, before mediation became popular with lawyers, mediators were often Indigenous elders or members of the clergy. For many disputants, a trusted elder or community member is preferable to a mediator neither party knows, and thus mediators do not necessarily have to be strangers to the parties. Nor do they have to be lawyers. All kinds of people act as mediators; neither a law degree nor any degree is required. All mediators assist parties so they can clarify their disagreements and explore options for resolution. All mediators are also forward-looking; they want to help the parties function better in the future. There are however different styles or approaches to mediation.

Some mediators take what they describe as a transformative approach, where the mediator fosters and supports positive interactions through techniques of empowerment and recognition (Bush & Folger, 2005). The Global Pound Conference, which studied mediation in 22 countries in 2016–2017, noted that Toronto lawyers said disputants' expectations are exceeded when they engage in processes that reinforce, build or preserve relationships and create opportunities for moments of transformation. (International Mediation Institute, 2019). It has been argued that preserving relationships and creating transformative opportunities corresponds with a "feminine" process, as opposed to, for example, fighting for justice. Mediation's focus on cooperation, consensus, and the parties' relationship contrasts with litigation's competitive discourse and individualistic goals of winning (Schulz & Turnbull, 2012).

For mediators who are legally trained, a problem-solving or facilitative approach often feels most intuitive. Focusing on problem-solving is important because as early as 1989 the Canadian Bar Association's task force report on alternative dispute resolution urged lawyers to see their role as problem-solvers rather than fighters. Indeed, research has shattered the myth that adversarial bargaining is more effective than a problem-solving approach (Schneider, 2002). Some mediators, for example retired judges, take an evaluative approach to mediation and offer their opinions about how a judge might rule, or provide suggestions as to viable options for resolution. Many mediators combine aspects of all these approaches, or change their approach depending on the nature of the dispute.

Areas of Law

Mediation was relatively unknown in legal practice before 1970. Labour and management disputes were among the first to be mediated. Today, mediation is used to resolve disputes and prevent conflicts in neighbourhoods, schools, government, businesses, families, and in international disputes. Mediation is recognized as the fastest growing method of dispute resolution and it is currently being used in all areas of law, including:

- Contracts
- Torts
- Property
- Criminal
- Commercial
- Labour and Employment
- Wills and Estates
- Family
- Environmental
- Professional malpractice
- Community and school disputes
- International disputes
- Human Rights
- Identity conflicts
- Cultural and ethnic disputes

Advantages of Mediation

Mediation has been such a popular dispute resolution mechanism for so long because it has many advantages. Key among those advantages is disputant self-determination. Parties have their say in mediation, get to choose their mediator, and have control over the outcome, because they themselves craft it. It is a much more informal process than court, and it is confidential: two things many disputants really appreciate. Disputants can tell their stories in confidence, express their emotions, and control the outcome of their disputes; all things that are not permitted in court. In so doing, disputants often find their relationships are less damaged than they are after litigation.

There are also important access to justice benefits to using mediation to resolve legal disputes. Mediation, as a more informal process, is less daunting for disputants. It is also cheaper than litigation, can be done without lawyers, and resolves disputes much more quickly than court processes. As such, it increases peoples' access to justice. In any three-year period, almost half the adult population in Canada experiences at least one justiciable civil or family problem (Farrow et al., 2016). Few, however, have the resources to resolve these legal problems. Mediation is a more cost effective and quicker way for most citizens to achieve their justice goals. Goal 16 of the 2030 United Nations Sustainable Development Goals commits nations to work toward ensuring equal access to justice for all by 2030 (A Roadmap for Change, 2013). Mediation will be one way many are able to resolve their legal disputes more accessibly. In particular, online dispute resolution (ODR), popular before the COVID-19 global pandemic and now flourishing, is very popular with mediation clients around the world, precisely due to its accessibility.

The cost-saving benefit of mediation is often highlighted. While this is vitally important, especially for access to justice, it is crucial not to forget about the true hallmarks of mediation: party self-determination and tailor-made agreements. To say that mediation is cheaper than litigation should not suggest that mediation is merely a way to cut costs. Rather, mediation can be an option of first choice for resolving complex disputes. Similarly, when the private and confidential nature of mediation is highlighted, it is generally to promote the monetary and business interests that are preserved because embarrassing situations (such as environmental disasters) can be kept secret. This means the mediation benefit of confidentiality is promoted in order to protect defendants' interests, rather than to showcase the true value of confidentiality to promote frank discussion and reach agreement in all types of cases.

Finally, research demonstrates that as compared to litigants, mediation participants report higher level of satisfaction (Lawrence et al. 2007; Boulle & Kelly 1998; and Brett et al. 1996). This satisfaction stems from mediation's efficiency and because disputants' needs and interests (not just their legal positions) are taken into account. Context, history, socio-economic situations and many other non-legal factors are examined in good mediation sessions. Consensus-based processes like mediation can generate more creative solutions than judges can, leading to more holistic, and even transformative, resolutions. This is true both in in-person and virtual mediation sessions. When good dispute resolution has been modelled for disputants in mediation, it can have a beneficial educative effect that lessens the chance of future conflicts between the parties. The only real disadvantages to mediation are that the process is confidential and does not set legal precedents. So, the few cases that require development of the law are still better served by reported court decisions.

The Mediation Process

Most cases begin with at least two disputing parties, who both agree to attempt mediation in a good faith effort to resolve their dispute. The parties, who can be unrepresented or represented by legal counsel, typically submit some kind of mediation brief to the mediator. Most mediators also like to meet with all parties individually before the mediation session. These individual meetings are an opportunity to build rapport with the parties and to help them plan how to put their best selves forward in the mediation session. The pre-mediation meetings are also an opportunity to assess whether mediation may be inappropriate, for example, due to an insurmountable power imbalance. The mediator will explain the terms of mediation to the disputants, have them sign the agreement to mediate, and indicate that they are ready to mediate in the agreed upon mediation venue.

Mediation agreements typically outline the fact that the mediation session is a confidential, without prejudice, settlement process. Information discovered in mediation cannot be used in any other legal proceedings and the mediator may not be called as a witness. The fact that the mediator will not provide legal advice is outlined, as is the fact that the parties have full authority to settle and will participate in good faith. The parties typically agree to indemnify the mediator from any claims for damages that may arise from the mediation and the mediation agreement outlines the mediator's fees for the session(s).

Throughout the process of mediation, the mediator must listen actively so that all parties feel heard. Mediators approach disputes with curiosity instead of judgment, provide equal airtime and caucus time to all participants, and manage and control the process, but not the outcome. Mediators must mediate ethically, with no conflicts of interest, bias, coercion, or undue pressure to settle. And, in some cases, mediators have to attempt to "balance power" between unequal negotiating parties. This is a contested part of the role of the mediator. Some feel that mediators lose their impartiality if they attempt to balance power. Others believe it is unethical to mediate when real power differentials exist, for example, between spouses in cases of domestic violence. Others feel that balancing power can be attempted, provided the mediator has sufficient training and the weaker party is participating completely voluntarily in the session.

Given the wide variety of areas of legal practice that incorporate mediation, and the diversity of individual approaches to practicing as a mediator, it is impossible to outline one mediation process that will be identical in each mediation situation. However, most mediation processes incorporate at least four stages:

Stage One/Introduction

The first stage, the introductory phase of the mediation session, begins with the mediator welcoming and introducing everyone. In their opening remarks, mediators outline what to expect, the mediator's role, and any ground rules, for example, no profanity, and no interruptions. The mediator sets a tone of positivity, obtains all parties' agreement to proceed, and then begins by inviting the plaintiff to tell their story.

Stage Two/Identify the Issues

In stage two of the process, the disputants have the opportunity to tell their stories, uninterrupted by the other side. The mediator will probe for both the facts and the parties' feelings. Mediators often restate or summarize what they heard after each disputant has spoken. This makes the disputant feel heard, allows the disputant to correct the mediator in case the mediator misunderstood anything, and enables the mediator to highlight important facts or feelings for the other side. Mediators employ active listening techniques, good eye contact, and paraphrasing skills throughout this phase of the process. Mediators will ask open ended and clarifying questions to help the speaker get the entire story out.

After the plaintiff has spoken, counsel, if present, can add anything that the client may have forgotten or that counsel wishes to stress. The mediator will summarize again, and then turn it over to the defendant to tell its side of the story. Thereafter, defence counsel, if present, will have an opportunity to speak. The mediator also reframes negative statements that any disputant made, which makes them easier to for the other side to hear. While the disputants and lawyers are describing the conflict from their perspectives, the mediator will be listening for the most salient issues in dispute. When all parties have finished speaking, the mediator will identify those issues, often by writing them out on a whiteboard. Mediators will try to use neutral language when listing the issues for discussion. For example, instead of saying "breach of contract," the mediator might describe it as "obligations under our contract." Those issues will then comprise the agenda for topics to be discussed in the next phase of the mediation process.

Stage Three/Discussion and Problem-Solving

This is the stage in the mediation process where most of the work is done. In this stage, the parties, together with the mediator, analyze the issues on the agenda, and discuss them with a view toward coming to a resolution. The mediator chooses an issue to begin with, and the disputants work on it, exploring their underlying interests and trying to find common ground. The mediator asks a lot of questions during this stage. Consequential questions encourage the parties to focus on the future and determine "what will happen if…?" Clarifying questions require the parties to be precise when outlining potential options for settlement. Probing questions help disputants reality-test options that are offered. The goal is to brainstorm possible settlement options in an open, non-judgmental way. If the mediator can help the parties find common ground and shared interests, durable resolutions can usually be crafted.

During the discussion phase, mediators often call for separate individual meetings, or caucuses. These are private meetings for each side with the mediator. Unless told to do so, mediators do not disclose what was said in private caucus to the other side. These private meetings are used to allow the disputant to vent, have a break, or to consult with the mediator or their lawyer. The mediator can also use the session to help coach a disputant, help the disputant prioritize issues, or to reality check expectations. Different jurisdictions differ greatly in how they employ caucuses.

In California, for example, the bar prefers mediations that are conducted almost totally through a series of private caucuses, rarely putting the two sides together for joint sessions (Stipanowich, 2016). In Manitoba, it is more common to begin and end in joint session, and to try to stay there for as much of the mediation session as possible, employing private caucuses only when necessary.

Stage Four/Agreement/Closure

The final stage of the mediation process is the agreement or closure stage. If the parties have not settled, it is still necessary to end the process respectfully, emphasizing and recording any progress that has been made. If a resolution has been reached, the lawyers, or the mediator if there are no lawyers present, must draft a clear, specific and detailed mediation agreement. Independent legal advice should always be recommended before parties sign any agreements. Simple, balanced language, framed positively and future-looking, is best. If the mediation was connected to a court process, all releases, claim withdrawals, and payment schedules must be finalized.

Lawyers in Mediation

Due to the prevalence of trials and courtroom storylines in popular culture, many citizens are not aware of the option of mediation when they have a legal dispute (Schulz, 2020). While American Fortune 1000 companies frequently use ADR processes such as mediation and find them better than litigation (Lamare, 2014), most clients have little to no experience of mediation. As a result, lawyers need to educate their clients about the existence of and advantages to mediation.

Many bar associations have codes of conduct for lawyers which require lawyers to recommend dispute resolution options such as mediation to all of their clients. For example, in 2002 the Canadian Bar Association added a requirement to its *Code of Professional Conduct* that legal counsel have a positive, continuing obligation to canvass with each client, in a fully informed manner, all available dispute resolution processes. This means lawyers should be thinking about the possibility of using mediation before litigation in all client disputes. Then, when representing clients in mediation, lawyers must do so competently and with integrity, and less adversarially than they might in litigation.

Lawyers can advise their clients to attempt mediation when negotiations have begun, but the parties have reached a stalemate, or, if the trial is really far off and the client wants immediate resolution. If the client acknowledges the weaknesses of the case, expresses concerns about going to court, has limited funds, wants to avoid publicity, or wants to tailor-make the remedy, mediation is an excellent option. When both sides agree to mediate, the chances of them resolving their dispute is much higher and each side will get at least some of what it wants.

Lawyers also have to make their clients aware that mediation is increasingly being mandated. Across the USA and Canada there are many state and provincial mandatory mediation programs, court-connected mediation programs, and statutes that mandate participation in mediation for particular types of disputes or disputants. In mandatory mediation, the parties have no choice but to attempt mediation. Sometimes this results in less satisfactory results because parties feel "forced" to negotiate. However, if lawyers advise and prepare their clients well, even when attendance is mandated, clients are able to participate in an open-minded, "voluntary" fashion.

Once a client has agreed to mediation, the lawyer can select the mediator. This is an advantage of mediation, unlike litigation, where one's judge cannot be selected. Lawyers choose and agree upon mediators for their clients' files. Elders and members of the clergy are often excellent mediators. Social workers and other non-lawyers also act as first rate mediators. Mediators with good settlement track records and mediators with subject matter expertise are often chosen. Mediation as a field is still unregulated and particular credentials are not essential in order to mediate. Because of the lack of regulation, many lawyers favour mediators who have highly regarded training (e.g. from the Program on Negotiation at Harvard) or some credentials (e.g. chartered mediator designations from the ADR Institute of Canada).

The lack of regulation and credentialization are tensions in the field. Many non-lawyer mediators would like to see mediation maintain its "alternative" status and remain unregulated, while lawyers would like to see credentialed practitioners and a regulated mediation field. Lawyers tend to favour mediators with legal expertise. As a result, most lawyers typically choose mediators who are also lawyers, or they choose retired judges. Choosing retired judges can be problematic because the retired bench is not diverse. Research shows that lawyers tend to choose lawyers whom they know and who look like them (Schulz, 2020 at 83–86), so the pool of mediators who obtain both the most work and the most lucrative work is neither diverse nor representative of the overall population. More needs to be done to ensure women, people of colour, and Indigenous mediators obtain paid mediation work. Some organizations have attempted this; they establish rosters of mediators who are randomly assigned to mediate files, thus ensuring a somewhat more equal distribution of work. The fact remains however, that most of the high-paying mediation work is in the hands of a few mediators, while the majority of mediators work as volunteers or are nominally paid.

Since most clients do not have a lot of experience with mediation, it is up to lawyers to ensure their clients receive good mediation services. Lawyers and clients can look to mediator codes of conduct to assess their mediator's performance. The American Bar Association, the American Arbitration Association, the Association for Conflict Resolution, and the ADR Institute of Canada have all developed similar codes of conduct that reflect the tenets of good mediation practice. Most organizations that keep a roster of mediators also ask their mediators to adhere to a code of conduct. However, as an unregulated practice that takes place in confidence, it can be difficult to determine if mediation services were properly provided. It is not enough for a disputant to be unhappy with the mediated agreement. A disputant must be able to show that the mediator breached a code or acted negligently, and that the mediator's actions resulted in provable damages. Thus far, no mediator in Canada, the United States, England, Australia, New Zealand or South Africa has been found liable for negligent mediation behaviour (Schulz, 2024). Mediator codes of conduct and case law concur that mediators have a duty to act impartially (*Furia v. Helm*, 2003), without conflicts of interest (*Chang's Imports Inc. v. Srader*, 2002), without bias (*McClintock v. Karam*, 2015), and in a manner that allows parties' rights to self-determination (*Vitakis-Valchine v. Valchine*, 2001). However, there are no decisions that definitively outline a duty of care for mediators. Instead, courts occasionally revoke agreements reached in mediations where the mediator behaved poorly. So, for example, mediator coercion in court-ordered mediation (*Vitakis-Valchine v. Valchine*, 2001); disputant incapacity occasioned by power imbalance (*Johannes Moleko Sejane v. Commission for Conciliation, Mediation and Arbitration*, 2001); and mediator bias (*T.H. Kasipersad v. CCMA Commissioner Linda Botha*, 2002) are reasons to set aside mediated agreements.

Conclusion

This chapter has described mediation as an advantageous process for clients and lawyers to use to resolve legal disputes. Mediators give disputing parties voice and help them problem-solve by focusing on their underlying interests in addition to their legal positions. Mediation provides affordable and timely access to justice for clients and is an important way for disputants to exercise self-determination in the resolution of their disputes. Mediators take different approaches; they practice in stylistically diverse ways and virtually any type of legal dispute can be mediated. Most mediators hold pre-mediation sessions with disputants, follow a four stage mediation model, utilize private caucuses, and encourage parties to be forward-thinking in the resolutions they reach. The lack of regulation in the field causes some tension between lawyer and non-lawyer mediators, who are currently only accountable to mediator codes of conduct.

Over time, courts will use mediator codes of conduct to formulate standards of care for mediators. The case law will develop and the tort law principle of custom will be utilized to establish how reasonable mediators in particular areas of mediation practice should mediate (Schulz, 2002, 2024). When the first mediator is found negligent for substandard mediation practice, not only will there be legal standards for mediators to reach and breach, mediation will have become a profession. Different schools of mediators will have diverse views about the desirability of professional status. Professionalization of the field will play out in a variety of ways cross-culturally, with varied credentialing and regulation responses, and all mediators will have to contend with the realities of AI for practice.

Future areas of research and development for mediation will centre around diversity; more diverse mediation practitioners, more diversity in the delivery of mediation services, and more diverse mediation models. Researchers will do more empirical work, attempting to gather evidence of mediation's effectiveness (Sinnadurai et al., 2023). Emphasis will continue to be placed on developing training and expertise in dealing with power imbalances. In Canada more work will be done to incorporate Indigenous mediation methodologies. Globally there will be a focus on designing more culturally appropriate mediation models.

Across the common law world more cases are settled than litigated. Mediation is a wonderful process for lawyers and clients to employ to help reach settlement of their disputes. Law schools' working assumptions will change. The focus on clients as opponents or adversaries will shift to understanding clients as disputants in search of mutually beneficial, creative agreements. Law schools will provide more extensive dispute resolution instruction (Lande, 2012) and students will graduate to become lawyers and dispute resolvers. This switch in curricular focus to problem solving, negotiation, and other mediative approaches will better reflect the realities of practice and the access to justice goals of clients.

Questions

1. How does popular culture shape public perception of mediation, and what responsibilities do legal professionals have in correcting or reinforcing these perceptions?
2. Identify a specific legal dispute (e.g. employment termination, Indigenous land dispute, family breakdown) and develop a mediation strategy. What role would legal representation play in balancing advocacy with collaborative problem-solving?
3. Under what circumstances should a mediator use private caucuses, and how might doing so impact perceptions of fairness and party autonomy?
4. Should professional regulation of mediators differ between legal and non-legal mediators? Propose a regulatory framework that balances access to justice with professional standards.
5. With the rise of online dispute resolution (ODR) and AI tools in conflict transformation, how should mediation training evolve to address future challenges, yet maintain core values?

Glossary

Access to Justice: A benefit of mediation. Mediation increases access to justice because it is a more informal process, less daunting, cheaper than litigation, can be done without lawyers, and resolves disputes more quickly than court processes. Mediation is a more cost-effective and quicker way for citizens to achieve their justice goals.

Caucus (Private caucus): Separate individual meetings between each side and the mediator. Mediators generally do not disclose what was said in private caucus to the other side unless told to do so. These meetings allow parties to vent, take a break, consult with counsel or the mediator, receive coaching, prioritize issues, or reality check expectations. Jurisdictions differ in how frequently caucuses are employed.

Confidentiality: Mediation is a confidential process. Information discovered in mediation generally cannot be used in any other legal proceedings, and the mediator may not be called as a witness.

Evaluative approach: A style of mediation where some mediators, such as retired judges, offer their opinions about how a judge might rule or provide suggestions for viable resolution options.

Facilitative approach: An approach to mediation where the mediator acts as a facilitator who helps disputants resolve their problems without offering them advice. The disputants are understood to have the best insights into the resolution of their dispute.

Mandatory mediation: Programs or statutes that require participation in mediation for particular types of disputes or disputants. Parties have no choice but to attempt mediation. Even when mandated, clients can participate in an open-minded way if well-advised and prepared by lawyers.

Mediation: The intervention into a dispute or negotiations by an acceptable, impartial, neutral third party who has no authoritative decision-making power.

The mediator controls the process, while the disputants control the outcome. Mediators assist disputants in voluntarily reaching their own mutually acceptable settlement. Mediators do not render a decision, unlike a judge or an arbitrator.

Mediation Stages: Most mediation processes incorporate at least four stages: Introduction, Identify Issues, Discussion, and Closure.

Mediator: An acceptable, impartial, neutral third party who intervenes in a dispute or negotiations. A mediator controls and guides the process, assists disputants in voluntarily reaching settlement, and has no authoritative decision-making power. Mediators are forward-looking and want to help parties function better in the future.

Mediator liability: Concerns whether a mediator can be held responsible for negligent mediation behaviour. No mediator in Canada, the USA, England, Australia, New Zealand or South Africa has been found liable for negligent mediation behaviour thus far. Courts occasionally revoke agreements when a mediator behaved poorly, such as through coercion, bias, or mediating with a significant power imbalance. Mediator codes of conduct and case law suggest duties to act impartially, without conflicts of interest or bias, and in a manner that allows parties' self-determination.

Pre-mediation process: This process is described in the source. It typically involves parties agreeing to attempt mediation, submitting a brief to the mediator, and the mediator

	meeting with parties individually before the session. These individual meetings build rapport, help parties plan, and assess if mediation is appropriate.
Problem-solving approach:	An approach to mediation where the focus is on helping parties solve their problems. Lawyers have been urged to see their role as problem-solvers rather than fighters. Research indicates this approach is more effective than adversarial bargaining.
Self-determination (Disputant self-determination):	A key advantage of mediation where parties have their say, get to choose their mediator, and have control over the outcome because they craft it themselves.
Stage One/Introduction:	The first stage begins with the mediator welcoming and introducing everyone. The mediator outlines expectations, their role, ground rules, sets a positive tone, and obtains agreement to proceed.
Stage Two/Identify the Issues:	In this stage, disputants tell their stories uninterrupted. The mediator probes for facts and feelings, uses active listening, restates or summarizes what they hear, asks clarifying questions, and reframes negative statements. The mediator identifies the most salient issues, often listing them neutrally to form the agenda for the next stage.
Stage Three/Discussion and Problem-Solving:	This stage involves analyzing the issues on the agenda with a view toward resolution. Parties explore underlying interests and find common ground. The mediator asks questions to encourage focus on the future, clarity on options, and reality-testing.

	Brainstorming options in an open way is the goal.
Stage Four/Agreement/ Closure:	The final stage. If settlement is not reached, the process ends respectfully, noting progress. If resolution is reached, a clear, specific, and detailed mediation agreement is drafted. Independent legal advice is recommended before signing.
Transformative approach:	A style of mediation where the mediator fosters and supports positive interactions through techniques of empowerment and recognition. This approach focuses on preserving relationships and creating transformative opportunities.

Competing Interests The author has no conflicts of interest to declare that are relevant to the content of this chapter.

References

Action Committee on Access to Justice in Civil and Family Matters, Access to Civil & Family Justice: A Roadmap for Change (Ottawa: Action Committee on Access to Justice in Civil and Family Matters, October 2013) at 6, online: CFCJ ["A Roadmap for Change"].

Boulle, L., & Kelly, K. (1998). *Mediation: Principles, process, practice*. Butterworths.

Brett, J. M., Barsness, Z. I., & Goldberg, S. B. (1996). Effectiveness of mediation: An independent analysis of cases handled by four major service providers. *Negotiation Journal, 12*(3), 259–269.

Bush, R. A. B., & Folger, J. P. (2005). *The promise of mediation: The transformative approach to conflict*. Jossey-Bass.

Chang's Imports Inc. v. Srader 216 F. Supp. 2d 325 (20 Aug. 2002).

Farrow, T. C. W., Currie, A., Aylwin, N., Jacobs, L., Northrup, D., & Moore, L. (2016). *Everyday legal problems and the cost of justice in Canada* (overview report). *Canadian Forum on Civil Justice*.. https://www.cfcj-fcjc.org/sites/default/files/Everyday%20Legal%20Problems%20and%20the%20Cost%20of%20Justice%20in%20Canada%20-%20Overview%20Report.pdf

Furia v. Helm 111 Cal. App. 4th 945, 2003 Cal. App. LEXIS 1343.

International Mediation Institute. (2019, December). The global pound conference (GPC) Toronto report: Local findings from North America GPC series 2016–2017. AAA-ICDR Foundation. https://imimediation.org/2020/01/14/a-snapshot-of-toronto-a-taste-from-the-gpc-toronto-report/.

Johannes Moleko Sejane v. Commission for Conciliation, Mediation and Arbitration, Case No: J2789/99, 2001-10-02.

Lamare, R. (2014, May 20). *The evolution of ADR systems at large US corporations*. Dispute Resolution Magazine.

Lande, J. (2012). Teaching students to negotiate like a lawyer. *Washington University Journal of Law & Policy, 39*, 109–155.

Lawrence, A., Nugent, J., & Scarfone, C. (2007). *The effectiveness of using mediation in selected civil law disputes: A meta-analysis*. Department of Justice Canada. https://www.justice.gc.ca/eng/rp-pr/csj-sjc/jsp-sjp/rr07_3/p3.html

McClintock v Karam 2015 ONSC 1024.

Schneider, A. K. (2002). Shattering negotiation myths: Empirical evidence on the effectiveness of negotiation style. *Harvard Negotiation Law Review, 7*, 143–198.

Schulz, J. L. (2002). Mediator liability: Using custom to determine standards of care. *Saskatchewan Law Review, 65*, 163–179.

Schulz, J. L. (2020). *Mediation and popular culture*. Routledge.

Schulz, J. L. (2024). Mediator liability 23 years later: The 'three c's' of case law, codes & custom. *Ottawa Law Review, 55*(1), 151–186.

Schulz, J. L., & Turnbull, J. (2012). Mediation: The 'girly' litigation? *Journal of Arbitration and Mediation, 2*, 43–74.

Sinnadurai, M., McMahon, P., Vanderwindt, B., & Farrow, T. (2023). A call for evidence-based research in ADR. *Canadian Arbitration and Mediation Journal, 32*(1), 13–16.

Stipanowich, T. J. (2016, Winter). Insights on mediator practices and perception. *Dispute Resolution Magazine, 4*, 7–8.

T.H. Kasipersad v. CCMA Commissioner Linda Botha Case No: D719/02, 24 October 2002.

Vitakis-Valchine v. Valchine, 793 So. 2d 1094 (Fla Dist. Ct. App 2001).

Negotiation

Laura E. Reimer

Abstract Negotiation is a problem-solving technique that helps lawyers resolve disputes with opposing parties. It is the process of reaching mutually agreeable terms for a settlement or transaction. There are common elements, stages and principles that apply across different situations and even cultures. This chapter introduces the basic principles of negotiation, including the common stages of the process, the key points of successful negotiation, the difference between interests and positions in the negotiation process, and the main criteria of Principled Negotiation. The chapter presents the three familiar models of negotiation, all of which are relevant to the practice of law: soft, distributive and principled negotiation, which are evident in the chapter about the Canadian National Negotiation Competition. The chapter concludes with some of the common errors of negotiation, criticisms of principled negotiation, and a brief commentary about the role of negotiation in international conflict.

Keywords Negotiation process · Positions and interests · Principled negotiation · Negotiation sequence · Soft negotiation · Hard

---

L. E. Reimer (✉)
University of Manitoba, Winnipeg, MB, Canada
e-mail: laura.reimer@umanitoba.ca

L. E. Reimer and R. Jochelson (eds.), *The Other Side of the Bar*,
https://doi.org/10.1007/978-981-96-9748-9_6

negotiation · Retributive negotiation · BATNA · EATNA · Negotiation errors

Introduction

Negotiation is a fundamental component of legal practice. Lawyers engage in negotiation routinely in practice—whether settling disputes, finalizing contracts, or advocating for client interests. Within the legal field, negotiation functions as a voluntary, strategic process of problem-solving and bargaining that enables lawyers to reach resolutions with opposing counsel or parties (Warters, 2000, 6). It is the mechanism through which legal professionals strive to achieve mutually satisfactory terms in both settlements and transactions. Previous chapters have introduced tools for legal practitioners to evaluate their own cognitive biases, conflict resolution styles, and personality traits—factors that also manifest in clients and significantly influence negotiation results. For lawyers, honing negotiation skills is essential to effectively advance client outcomes and achieve favorable legal resolutions.

Beyond the legal sphere, the foundational principles of negotiation remain consistent across civil and criminal cases, as well as in global and international dispute contexts. These principles, discussed throughout this chapter, are exemplified in forums like the Canadian National Negotiation Competition, which illuminates both the pedagogy and application of legal negotiation. Within these settings, legal professionals engage in structured dialogues aimed at achieving compromise without resorting to litigation or hostility. This iterative, communicative process is often facilitated by legal representatives acting on behalf of individual or collective interests. Negotiation, in legal contexts, involves a deliberate exchange intended to align divergent perspectives through collaboration and skilled advocacy.

In their 1981 publication, *Getting to Yes: How to Negotiate Agreement without Giving In*, Roger Fisher and William Ury introduced the legal profession to the concept of principled negotiation (Fisher and Ury, 1981). This framework offers a systematic approach to resolving disputes and forming agreements based on objective criteria, mutual interests, and effective communication—principles particularly relevant to legal practitioners. With Bruce Patton joining as co-author in later editions

(2011), the text has become a cornerstone in legal negotiation literature. Derived from the Harvard Negotiation Project, the methodology promotes a structured, ethics-based strategy for resolving conflicts in legal settings. The widely adopted term "win-win"emerged from this work, encapsulating the goal of equitable outcomes through cooperative negotiation. Mastering these techniques equips lawyers—especially those in corporate law—with essential skills for both domestic and international practice. As Fisher, Ury, and Patton aptly note, "however unsavoury the other side…the question you face is not whether to negotiate, but how!" (Fisher, Ury, and Patton, 2011, 163).

Negotiation Process

One of the most compelling aspects of negotiation within the context of legal conflict transformation is its inherent nature as a constructive dialogue, designed to help parties reach agreements or compromises while minimizing adversarial disputes and emotional escalation. Negotiation is aptly described as "back-and-forth communication" (Fisher and Ury 1981, xxvii), a process that may be undertaken personally, on behalf of others, or through legal representation. Legal practitioners frequently negotiate not only for their clients but also in collaborative legal settings such as settlements, mediations, labour disputes, and international arbitration. The relevance of negotiation spans across multiple domains—including professional sports, employment law, business contracts, and international diplomacy—where the legal framework for resolving disputes often mirrors or complements the same negotiation principles.

Getting to Yes sets forth three key criteria for evaluating successful and sound legal negotiations. These measures are particularly valuable for lawyers in assessing the validity and integrity of both the agreement and the negotiation process:

1. The negotiation should result in a wise agreement, if an agreement is possible.
2. The process should be efficient.
3. The agreement and process should maintain or improve the relationship between the negotiating parties (Fisher et al., 1981, 4).

In legal conflict resolution, certain conditions tend to support successful negotiations. These include scenarios where multiple parties must make decisions affecting shared or interdependent interests, where there is mutual commitment to resolving conflict through peaceful means, and where no established legal procedure exists to guide the resolution (Lewicki, Saunders, and Minton, 1999, 1). Legal negotiation typically follows a sequence of stages (Nolan-Haley, 2013, 27):

1. Preparation and planning
2. Discussion and exchanging information
3. Clarification of goals
4. Negotiating toward a win-win outcome through concession and compromise
5. Agreement
6. Implementation of a course of action

In real-world legal settings, however, these phases are fluid rather than linear. Legal negotiations often unfold unpredictably, shaped by the unique dynamics of each case and the behavior of the parties involved. Departures from a rigid sequence are not indicative of a failed negotiation, but rather, they highlight the nuanced and iterative nature of legal dispute resolution. Each stage—even if momentarily or briefly encountered—contributes to the progress of the negotiation and may recur as parties reassess their positions.

Numerous factors can influence legal negotiation outcomes, and not all serve the process constructively. Lawyers may encounter parties who adopt positional or defensive tactics, prioritizing personal advantage over collaborative resolution. Additionally, within institutional or governmental environments, those in leadership roles may resist negotiation, viewing it as a threat to authority rather than a legitimate form of dispute resolution. Nonetheless, negotiation remains a critical tool in the legal practitioner's skill set—an indispensable method for resolving conflicts and advancing legal solutions in an effective, principled, and human-centered manner.

Positions and Interests

Two core principles in negotiation theory are positions and interests, both of which must be thoroughly understood to facilitate effective dispute resolution. A *position* represents a party's stated demand or stance, while an *interest* encapsulates the underlying motivations, concerns, or needs that drive a party to adopt that position. Positions tend to be explicit, making them easily identifiable, whereas interests are often implicit, intangible, and subject to fluctuation, because they are rooted in concerns, aspirations, and fears. Given their significance in fostering mutually beneficial outcomes, and that they contain the keys to a good, wise, satisfactory agreement, interests are considered the cornerstone of a principled negotiation strategy.

The most prevalent form of negotiation is positional negotiation, or positional bargaining, in which parties iteratively assert and modify their positions (they bargain), until an agreement is reached. However, this method frequently leads to inefficiencies and strains relationships due to its adversarial nature. Illustratively, positional statements such as "I want the car" followed by "No, I want the car" exemplify the rigid contest that often arises. Scholars Ury, Fisher, and Patton critique positional bargaining, emphasizing that it typically results in suboptimal outcomes. In international diplomacy, an undue focus on positional stances has historically contributed to protracted conflicts and even violence. Such an approach inherently places substantive interests and relationships at odds with one another. While articulating positions can provide clarity, an adversarial stance is not the sole means of achieving an equitable agreement.

Conversely, interest-based negotiation, also referred to as integrative or cooperative bargaining, seeks to reconcile the underlying interests of all parties rather than merely contesting positions. Fisher, Ury, and Patton (2011, 21) argue that negotiators ultimately strive to reach agreements that address their substantive interests, as these interests define the core issues requiring resolution. Interests, encompassing desires and concerns, drive negotiations and hold the key to sustainable agreements. As they assert, "The basic problem in a negotiation lies not in conflicting positions, but in the conflict between each side's needs, desires, concerns, and fears… Interests motivate people; they are the silent movers behind the hubbub of positions"(Fisher, Ury, and Patton, 2011, 43). Accordingly, prioritizing the identification and consideration of interests fosters a negotiation process that is more constructive and results in more satisfactory, durable agreements that reflect the best interests of each party, and leads to a better process and much better outcomes.

Most of the negotiation literature focuses on one of the interest or positional strategies, with a number of different names (Burgess, 2004, online). Prior to the advent of Fisher and Ury's work, negotiation strategies had been categorized into two predominant approaches: interest-based (integrative or cooperative) bargaining and positional (distributive or competitive) bargaining (Burgess, 2004, online). These approaches are often described in terms of "hard" and "soft" negotiation styles, each of which entails distinct strategic considerations and implications for the negotiation outcome.

Soft Negotiation

According to the literature, soft negotiation is extreme integrative bargaining. Soft negotiation is so integrated in terms of satisfying the other party that the negotiator wants to avoid conflict, if at all possible (Burgess, 2004, online). Although the parties bargain over positions, soft negotiators are usually highly relational, and their efforts are directed toward preserving the relationship. They treat the other participant in the negotiation as a friend, trusting for a good outcome, and open up about what they really need from the negotiation. Soft negotiators will make concessions, give in, and in general want agreement to come quickly. Like conflict avoiders, soft negotiators will abandon their own interests in an effort to satisfy the interests of the other party. Soft negotiators are vulnerable to competitive negotiators and often end up feeling unsatisfied with the negotiation process.

Almost all negotiation processes are combinations of hard and soft approaches. *Beyond Intractability* (2025), a well-used conflict resolution web resource, explains: "First negotiators try to 'create value' by enlarging the pie as much as they can. (This is the approach advocated by interest-based and principled negotiation.) But inevitably, the pie will then need to be divided up, which calls for distributive negotiation. So they claim that all negotiation is a combination of creating and claiming value, not one or the other as other theorists suggest" (Burgess, 2004). To more clearly understand the influences of soft negotiation, hard negotiation is explained below.

Hard Negotiation

In legal conflict resolution, hard negotiation represents a highly competitive and adversarial approach to bargaining. Known by various terms—such as positional, power-based, adversarial, or "hard-ball"—it is most referred to in legal literature as distributive negotiation. This model operates under a zero-sum framework, where the presumption is that only one party can prevail or attain meaningful gains. In contrast to interest-based or integrative bargaining, distributive negotiation is focused solely on securing unilateral advantage rather than pursuing mutually beneficial outcomes. For legal practitioners, this type of negotiation is a battle of endurance and tactics, where the party most resistant to compromise is often viewed as the victor (Fisher, Ury, and Patton, 2011). The primary objective in this context is to secure maximum benefit with minimal concession—often at the expense of long-term relationships or reputational integrity.

In distributive legal negotiations, the dialogue centers around fixed positions rather than underlying interests. Lawyers employing this method may utilize coercive tactics, including the exertion of power, strategic use of silence, or deliberately inflated demands—all intended to manipulate the negotiation process. These tactics aim to wear down opposition, often through prolonged engagement or psychological pressure. Distributive negotiators are advised to avoid disclosing their opening positions prematurely or accepting the first offer on the table. Tactics such as feigned reluctance or maintaining prolonged discussions are designed to increase leverage and extract concessions. In scenarios where one party adopts a hard approach and the other a soft, the hard negotiator typically secures the upper hand but at the cost of damaging, if not entirely severing, the relationship—yielding a "win-lose" outcome. When both parties rely on hard negotiation, the process often deteriorates into a "lose-lose" scenario, undermining both the agreement and the parties involved. By contrast, when two soft negotiators engage, they often reach a quick consensus that favours relationship preservation over positional dominance, achieving a "win-win" result.

A compelling case study of conflict resolution through legal negotiation is the Camp David Accords of 1978, involving US President Jimmy Carter, Israeli Prime Minister Menachem Begin, and Egyptian President Anwar Sadat. In a moment of hard-line posturing, Prime Minister Begin is said to have declared he would sever his own right hand before conceding land in the Sinai Peninsula—a classic example of hard negotiation rhetoric. Recognizing the impasse and the risks posed by entrenched positions, President Carter skillfully redirected the negotiation toward mutual interests. By suggesting that Israel's parliament—not Begin personally—could authorize the concessions, Carter allowed both leaders to maintain their dignity while shifting the process toward a more collaborative, interest-based framework. This pivotal moment exemplified a successful transition from positional, hard bargaining to a principled negotiation model, one that safeguarded the core interests of both nations and preserved critical political relationships (Wilmot and Hocker 2014).

Principled Negotiation

Principled negotiation, developed by the Harvard Negotiation Project, offers legal practitioners a framework for resolving disputes by focusing on the merits of the issues rather than engaging in positional bargaining. This approach emphasizes reaching outcomes that are fair, efficient, and mutually beneficial—an essential strategy in legal practice where sustained relationships and ethical outcomes often matter as much as legal victories. Unlike traditional adversarial tactics, principled negotiation seeks common ground and mutual gains, which can be particularly useful in contract discussions, settlements, and mediation (Fisher, Ury, and Patton, 2011, xvii). According to Fisher, Ury, and Patton (2011, 17–95), four core principles guide this approach:

1. Focus on People, not Problems
2. Focus on Interests, not Positions
3. Invent Options for Mutual Gain
4. Insist on Using Objective Criteria

This methodology—also known in legal circles as integrative, interest-based, or problem-solving negotiation—applies across a broad spectrum of legal contexts, including multi-party disputes, complex litigation, and transactional law. It accommodates parties of unequal negotiation experience and assumes that mutual benefits are achievable. Lawyers engaging in principled negotiation must demonstrate both active listening and clear communication to achieve resolutions that meet client interests without sacrificing integrity. The model presumes that legal negotiators understand both their own clients' priorities and those of the opposing party, recognizing that interests may differ but are not inherently antagonistic (Fisher, Ury, and Patton, 2011, xvii).

Principled negotiation eschews deceptive tactics and posturing, instead favoring transparency, trust, and strategic collaboration. In practice, lawyers using this model aim to secure what their clients need while facilitating favorable terms for opposing parties when possible, ensuring durable and implementable agreements (Wilmot and Hocker, 2014). Trust, interdependence, and openness—key components often absent in hard bargaining—are fundamental to this legal negotiation style.

BATNAs and EATNAs

In the context of legal negotiation, BATNA—Best Alternative to a Negotiated Agreement—is a fundamental principle that underpins the strategy of principled negotiation. Developed by Fisher and Ury (1981), BATNA enables lawyers and their clients to assess whether a proposed settlement is preferable to proceeding with litigation or another course of action. In legal practice, understanding one's BATNA is critical; it serves not only as a fallback plan but also as a benchmark against which any negotiated outcome should be evaluated (Lax and Sebenius, 1991, 99).

At its core, the BATNA framework allows legal professionals to test the value of a negotiated agreement against available alternatives. For instance, if a client is confident of a favorable and expedient court ruling, that litigated outcome may be deemed superior to any negotiated resolution. In high-stakes legal matters such as international treaty enforcement or regulatory disputes, the most viable alternative may be to extend negotiations rather than prematurely accept a suboptimal settlement. Similarly, in sports law or contract negotiations, free agency functions as a legal BATNA—players can explore competing offers, thereby strengthening their negotiation position (Glaser, 2005, np).

Building upon this concept, negotiation experts Guy Burgess and Heidi Burgess (1998, online) introduced the term EATNA—Estimated Alternatives to a Negotiated Agreement—to highlight the psychological aspect of alternatives in negotiation. In the legal realm, this notion is highly relevant, as clients often make decisions based on perceived, rather than actual, legal outcomes. EATNAs suggest that perception can drive parties toward or away from resolution. For legal negotiators, this underscores the importance of managing client expectations and thoroughly assessing not only the strengths of a case but also how alternatives are interpreted by all parties.

Recognizing both one's own BATNA or EATNA and accurately estimating that of the opposing party enhances the strategic use of principled negotiation. This awareness allows legal professionals to steer discussions in a direction that fulfills both parties' underlying interests and supports the development of an agreement that meets the accepted standards of a successful legal negotiation—efficiency, fairness, and relationship preservation.

Brainstorming

A vital element of integrative negotiation, particularly within legal dispute resolution, is the practice of brainstorming. In legal negotiation settings—whether mediating civil disputes, drafting settlement agreements, or resolving family law conflicts—brainstorming allows legal professionals and their clients to creatively explore options without immediate judgment. Lawyers must encourage clients to generate as many ideas as possible, free from the constraints of assessing feasibility or value at the outset. This strategy fosters creativity, increases engagement, and avoids prematurely discarding potentially valuable options. Emphasizing quantity over quality initially, legal negotiators can then guide clients to analyze, refine, and prioritize options, aiming for outcomes that address the interests of all parties.

An enduring illustration of this concept is the classic "orange story," frequently used in legal negotiation training. Imagine two parties each demand the same orange, and the legal practitioner is called to resolve the dispute. Many intervenors would suggest cutting the orange in half or finding a substitute—seemingly fair, but often unsatisfying. However, a lawyer practicing principled negotiation would explore the underlying interests: one party seeks the fruit to satisfy hunger, the other needs the zest for baking. By peeling the orange and dividing it accordingly, both parties receive 100% of what they need. Though simple, this example demonstrates the power of asking why a party wants what they want—a skill essential for lawyers resolving more complex, interest-based legal disputes.

Principled negotiation scales to cases involving custody arrangements, business dissolutions, or property disputes. In such matters, the ability to delve into parties' true motivations allows legal negotiators to craft durable solutions that protect interests and preserve relationships. The use of integrative strategies like brainstorming can lead to outcomes that satisfy all parties, strengthening client satisfaction and ethical practice in law.

Nevertheless, legal negotiators must also emphasize the development of a strong BATNA—Best Alternative to a Negotiated Agreement. Legal education and practice teaches that a well-defined BATNA serves as a safeguard, preventing clients from agreeing to unfavorable settlements and empowering them to walk away when necessary. Unlike rigid bottom lines, BATNAs offer strategic flexibility, enabling lawyers to negotiate with confidence, even under pressure.

When the four foundational principles of principled negotiation—separating people from the problem, focusing on interests over positions, generating options for mutual gain, and using objective criteria—are implemented effectively, outcomes are often optimal. Lawyers find these approaches especially valuable in emotionally charged fields such as family law, where preserving relationships is critical. By transforming adversarial conflict into collaborative problem-solving, principled negotiation allows legal professionals to not only resolve disputes but also to do so in a way that respects all involved.

Criticisms of Principled Negotiation

As a legal practitioner engaged in the art and application of conflict resolution, it is essential to approach even the most well-regarded negotiation frameworks with a critical lens. As presented above, principled negotiation, developed at the Harvard Negotiation Project, is a foundational model widely utilized in North America and beyond. Its emphasis on mutual interests, objective standards, and collaborative problem-solving has proven valuable in a range of legal contexts—from mediation and civil litigation to family law and contract disputes. However, it is important to acknowledge and explore the critiques that have emerged regarding its theoretical underpinnings and practical limitations.

One significant critique centres on the method's Western origin and cultural assumptions. While principled negotiation offers a systematic and rational approach to reaching agreements, some scholars argue that it tends to trivialize the complexities of conflict. Critics suggest that the model risks reducing nuanced, context-specific disputes into standardized procedures, potentially overlooking cultural, emotional, and relational dynamics that are often central to legal conflicts (Funken 2002, 3). This routinization of conflict resolution methods may be less effective in legal settings where power disparities, historical injustices, or identity-based tensions are prominent.

UK labour negotiator Lord William McCarthy (1985), offers pointed critiques of principled negotiation's limitations in addressing power dynamics. From a legal perspective, this is especially relevant. In negotiations involving vulnerable clients, such as victims of domestic violence, marginalized communities, or individuals in disputes with large institutions, the distribution of power significantly shapes the negotiation landscape. McCarthy (1991, 119) contends that the development of a strong BATNA (Best Alternative to a Negotiated Agreement), while useful, does not fully address the core issue of unequal power relations. He asserts that a realistic analysis of the balance of power is often more determinative of a settlement's feasibility than the presence of objective criteria or interest-based bargaining.

Furthermore, McCarthy critiques the implicit assumption within principled negotiation that the same methods apply uniformly across diverse negotiation arenas. From a legal education standpoint, this is an important teaching point. Whether handling labour negotiations governed by union politics, international disputes steeped in diplomatic strategy, or family disagreements marked by emotional history, the context fundamentally alters the dynamics at play. Political, ideological, and relational variables differ drastically across domains, and legal negotiators must be trained to adapt their approach accordingly.

In sum, while principled negotiation remains a valuable framework within legal practice, particularly for its emphasis on fairness and structured dialogue, its limitations must be addressed in legal training and practice. Lawyers should be equipped not only to apply this model but also to recognize when its assumptions may not hold, and when power analysis, cultural sensitivity, recognition of trauma responses, and contextual judgment must take precedence to achieve just and sustainable outcomes.

Negotiation Errors

David Lax and James Sebenius, widely respected scholars in the field of negotiation theory, have outlined a critical dilemma faced by negotiators: the tension between choosing a cooperative or competitive approach. This fundamental choice often gives rise to errors, which can exacerbate conflict if left unaddressed (Glaser, 1992, pp. 49–62). Particularly relevant to the legal profession, where negotiation is a frequent and essential part of practice, these insights help frame a more thoughtful approach to resolving disputes.

In his 2001 article, James Sebenius offered a detailed summary of common negotiation mistakes, drawing from both empirical observation and theoretical research (Sebenius, 2001, pp. 87–95). According to Sebenius, the most effective way to avoid these pitfalls is to maintain a clear focus on solving the correct problem—a task that often becomes obscured in high-pressure scenarios. Whether in business transactions, litigation settlements, or international diplomacy, negotiators working in legal and regulatory frameworks can find themselves under immense pressure. In such conditions, practitioners may fixate on procedural stages or tactics, losing sight of the overarching aim: to transform conflict into a constructive outcome.

Sebenius attributes these errors to deeply rooted bad habits, which in turn impede the development of constructive negotiating behaviors. He emphasizes a foundational principle: "Your negotiation problem is to understand and shape your counterpart's perceived decision so that the other side chooses in its own interest what you want" (Sebenius, 2001, p. 88). Although this may initially appear manipulative, in practice, it reflects a deeper strategic empathy—framing proposals in a way that satisfies both parties' core interests, thereby fostering sustainable agreements.

Sebenius (2001) identifies six primary negotiation errors, along with their more productive counterparts, which are particularly relevant to lawyers, mediators, and judges involved in dispute resolution. He identifies six "bad habits" (Reimer et al., 2015, 94). These are neglecting the other side's problem, letting cost concerns in its many forms overtake other interests, letting positions drive out interests, searching so hard for common ground that it is missed, fail to correct for bias, and finally, neglecting the BATNA.

Conversely, Sebenius identifies six good habits of successful negotiation (Reimer et al., 2015, 94). These are: solve the other side's problem as a means of solving one's own; work with the interests of the parties as a whole and focus on relationship; recognize and balance the tension between cooperation and competition; recognize that differences can also transform conflict; recognize that the potential deal and the BATNA work together like two blades on scissors; and prepare extensively, including research about the other party's interests.These behaviors and assumptions commonly emerge during negotiation and often lead to suboptimal results. While "bad habits" may arise naturally in the course of negotiation, practitioners are urged to instead cultivate "good habits." As with any professional practice, the quality of outcomes in negotiation often depends on the habits that guide decision-making. In legal negotiation, where rights, obligations, and relationships are at stake, awareness and correction of these errors are essential for achieving fair, efficient, and durable resolutions.

International Negotiation

Negotiation is a fundamental mechanism in managing international conflict, and its relevance extends directly to legal negotiations within the realm of international law and diplomacy. While a significant body of research in strategic conflict resolution focuses on interpersonal dynamics, legal scholars and practitioners recognize that the principles underpinning legal negotiation also apply within the international conflict arena. In these important ways, opportunities are identified for potential positive or constructive change on the path to shared futures and respect for multiple voices (Reimer and Schmitz 2022). William Zartman (1981) identified essential preconditions for the initiation of negotiations in international disputes. Bercovitch and Jackson (2001, 2) further articulated these legal-analytical conditions as follows:

1. A low or decreasing probability of achieving conflict objectives through unilateral means such as violent confrontation, withdrawal, or non-engagement;
2. A decline in the perceived value of conflict goals in comparison to the tangible and intangible costs of continued pursuit, and in comparison to alternative legal or diplomatic objectives;

3. The presence of shared or at least non-conflicting interests between parties, or a scenario in which a negotiated settlement offers more mutual benefit than ongoing conflict;
4. Sufficient political and legal flexibility within each party's leadership to consider negotiation as a viable resolution mechanism.

Under these preconditions, the methodologies and tactics that apply to legal negotiation—such as interest-based bargaining, use of leverage, legal precedent, and treaty interpretation—serve as vital tools in the transformation of international conflict into structured legal agreements.

Although this volume does not delve deeply into the specifics of international legal negotiations, it is evident that negotiations on both bilateral and multilateral levels occur daily. A notable example is the ceasefire negotiation between Russia and Ukraine following the 2014 incursion of Russian forces into Ukrainian territory. The diplomatic summit held in Minsk, Belarus on February 12, 2015, included representatives from Russia, Ukraine, France, and Germany. These 17-hour negotiations culminated in a ceasefire agreement and addressed complex legal and constitutional issues, including federal reform in Ukraine to accommodate ethnic Russians in the Donbas region, demilitarization efforts, and the resolution of border and humanitarian concerns. Each element followed a structured negotiation format similar to those employed in legal settings. Despite the agreement, Russia launched a renewed invasion in February 2022, escalating the conflict and illustrating the fragility of legal agreements without robust enforcement mechanisms.

Another illustrative case of international legal negotiation involves the protracted conflict over Iran's nuclear program. Although Iran has maintained that its nuclear endeavors are peaceful, Western legal and diplomatic authorities have raised concerns over its activities in uranium enrichment and weapons delivery capabilities. Negotiations spanning two decades have centered on creating a legally binding framework to ensure non-proliferation. A key breakthrough occurred in November 2013, when Iran reached an interim agreement with the United Kingdom, France, the United States, China, and Germany. This accord resulted from extensive negotiation, during which Iran agreed to scale back nuclear activities in exchange for the easing of international sanctions. The terms and obligations under this agreement reflected not only political compromise but also complex legal commitments grounded in international norms.

Legal negotiation, particularly in the international sphere, is crucial for ceasing hostilities and setting the terms of peace within a legal framework. While transforming conflict and cultures is an ongoing, circular process, the backbone for the process is grounded in developing personal and interpersonal skills, building capacity, and transforming relationships (Reimer and Schmitz 2022, 16). Once agreements are established, post-conflict legal systems can begin reconstruction processes, emphasizing the importance of durable legal institutions over continued violence. Additionally, lawyers engaged in international negotiation must possess a thorough understanding of treaty law, customary international legal principles, and procedural diplomatic norms to secure agreements that are not only effective but legally enforceable under international law.

Conclusion

In the context of legal negotiations, the process of resolving disputes through dialogue and bargaining is enriched by applying the principles of negotiation as outlined by Roger Fisher and William Ury in the various published editions of Getting to Yes. According to them, successful negotiation is measured by three core criteria: producing a wise agreement (if agreement is possible), efficiently resolving the conflict, and improving—or at least not damaging—the relationship between the parties. Legal professionals are particularly encouraged to pursue principled negotiation, which focuses on separating people from the problem, focusing on interests rather than positions, generating options for mutual gain, and using objective criteria.

Understanding the distinction between positions—what a party says they want—and interests—why they want it—is crucial to transforming conflict in legal practice. Positional bargaining, whether in a hard (adversarial and competitive) or soft (accommodating and yielding) form, often undermines relationships and leaves at least one party dissatisfied. In contrast, principled negotiation seeks durable outcomes that respect each party's underlying interests.

Fisher and Ury introduced the concept of BATNA (Best Alternative to a Negotiated Agreement), which empowers negotiators to walk away if a proposed agreement is inferior to their alternatives. Expanding on this, Guy Burgess and Heidi Burgess introduced EATNAs (Estimated Alternatives to a Negotiated Agreement), emphasizing the collective perceptions and expectations of groups, particularly in complex or large-scale disputes.

To further enrich negotiation practice, it is essential to view negotiation not merely as a transactional tool, but as a space for relational justice—a process that attends to recognition, dignity, and the repair of strained relationships. Negotiation is often one of the few moments in legal practice where parties interact directly, and that encounter can either reinforce disconnection or open the door to renewed respect and understanding. When legal professionals approach negotiation with an awareness of the human and relational dimensions at play, the process becomes more than a means to an end; it becomes a mechanism for building trust, fostering accountability, and acknowledging harm.

Moreover, meaningful negotiation requires attention to epistemic repair: addressing whose experiences and knowledge are given weight during the process. Traditional legal negotiation frameworks often center a narrow set of communication styles and cultural norms, which may inadvertently marginalize parties whose ways of knowing and expressing interests differ. A more inclusive approach to negotiation invites reflection on how structure, culture, and history shape the terms of engagement—and how systemic imbalances can be replicated if left unexamined. By actively creating space for diverse voices and alternative epistemologies, negotiation can serve as a corrective force rather than a site of continued exclusion.

Integrating these commitments also aligns with a vision of transformative practice, in which the goal of negotiation extends beyond resolution alone. In this view, effective negotiation not only solves the immediate problem but also shifts how parties relate to one another going forward. It encourages legal practitioners to consider how procedural choices, tone, and framing can support more equitable relationships and durable outcomes. This orientation transforms negotiation from a tactical exercise into a practice of justice itself—one that models the kind of legal culture that values both outcome and process, both agreement and dignity.

While principled negotiation provides a valuable framework, it has faced criticism for being "too Western," particularly in its emphasis on individualism, rationality, and direct communication styles, which may not align with cultural norms in other parts of the world. This does not, however, lessen its value for common law lawyers engaged in negotiations. Additionally, negotiation errors such as failure to prepare adequately, ignoring interests, or resorting to positional strategies are pitfalls outlined in the preceding chapter.

In international contexts, negotiation is an indispensable tool for diplomacy, conflict resolution, and legal settlement, offering structured means to bridge cultural, political, and legal differences. It fosters cooperation and mutual understanding, serving as a critical mechanism in both bilateral and multilateral interactions.

Questions

1 Reflect on a past personal negotiation—such as resolving a dispute, making a purchase, or arranging a collaboration. How might the outcome have differed if you had applied the negotiation strategies and models (e.g., positional vs. interest-based, hard vs. principled) now covered in your legal negotiation studies?
2. Simulate a legal negotiation within a mock group project (e.g., forming a legal team to prepare a case). Identify five distinct responsibilities (such as research, drafting, oral advocacy, coordination, and peer review). Negotiate role assignments and reflect on the process by answering the following:

- How did the negotiation unfold, and what procedural steps were taken to manage the legal aspects of the dispute?
  (This emphasizes structure, which is crucial in legal negotiations.)
- What legal interests and underlying concerns did each party bring to the negotiation, and how were they identified and addressed?
  (This focuses on distinguishing between legal positions and interests—a key concept in principled negotiation.)
- Were there any legal or ethical challenges during the negotiation, and how were they resolved to maintain professional standards and fairness?
  (Highlights the importance of ethics and legal propriety in practice.)
- In hindsight, how could the negotiation process have been improved from a legal strategy standpoint to yield a more effective or just outcome?
  (Encourages reflection through a legal lens, aimed at improving future negotiations.)

3. Choose a well-known children's story and rewrite it to include legal negotiation principles. Focus on embedding elements such as separating people from the problem, focusing on interests over positions, and proposing mutually beneficial outcomes.
4. Analyze a film or television episode that features a legal or quasi-legal negotiation (e.g., contract dispute, courtroom settlement, or diplomatic dialogue). Identify how the principles of principled negotiation were demonstrated. What key elements were effective or missing, and how could the resolution have been improved by applying concepts such as BATNA, objective criteria, or mutual gains?

Glossary

Negotiation. A problem-solving technique that helps parties resolve disputes or reach agreements on mutually agreeable terms for a settlement or transaction. It is a voluntary, strategic process of problem-solving and bargaining. Negotiation is described as "back-and-forth communication" and is a fundamental component of legal practice used for settling disputes, finalizing contracts, and advocating for client interests.

Principled Negotiation. A framework developed by the Harvard Negotiation Project for resolving disputes by focusing on the merits of the issues rather than engaging in positional bargaining. This approach emphasizes reaching outcomes that are fair, efficient, and mutually beneficial. It is guided by four core principles: focusing on people (not problems), focusing on interests (not positions), inventing options for mutual gain, and insisting on using objective criteria. It is also known as integrative, interest-based, or problem-solving negotiation.

A framework developed by the Harvard Negotiation Project for resolving disputes by focusing on the merits of the issues rather than engaging in positional bargaining. This approach emphasizes reaching outcomes that are fair, efficient, and mutually beneficial. It is guided by four core principles: focusing on people (not problems), focusing on interests (not positions), inventing options for mutual gain, and insisting on using objective criteria. It is also known as integrative, interest-based, or problem-solving negotiation.

Positions. A party's stated demand or stance in negotiation. Positions tend to be explicit and easily identifiable. Focusing on positions is the basis of positional bargaining, which can lead to inefficiencies and strain relationships.

Interests. The underlying motivations, concerns, or needs that drive a party to adopt a position. Interests are often implicit, intangible, and rooted in concerns, aspirations, and fears. They are considered the cornerstone of a principled negotiation strategy because they hold the keys to a good, wise, satisfactory agreement. Interests motivate people and are the "silent movers behind the hubbub of positions."

Soft Negotiation. An extreme form of integrative bargaining where the negotiator prioritizes avoiding conflict and preserving the relationship. Soft negotiators are highly relational, treat the other party as a friend, and are open about their needs. They will make concessions and abandon their own interests to satisfy the other party's interests.

Hard Negotiation. A highly competitive and adversarial approach to bargaining. Also known as positional, power-based, adversarial, "hard-ball," or most commonly in legal literature, distributive negotiation. This model operates under a zero-sum framework, where the goal is securing unilateral advantage rather than mutual benefit. Hard negotiators focus on fixed positions and may use coercive tactics like strategic silence or inflated demands to gain leverage.

Distributive Negotiation. The most common term in legal literature for hard negotiation. It is a competitive and adversarial approach focused on securing maximum benefit with minimal concession, often at the expense of relationships. The dialogue centers around fixed positions.

Interest-BASED **Negotiation**. Also known as integrative or cooperative bargaining, this approach seeks to reconcile the underlying interests of all parties rather than just contesting positions. It aims for satisfactory, durable agreements that reflect the best interests of each party.

BATNA (Best Alternative to a Negotiated Agreement). A fundamental principle in principled negotiation developed by Fisher and Ury. It allows parties to assess whether a proposed settlement is preferable to proceeding with litigation or another course of action. Understanding one's

	BATNA is critical as it serves as a fall-back plan and a benchmark to evaluate any negotiated outcome. A well-defined BATNA prevents clients from agreeing to unfavorable settlements and empowers them to walk away when necessary.
EATNA (Estimated Alternatives to a Negotiated Agreement).	Introduced by Guy Burgess and Heidi Burgess. This term highlights the psychological aspect of alternatives, suggesting that clients often make decisions based on perceived, rather than actual, legal outcomes. EATNAs indicate that perception can influence parties towards or away from resolution.
Brainstorming.	A vital element of integrative negotiation used to creatively explore options without immediate judgment. In legal negotiation settings, it allows professionals and clients to generate as many ideas as possible, fostering creativity and engagement before assessing feasibility.

Competing Interests This work was funded by the Marcel A. Desautels Centre for Private Enterprise and the Law at the Faculty of Law, University of Manitoba at which Dr. Reimer is the Director.

The author has no conflicts of interest to declare that are relevant to the content of this chapter.

References

Bercovitch, J., & Jackson, R. (2007). Negotiation or mediation?: An exploration of factors affecting the choice of conflict management in international conflict. *Negotiation Journal*. https://doi.org/10.1111/j.1571-9979.2001.tb00227.x

Burgess, H. (2004). Negotiation strategies. *Beyond Intractability*. http://www.beyondintractability.org

Burgess, G., & Burgess, H. (1998). Limits to agreement: Better alternatives. *Conflict Research Consortium.*. http://www.colorado.edu/conflict/peace/problem/batna.htm

Fisher, R., & Ury, W. (1981). *Getting to yes!: Negotiating agreement without giving in*. Penguin Group.

Fisher, R., Ury, W., & Patton, B. (2011). *Getting to yes: Negotiating agreement without giving in* (3rd ed.). Penguin Books.

Funken, K. (2002). The pros and cons of getting to yes-shortcomings and limitations of principled bargaining in negotiation and mediation. *SSRN*. https://doi.org/10.2139/ssrn.293381

Glaser, T. (2005). Conflict research consortium. Book review: Lax, D., & Sebenius, J. David Lax. The power of alternatives or the limits to negotiation. In W. J. Breslin & J. Z. Rubin (Eds.), *In negotiation theory and practice*. The Program on Negotiation at Harvard Law School.

Beyond Intractability. (2025) May 8. https://www.beyondintractability.org/about/citing-beyond-intractability-resources.

Lax, D., & Sebenius, J. (1991). The power of alternatives or the limits to negotiation. In W. Breslin & J. Z. Rubin (Eds.), *In negotiation theory and practice*. The Program on Negotiation at Harvard Law School.

Lewicki, R. J., Saunders, D. M., & Minton, J. W. (1999). *Essentials of negotiation*. McGraw Hill.

McCarthy, W. (1985). January. The role of power and principle in getting to yes. *Negotiation Journal*, 59–66. https://doi.org/10.1111/j.1571-9979.1985.tb00292.x

McCarthy, W. (1991). The role of power and principle in getting to yes. In J. W. Breslin & J. Z. Rubin (Eds.), *Negotiation theory and practice* (pp. 115–122). The Program on Negotiation at Harvard Law School.

Nolan-Haley, J. M. (2013). *Alternative dispute resolution in a nutshell*. West Publishing.

Reimer, L. E., & Schmitz, C. L. (2022). International conflict transformation: The pursuit of positive peace. In K. Standish, H. Devrere, A. Suazo, & R. Rafferty (Eds.), *The Palgrave handbook of positive peace*. Palgrave Macmillan. https://doi.org/10.1007/978-981-15-3877-3_17-1

Reimer, L. E., Schmitz, C. L., Janke, E.M., Askerov, A., Strahl, b. T., Matyók, T. G. (2015). Transformative change: An introduction to peace and conflict studies..

Sebenius, J. K. (2001). Six habits of merely effective negotiators. *Harvard Business Review:87–95*.

Warters, W. C. (2000). *Mediation in the campus community: Designing effective programs*. Jossey-Bass.

Wilmot, W., & Hocker, J. (2014). *Interpersonal conflict*. McGraw-Hill.

Zartman, W. (1981). Explaining disengagement. In J. Rubin (Ed.), *Dynamics of third party intervention: Kissinger in the Middle East*. Praeger.

The Pedagogical Value of the Canadian National Negotiation Competition

Bruce J. Curran, Michaela Keet, John C. Kleefeld, and Gemma Smyth

Abstract The skill set required of lawyers is evolving, and the ability to creatively and expeditiously resolve client concerns through effective negotiation is increasingly important. In this chapter, we argue that negotiation competitions are an excellent method to nurture the knowledge, skills, attitudes, judgment, and values—or competencies—that are vital to law students' success in legal practice. Such competencies include knowing key negotiation concepts; managing information and process; communicating and relationship-building; advocating for client interests in a problem-solving environment; being aware of and managing one's own biases; internalizing ethical decision-making in negotiation, and engaging in reflective practice. These competencies are not the focus

B. J. Curran (✉)
University of Manitoba Faculty of Law, Winnipeg, Canada
e-mail: bruce.curran@umanitoba.ca

M. Keet
University of Saskatchewan College of Law, Saskatoon, Canada

J. C. Kleefeld
University of New Brunswick Faculty of Law, Fredericton, Canada

G. Smyth
University of Windsor Faculty of Law, Windsor, Canada

L. E. Reimer and R. Jochelson (eds.), *The Other Side of the Bar*,
https://doi.org/10.1007/978-981-96-9748-9_7

of certain other kinds of law student competitions, such as appellate and trial moots, which are designed to sharpen legal analysis and rights-based advocacy in an adversarial model. The Canadian National Negotiation Competition (CNNC) departs from that model. It gives law students the opportunity to engage in negotiations like those that lawyers experience in practice and to receive feedback from experts, in either English or French streams. It also invites students to wrestle with complex scenarios that feature both business and broader social policy tensions and objectives. In this chapter, the authors recount their experience with developing, running and growing the CNNC for nine years and highlight some of the key pedagogical lessons learned.

Keywords Experiential learning · Problem-solving · Professional identity · Expert practice · Reflective practice · Negotiation phases · Negotiation competencies

Introduction

Experiential education is an effective pedagogy to provide law students with the knowledge, skills, attitudes, judgment, and values—jointly, "competencies" (Govaerts, 2008)—that are critical to their success as lawyers (Stuckey et al., 2007; Sullivan et al., 2007). "Experiential education" has been described as "integrating theory and practice by combining academic inquiry with actual experience" (Stuckey et al., 2007, p. 121). It helps students adjust to their professional roles, become better legal problem-solvers, develop interpersonal and professional skills, and learn how to learn from experience (Stuckey et al., 2007).

Proficiency in dispute resolution and negotiation is critical to success in law study and legal practice and is in demand in the job market, yet most lawyers are inadequately trained in it (Folberg & Reynolds, 2022; Sullivan et al., 2007). Negotiation is at the core of what lawyers do, which is to solve a client's problems (Macfarlane, 2017; Menkel-Meadow, 1999; Stuckey et al., 2007). In short, negotiation is "everywhere" and "is a lawyer's 'bread and butter'" (Farrow, 2008, p. 12). The lawyer's skill set is evolving, and the ability to creatively and expeditiously resolve client concerns is increasingly important (Macfarlane, 2017). The Federation of Law Societies' amended National Requirement requires that Canadian law schools commit to integrating experiential learning, and that graduates demonstrate problem-solving competencies directed at exploring resolutions to legal problems (Federation of Law Societies of Canada, 2024).

Lawyers may think they are skilled negotiators because they negotiate often. But negotiating often doesn't necessarily mean negotiating effectively. Negotiation is usually done in private without the opportunity to compare results or benefit from a critique. We shouldn't expect our negotiation counterparts to frankly assess how we did: it is most often in their interest for us to believe we did well. While some individuals may be naturally better at negotiating, negotiation skills and results can be improved with analysis, understanding, and practice—regardless of inherent ability and learned bad habits (Folberg & Reynolds, 2022).

We argue that negotiation competitions are an excellent way to teach students competencies that are vital to success in legal practice. When done well, negotiation competitions let students learn by doing, be observed, try different approaches without harming clients, and develop reflective skills to learn from both successes and mistakes.

The competition we focus on is the Canadian National Negotiation Competition (CNNC). In the CNNC, teams of two students are given a mock problem with some generally known facts and some confidential information about their client's situation and settlement preferences. They then attempt to negotiate a resolution with other teams. Each team participates in three negotiation rounds, and after each round expert judges score the teams and give them feedback. Students reflect on their preparation and experience before and after each round (Canadian National Negotiation Competition, 2025). There are key differences between the CNNC and certain other kinds of law school competitions, such as appellate and trial moots. Such differences, along with similarities to other recently added competitions, are explored below.

Experiential Education

The competencies needed to succeed in practice have dramatically changed. As Menkel-Meadow says,

> The lawyer of the next century will need to be able to diagnose and analyze problems, to talk to and listen to people, to facilitate conversations, to negotiate effectively, to resolve disputes, to understand and present

> complex material, to use ever-changing technologies, to plan, to evaluate both economic and emotional components and consequences of human decision-making, and to be creative – to use tried and true methods when they are appropriate, but not to fear new and category-smashing ideas or solutions. (1999, p. 14)

Macfarlane has a similar view of the modern lawyer's role, while placing heightened emphasis on achieving expedient results: "The New Lawyer of the twenty-first century must find creative, practical, and affordable ways to meet his or her clients' expectations and aspirations. This means a shorter time frame for achieving effective, appropriate, and sustainable outcomes" (2017, p. 5). Students should anticipate a wider variety of future professional roles than that of a litigator (Macfarlane, 2017; Sullivan et al., 2007). Negotiation skills play a prominent role for the modern lawyer: "The New Lawyer's effectiveness as a negotiator, and his or her ability to develop expeditious and fair outcomes, lie at the heart of a renewed professional role" (Macfarlane, 2017, p. 84). The traditional law school curriculum produces students well-versed in legal analysis, but fewer of the other skills demanded in modern law practice (Stuckey et al., 2007).

The Carnegie Report posits that there are three apprenticeships in professional education, and that they must begin in law school. The first is the intellectual or cognitive, "focus[ing] the student on the knowledge and way of thinking of the profession" (Sullivan et al., 2007, p. 28). The second is "the forms of expert practice shared by competent practitioners" (Sullivan et al., 2007, p. 28). The third is professional identity formation, "introduc[ing] students to the purposes and attitudes that are guided by the values for which the professional community is responsible" (Sullivan et al., 2007, p. 28). An excellent way for law schools to provide the second and third apprenticeships is through experiential education, particularly simulations (Sullivan et al., 2007). Actual experience with client situations facilitates ethical engagement, a pivotal aspect in lawyer formation (Sullivan et al., 2007). Students must experience legal practice, whether real or simulated, to internalize and make their own moral and ethical judgements that are at the core of practice (Stuckey et al., 2007).

Law school pedagogy has traditionally used the Socratic case-dialogue method or something akin to it. That method has at least two deficiencies. First, it doesn't fully teach students to think like apprentice practitioners, solving clients' problems. Second, it is less effective at helping students develop ethical and social skills, particularly opportunities to learn about the "practice responsibilities of legal professionals" (Shariff et al., 2016, p. 314). Experiential education has become increasingly prominent in law schools as a supplement to case-dialogue pedagogy (Stuckey et al., 2007; Sullivan et al., 2007).

Experiential education can impart many of the modern lawyer's competencies. It is "student centered, takes clients seriously, and values feelings as much as thinking, whereas the Socratic dialogue and case method is teacher centered, gives little consideration to clients, and treats feelings as irrelevant," according to the influential Stuckey Report (Stuckey et al., 2007, p. 26). To develop, law students need significant involvement in performing the tasks of practising lawyers (Stuckey et al., 2007). Studies of professional education programs have shown that simulations help students improve their performance of key components of professional practice through targeted instruction and feedback (Grossman et al., 2005).

The optimal method of experiential instruction is to integrate theory, doctrine, and practice (Stuckey et al., 2007). Students need opportunities to experience practice under expert supervision, because the development of expertise is facilitated by feedback from experts (Sullivan et al., 2007). Often, the best practice is to integrate lawyers and judges into the instruction (Stuckey et al., 2007). Law school experiential programs should also use simulations with appropriate debriefing, which can help cultivate students' practical wisdom and professional values, and cultivate commitment to lifelong learning (Stuckey et al., 2007). The CNNC adopts this approach.

To succeed in practice, students must develop self-reflection and lifelong learning skills, best taught by experiential education (Shariff et al., 2016; Stuckey et al., 2007). According to Smyth, "[R]eflective practice is increasingly understood as a core competency in Canadian legal education and practice. Law schools (and, indeed, law practice regulators) have begun incorporating [it] in various classes and clinical and experiential contexts" (2024, c. 4.1). Self-reflection integrates theory and practice (Leering, 2014), thereby teaching students how to analyze performance, think critically about it, and generalize from their experience (Shariff et al., 2016). In other words, reflective practice helps students "learn how to learn" from experience (Shariff et al., 2016; Stuckey et al., 2007). The technique also "provides the new professional with a process to develop professional judgment" (Casey, 2014, p. 319). As summarized by

Leering: "An aspirational conceptualization [of reflective practice] would be an integrated reflective practitioner who is self-aware and critically reflects on practice and theory as a self-directed lifelong learner, reflects collectively and in community[,] and takes action to improve his or her practice." (2014, p. 85). In this way, reflective practice can be viewed as a meta-competency that deepens development of a wide range of other capacities and skills.

Having discussed experiential education in legal education generally, we now focus on it for negotiation skills specifically.

Experiential Teaching of Negotiation

There are supply and demand pressures for improved negotiation skills. On the demand side, pressure for increased use of dispute resolution processes other than litigation (e.g., mediation, negotiation) have come from government, from a public disenchanted with adversary-based legal service, and from influential members of the bench and bar—all arising from a growing realization of the adversary system's inadequacy to best settle all disputes (Macfarlane, 2017; Sullivan et al., 2007). On the supply side, negotiation services have increasingly been marketed by law firms, with advanced negotiation training becoming attractive in the job market for young lawyers (Sullivan et al., 2007).

Lawyers, including civil litigators, administrative lawyers, and corporate-commercial counsel, are increasingly involved with dispute resolution outside the adversarial model. Legal culture has become more attuned to the need to offer practical problem-solving and expedient resolution (Macfarlane, 2017).

Negotiation skills are a core dimension of modern law practice. According to Macfarlane, they "are critical to the effectiveness of the New Lawyer, and she will place a far greater emphasis than her predecessors on becoming a good (intentional, educated) negotiator. The old tools of positional bargaining, often ritual bluff and bluster represented by a terse exchange of offers, are ineffective in building a consensus. They are being replaced by problem-solving strategies and more effort to directly include the client in face-to-face negotiation" (2017, pp. 25–26).

Simulations are a critical part of the experiential teaching of negotiation skills, broadening law students' awareness of the multiple dimensions of legal actions (Sullivan et al., 2007). These exercises help students learn by doing, be observed and receive feedback, try different approaches without detriment to clients, and learn from mistakes (Folberg & Golann, 2016). Experiential negotiation exercises can be more valuable than negotiating actual legal cases for two reasons. First, students practice in a consequence-free environment. Second, they get feedback on their performance, including post-negotiation insight into their negotiation counterparts' strategy and confidential instructions (Folberg & Golann, 2016). Students learn from comparing their actions, approaches, and results with those of fellow students (Folberg & Golann, 2016).

Experiential negotiation exercises help students recognize the influence that biases have on negotiation process and outcome. These biases can affect a client's thinking and an advocate's assessment of the value of a case and an appropriate settlement range (Folberg & Reynolds, 2022; Keet, 2017). Students also learn about the impact of emotions, biases, and identity considerations (Folberg & Reynolds, 2022). Learning about these through theory, experience, and self-reflection develops more nuanced understandings of ourselves and others, making us more creative, successful bargainers (Folberg & Reynolds, 2022).

Description of CNNC

This section outlines the competition's background, its educational emphasis, format, problems used, and criteria for evaluating competitors. The CNNC was started in 2017 and has run each year since, with two competitions held online during the COVID-19 pandemic. Hosting has rotated among law schools.[1] The competition has grown each year, both in the number of teams participating and the number of law schools represented. Any accredited Canadian law school can send up to two teams to compete in each of the language streams, English or French.[2] Each team has two students who work with a coach, typically a practitioner who has competed in the CNNC or a faculty member at the school in question. While each law school varies in how they select students for their teams,

[1] CNNC hosts to date: University of Manitoba (2017); University of Saskatchewan (2018); Osgoode Hall Law School of York University (2019); University of New Brunswick (2020); University of Saskatchewan (online) (2021); University of Ottawa (online) (2022); McGill University (2023); McGill University/Sustainable Growth Initiative (2024); University of Windsor/Centre for Cities (2025); Université de Sherbrooke (scheduled, 2026).

[2] The French stream was added in 2022. The problem set is the same in English and French, and judges are fluent in the language in which students negotiate.

competitors have usually completed and excelled in a negotiation course at their law school, and in many cases have won (or were runners-up) in an internal negotiation competition at their school. This is to say that these students have already had some experience with learning negotiation skills and theory, and come to the competition having been coached and judged by individuals with negotiation expertise.

Although the CNNC is a competition, the educational component is paramount. The educational emphasis is made clear to students at the outset, and the competition organizers have fostered a collegial atmosphere among teams. As part of the educational mandate, the students participate in a group educational activity on some aspect of negotiation during the competition. For example, the 2025 CNNC negotiation problems addressed the housing crisis in Canada, and there was a pre-competition symposium on this topic with experts in the field. We have, over time, expanded the vision of this competition to include more dialogue around public policy issues, focusing on the roles of negotiation and problem-solving in addressing them. The CNNC aims to educate future lawyers about the centrality of negotiation and collaborative approaches in exploring and resolving complex social problems.

The CNNC's current format is three negotiation rounds, with each team competing in each round before several judges. The first two rounds are bilateral: two teams from different schools negotiate with one another. The third round is multilateral, with at least three, sometimes four, teams participating (again, all from different schools).[3]

The CNNC problems are key to its success. In recent years, we have developed and drafted the problems and released them to the participants about one month before the competition. A sample problem, attached as Appendix A, was one of the two-party rounds for the 2020 CNNC. As this sample shows, problems are typically written so that the parties have relatively equal bargaining power to ensure that one party does not have an unfair advantage over the other.

Sometimes there is one meta-problem or overarching topic, with rounds building on the factual foundation of previous rounds; sometimes there are three distinct problems, with no relationship among the

[3] The number of teams registered can play a role in how the third round is structured. For example, with 20 teams, the optimum structure is a four-party problem with five concurrent negotiations; with 18 teams, the optimum structure is a three-party problem with six concurrent negotiations.

topics, facts or parties between rounds. In recent years, we have tried to create one meta-problem, raising social or policy issues like sustainability or housing—with aspects of the problem being addressed (and resolved) incrementally, closer to real life. For example, the 2024 theme was environmental policy: specifically, the construction of an electric-vehicle battery plant with governmental, industry, and public policy interests at stake. A problem is chiefly of one of two varieties: a dispute with the potential for a legally imposed solution in the absence of agreement; or transactional problems, with more of a deal-making/future-focused approach.

Each problem provides certain information to the two-student teams. There are general facts for each round, and there may be general facts applicable to all three rounds. General facts are given to all teams and intended to be adopted as fact or authentic perspective. Each team also has confidential information, including client settlement preferences or instructions, which are not known to the other teams. Typically, the parties and events prompting the negotiation are in a fictional or mock jurisdiction, and the general facts usually provide the relevant applicable law. The problem may also provide information that everyone must know to negotiate effectively (standard pricing, business norms, etc.) and perhaps the objective criteria to use. The point is for the students to demonstrate negotiation skills and abilities, rather than conduct a substantial amount of research for the legal or factual foundation. Negotiations can quickly get derailed if the parties ambush each other with outside factual or legal research! Judges receive all materials provided to competitors, as well as a judges' summary developed by the organizers. Only judges have all the facts to understand how the problem could be resolved.

Each round raises several issues, and each issue may have integrative or distributive aspects, typically calling for a mix of bargaining styles, rather than an exclusively adversarial or cooperative one. There are possibilities for creative solutions. The problems are typically written so that each issue has a "zone of possible agreement" ("ZOPA"), and is thus capable of resolution. The parties often place different priorities on the issues, usually in accordance with the confidential instructions. These different priorities often enable trade-offs and mutual gains: a party can concede on a low-priority item in exchange for a "win" on a high-priority item. One of the learning points here is that "it isn't done until it's all done." That is, the different valuations that parties put on issues can yield packages that enhance value for both parties, compared to negotiating on an issue-by-issue basis.

Each negotiation round has structured opportunities for planning and reflection. First, teams present their negotiation plans to their judging panel, practitioners who have negotiated extensively and have knowledge of negotiation theory. After the plans are presented, the negotiation starts, taking place under the judges' scrutiny. The negotiations in the first two rounds are 50 minutes; in the third round, 70 minutes. After the negotiation, each team reflects and prepares a "self-analysis," then has five minutes to present it to the judges in the absence of other teams. The teams answer two questions: (1) In reflecting on the entire negotiation, if you faced a similar situation tomorrow, what would you do the same and what would you do differently? and (2) How well did your strategy work in relation to the outcome? The teams then withdraw while the judges rank, score and write comments. On returning to the negotiation room, the teams receive detailed feedback from the judges about what they did well and potential areas for improvement.

After each round, judges "rank" and "score" the teams. The judges first rank the teams that competed against each other in order of effectiveness in the negotiating session. The aggregated values of the rankings primarily determine the first-, second- and third-place winners. The judges also score the teams on certain criteria, such as their skill in providing (or protecting) information, their adaptability, and their capacity for building relationships with their negotiating counterparts: see Appendix B. The scores are used to break ties and determine skill-based prizes. The negotiated outcome itself is de-emphasized in the scoring, to keep the focus on learning and to encourage negotiating quality over speed. Judges are told that parties needn't reach an agreement, and that in some situations, the best outcome might be no agreement at all.

Several things happen at the close of the competition. A winning team is named based on aggregate rankings, and that team gets to represent Canada in the International Negotiation Competition (INC) (International Negotiation Competition, 2025). Awards are also given to teams that best demonstrated certain skills, such as process management or relationship-building. Afterwards, all teams receive their ranking and scoring sheets, in addition to their overall rank.

Comparisons to Other Canadian Competitions

Some competitions are unlike the CNNC in terms of the competencies they develop; others are more similar. Two longstanding competition types that are most unlike the CNNC are appellate and trial advocacy moots. Appellate moots excel at giving students legal knowledge and teaching them to theorize and argue complex and contentious points of legal doctrine. However, such moots are but a small part of the day-to-day experience of most legal practice, tend not to raise issues of professional ethics, and don't enable students to engage in multiple dimensions of legal cases (Kozinski, 1997; Stuckey et al., 2007; Sullivan et al., 2007). There is little scope to focus on a client's non-legal interests or to develop skills like exploring interests, building relationships, and solving problems creatively (Kozinski, 1997). Appellate moots also differ in that they require intensive legal research on specific points of law, typically followed by writing a factum and making formal legal arguments on what the law is or ought to be and how it applies to a specific fact pattern.

Trial advocacy competitions like the Sopinka Cup, honouring the memory of the late Supreme Court of Canada judge John Sopinka, develop the skills of litigating a case before a judge or a judge and jury, including presenting documentary and witness evidence in court and engaging in trial-level advocacy. While these competitions develop skills commonly used by litigators, they do not develop many skills necessary for the lawyer of the future, such as interest-based problem-solving.

Critiques of appellate and trial advocacy moots observe that these moot experiences suffer a lack of connection to real clients (Kozinski, 1997). Visions of the elite rhetorical tradition can also obscure criteria for good advocacy, and, especially in the courtroom, notions of the 'strong advocate' can channel the profession's historic lack of racial, cultural, and gender diversity (Morrison, 1995). The traditions and design of these moots mean that a limited number of competencies are therefore taught and rewarded.

Some other Canadian competitions do highlight problem-solving skills. The National Family Law Negotiation Competition (NFLNC) is an example. It gives students the opportunity to experience first-hand how effective negotiation skills can help families navigate difficult life transitions and address sensitive issues like parenting time and division of marital assets (University of Manitoba Faculty of Law, 2023). The Kawaskimhon Moot, which unfolds through roundtable negotiations on a topic in Indigenous or Aboriginal law, uses facilitators to guide discussions. Unlike the CNNC, it is not run as a competition, and has no "winner" (Bora Laskin Faculty of Law, 2025). The Canadian Client Consultation Competition (CCCC), which feeds into the international event (ICCC), puts competing teams in a consultation with a client about whom they have very limited information (Canadian Client Consultation Competition, 2025). Because this event is focused on consultation and advice-giving in the first client interview, rather than involving opposing parties in a direct problem-solving process, it is only intended to capture competencies (albeit important ones) that shape the initial lawyer-client relationship.

Competencies Developed by the CNNC

Across this range of moot opportunities, the CNNC's focus remains unique. It centres on a process that is key to the lawyer's day-to-day work and, in so doing, welcomes diverse modes of lawyering that avoid some of the more problematic aspects of traditional mooting experience. In this section, we discuss the higher-level knowledge and values developed by the CNNC, and the accompanying skills cultivated by the competition. Many of these competencies are assessed by the judges using the competition's scoring rubric; indeed, the coaching, judging and self-analytical attention placed on these competencies is what allows students to *integrate* them in a way that is rare in law school.

Knowledge of Key Negotiation Concepts

The competition teaches students critical negotiation concepts such as assessing their own "best alternative to a negotiated agreement" (BATNA) and "worst alternative to a negotiated agreement" (WATNA) and the other party's BATNA and WATNA. The BATNAs impact their own and the other side's resistance points. The resistance point is "a negotiator's bottom line, or the point at which they are indifferent to a deal" (Lewicki et al., 2011 at p. 19). Between the parties' resistance points lies a ZOPA, defined earlier. At least for distributive issues, it is often to one party's advantage to persuade the other side to agree to a point within the ZOPA as close as possible to the other party's resistance point (Lewicki et al., 2011).

Students also learn to adopt negotiation styles that accord with the "value climate" they face. These include both distributive and integrative bargaining. If the value climate is one of scarce resources, a predominantly distributive style is likely more appropriate. But if the value climate is one where there appear to be sufficient resources to satisfy all parties' needs, a predominantly integrative style is probably preferred (Hanycz, 2008). CNNC problems present a mix of distributive and integrative elements, with value climates that allow both dimensions to be explored and leveraged.

Judgment around Information Management

To discover the value climate in any CNNC problem, students must strategically assess the benefits and risks of information exchange. Competitors must adapt as they receive new information or when the other team makes unforeseen moves. Teams must continually re-assess BATNAs and WATNAs—their own and the other team's—and adjust strategy accordingly.

Some decisions on information management invite students to wrestle with professional responsibilities, and one of the CNNC's purposes is to instill ethical decision-making in negotiations. As previously noted, students must experience the reality of practice to form and internalize ethical judgements (Stuckey et al., 2007). Under the CNNC rules, the Federation of Law Societies of Canada *Model Code of Professional Conduct* governs competitor conduct. Through the competition, students learn to keep a client's confidences, honour a client's settlement instructions, and make difficult decisions on how to represent (or refrain from representing) material facts and settlement authority. Outright lying is unethical, but reframing, partial disclosure, and evading some questions may be not only permissible but advisable or required in certain circumstances.

Students also learn to deal with the negotiator's dilemma: "the tension ... between the behaviors that tend to create value and that individually claim the value that was jointly created" (Folberg & Reynolds, 2022, p. 39). In a negotiation's early stages, some information must be shared to "expand the pie." However, negotiations often later enter a distributive phase, and the very information that negotiators have shared may be used against them (Folberg & Reynolds, 2022). The balance that competitors must strike is that information or interests may on their face be risky to disclose, but such risk-taking could pay off with large dividends in the form of solutions that are tailored to meet those interests.

Problem-solving Attitudes and Capacities

Through the CNNC experience, students learn that a problem-solving framework is essential to the pursuit of those creative solutions. The underlying skills involved in problem-solving processes include sensitivity to client needs, the ability to think beyond a counterpart's positions and explore their interests, a capacity to think critically about the outcome (including the social policy dimensions or community impact), and the ability to embrace visions of advocacy that escape old "war models." These skills are critical for lawyers but hard to otherwise acquire in law school. Students also learn to use creativity in overcoming impasses, adding value, and crafting settlement terms to form a durable agreement— one that is fair to both parties and that lasts (Fisher et al., 2011).

Communication and Relationship-Building

Communication and relationship-building skills are the vehicle for reaching such outcomes. As Macfarlane says,

> [C]ommunication skills such as listening, explaining, questioning, and establishing rapport and trust have always been important for lawyers who work directly with clients or as oral advocates. In the litigation model, however, effective interpersonal communication takes second place to making substantive and procedural arguments. Courtroom eloquence – the convincing presentation of arguments – has been regarded as the pinnacle of communication. For the New Lawyer, a different type of communicative eloquence is necessary. Interpersonal communication is the primary vehicle for the resolution of conflict, whether through negotiation, mediation, or another settlement process. In this model, interpersonal communication skills have the potential to set one lawyer apart as particularly skillful and ultimately successful. This model also elevates the importance of so-called emotional intelligence, as well as legal knowledge, including attributes such as empathy, self-awareness, optimism, and impulse control – all important qualities in an effective negotiator". (Macfarlane, 2017, p. 26)

The CNNC facilitates development of communication and relationship-building skills, which form part of the scoring rubric. Students learn the importance of asking questions of their negotiation counterparts. The form of questioning may be very different from, e.g., that used in cross-examination. Open-ended questions—"Can you tell me more about why that's important to you?"—typically yield the most information about party interests. Teams are also assessed for how perceptive and skillful they are at reading the other negotiating team's cues. Relationships are built on two different levels. First, teammates must engage with one another. They need to back each other up and share responsibility for managing the negotiation, developing proposals, and deciding whether potential solutions are acceptable. Second, a team must also establish a relationship with the counterpart team, and must maintain an appropriate level of courtesy and professionalism.

The third round also lets competitors learn about more complex multi-party bargaining situations, especially forming coalitions and sequencing dialogue where multiple issues, parties and interests are involved. The potential for a coalition exists when two or more parties discover that they have complementary interests, particularly when they perceive themselves as lacking power. They can then leverage their combined bargaining strength against the others to achieve certain ends, or to reach a deal on an issue that leaves out another party (Folberg & Reynolds, 2022). In real time, students learn how to make strategic assessments about the benefits and risks of these dynamics, and how to employ clear and organized communication frameworks.

Process Management and Analysis

To balance objectives around information management and relationship-building, lawyers must be expert process managers (Wiggins & Lowry, 2005). The competition teaches students how to manage a negotiation's various phases, wisely using the time available in light of client interests and goals. As discussed in the previous chapter, negotiation phases can be conceptualized as follows (even though not all negotiations follow the same linear staging):

1. Preparing and setting goals
2. Initial interaction, agenda-setting, offers
3. Exchanging and refining information
4. Bargaining
5. Moving toward closure

6. Reaching impasse or agreement
7. Finalizing agreement (Folberg & Reynolds, 2022).

The CNNC also teaches that managing such a process requires careful preparation (Fisher et al., 2011). Each team prepares a negotiation plan and presents it to the judges before the negotiation. A team must explain how their process will advance their client's goals: how they will prioritize interests (both the client's and those anticipated of the counterpart), respect and explore BATNAs and WATNAs for the client and the other parties, and employ and justify their overall negotiation strategy.

Advocating for Client Interests

Within such a structure, students are encouraged to expand their views of advocacy—bringing strength and insight to advocate for client interests *outside* the courtroom context and the bounds of legal argument. Teams must be reasonable, realistic, persuasive, and convincing. A good negotiation outcome, from the perspective of a team being judged, is evaluated on the following criteria:

- It is better than the best alternative to a negotiated agreement.
- It satisfies the interests of:
    - the client—very well
    - the other side—acceptably (enough for them to agree and follow through)
    - third parties—tolerably (so they won't disrupt the agreement).
- It adopts a solution that is the best of all available options.
- It is legitimate—no one feels "taken."
- It has commitments that are clear, realistic and operational.
- It involves communication that is efficient and well understood.
- It results in an enhanced working relationship or agreement to negotiate further.

Reflective practice and Awareness of Cognitive Biases

Above all, the CNNC requires students to engage in the meta-competency of reflective practice under expert guidance. After each competition round, students engage in self-reflection and present the results to the judges, who are themselves expert negotiation practitioners. The students evaluate how well their strategy worked in achieving the outcome and explore what they would do the same and differently in the future. Students get feedback from the judges about the efficacy of their strategy and tactics. This helps them improve, both in subsequent competition rounds and in future real-world negotiations. During the feedback sessions, the competitors also learn about the other side's instructions and goals, allowing them to better assess how their strategies worked—an invaluable educational experience that is not available for actual cases.

At a deeper level, students learn to acknowledge and understand biases that can impede negotiation and professional identity development. Such biases fall under two categories: cognitive biases unrelated to stereotypes; and those related to stereotypes (Folberg & Reynolds, 2022; Smyth, 2024; Stabler, 2023). An example of the former type is the anchoring-and-adjustment bias, in which "we are often unduly influenced by the initial figure we encounter when estimating the value of an item [which] serves as a kind of reference point or benchmark that anchors our expectations about the item's actual value" (Guthrie & Orr, 2006, p. 597; Tversky & Kahneman, 1974). The competition, and the training preceding it, can encourage students to consider anchoring's ethical implications, as well as strategies to safeguard against being anchored (Kleefeld & Pohler, 2019). Other examples of biases unrelated to stereotypes include confirmation bias, framing, loss aversion, and self-serving bias (also called attribution error) (Folberg & Reynolds, 2022).

Students also learn that they operate on implicit biases based on stereotypes—"the automatic stereotyping that people do unconsciously, drawing on deep cultural notions of the familiar and the normal" (Folberg & Reynolds, 2022, p. 17). For example, students should consider the impact of identity considerations (e.g., race, gender, sexual orientation, class, religion, disability, etc.) on negotiations. Studies have shown that increased awareness can reduce implicit bias (Folberg & Reynolds, 2022). Even the CNNC's shift to a dual language stream, with teams competing from both English and French law schools, directly invites teams into a cross-cultural bargaining and learning environment. Some of the most powerful feedback from competition judges comes from ethical, contextual and critical judgments they have wrestled with in their professional lives. In that way, the competition continues to be as much about relational and professional identity competencies as it is about task-related skills.

Conclusion

Negotiation theory and practice is not static, nor is the CNNC. The competition has evolved and will continue to do so. We are striving to elevate the importance of equity, diversity, and inclusion at the CNNC. To this end, we have been trying to offer a more inclusive and inviting competition in a setting that embraces cross-culturalism,[4] as well as creating scenarios that encourage students to think about advancing social justice goals in a problem-solving framework.

We have also grappled with challenges in evaluating competitors. Evaluations are difficult for experiential education activities, given the subjectivity involved. The CNNC is no exception, particularly because of the large array of approaches, arguments, and negotiation styles employed. One aspect of this subjectivity is the risk of bias in CNNC judges. Bias can arise in various ways—for example, the way a judge personally relates to a student, unexamined views about what legal professionalism 'looks like,' perceptions of leadership, and types of negotiation outcomes thought to be desirable. As for implicit bias based on stereotypes, the same forces that create risks for lawyer negotiators and their clients also create dangers for competition judges. We are taking steps to mitigate these dangers, including striving to enhance the diversity of our judging pool, educating judges to guard against implicit bias, and improving the evaluation forms.

We recognize that the CNNC is an imperfect proxy for the representation of clients in a legal practice. The simulations necessarily use a fictitious scenario without real clients. This might make the students behave in a different, perhaps less adversarial, way than lawyers would in an actual dispute. Additionally, litigation expenses such as counsel fees do not typically form part of the simulation, which might impact the negotiation process.

Despite the shortcomings, we think that negotiation competitions like the CNNC are an excellent way to teach students critical competencies. These competencies will help students to creatively and expeditiously solve clients' problems. The dominant litigation model emphasizes a very different set of skills, ones used less frequently in practice. The skills that the CNNC builds are closer to the fundamental skill sets for "lawyers

[4] For example, participants are invited "to wear clothing appropriate to their gender identity or expression, or to their religious or cultural identities." (Canadian National Negotiation Competition, 2025).

of the future." The CNNC provides two forms of the Carnegie Report apprenticeships: the "apprenticeship of practical skills" and the "apprenticeship of professional identity and values." The competencies students learn in negotiation competitions can smooth the transition from law school to practice.

Lastly, the competition builds practice communities of negotiation, somewhat lacking in the legal profession. The CNNC brings together law students interested in negotiation, enabling them to form professional networks that we hope last long into their careers. Additionally, the CNNC facilitates the building of networks among experiential education programs at Canadian law schools. Our collaboration on this chapter is ample proof of that.

Appendices

Appendix A: 2020 CNNC Round 1 Problem—Leonardo & III[5]

General Information for Both Parties

This negotiation is between the artist Leonardo (who goes by that name alone) and the non-profit International Ideation Institute/Institut international d'idéation ("III" or "the Institute"). The purpose is to commission a multi-media art installation for III's planned new facilities.

The Institute is a combined think tank, museum, gallery and innovation lab that houses an ever-changing and eclectic mix of scientists, artists, writers, film makers, social engineers and others—"ideationists" as they call themselves. The shared vision of this disparate group and of III's board is to "turn ideas into futures." Challenges taken up by the group include climate change, human rights violations, the Ebola virus, and space exploration; in each case, the goal is to develop innovative, cross-disciplinary solutions to these challenges.

Leonardo is renowned for his startling multimedia installations (or "interventions," as he calls them). For instance, "War" combines, among other things, documentary footage of bombing with the sounds of air raid sirens, speeches by Hitler and Churchill, and love letters to military personnel in active service in wars around the world; "Sea" is a virtual-reality experience in which the viewer has the impression of being below

[5] Published with permission from the Canadian National Negotiation Competition ("CNNC"). All rights reserved.

sea level and surrounded by coral, jellyfish, whales and sharks; "Cerebrum" is an imaginary inner journey that explores and vivifies the effect of the senses on the brain.

The Institute wants its donors and others to connect with its work and thinks that Leonardo's style would serve that purpose well; Leonardo in turn is attracted by III's vision and would be honoured to create a commissioned work for it. The parties have agreed that the work will be in a wing of the building that will house the donor's lounge and meeting rooms and will be installed no later than one month before the building's opening, expected two years from now. The parties have authorized their representatives to work out the remaining details.

Confidential Information for Leonardo's Representatives

Leonardo, 69, thrives on ideas, inventions, and creativity. He has fuelled that appetite with extensive travels and by engaging with a wide range of artistic media. Early in his career, he was a journalist, and is intrigued with the idea of the artist as journalist. Indeed, he puts as much time and effort into researching one of his "interventions" as he does in its actual formation, and that is an important part of his sense of fulfillment.

Leonardo has produced several hundred works, including about 60 large-scale ones of the type that might be envisioned for the Institute. Most are in museums, corporate settings, or private collections around the world. For example, one of his recent works, *Collegium*, was sold to an anonymous buyer for the equivalent of CAD $350,000, and two of his earlier works have recently been acquired by the Smithsonian Institution in Washington DC for an undisclosed sum.

Several years ago, Leonardo suffered a great personal loss that devastated him emotionally. He went into a state of depression, began using drugs, and ended up in rehab. Fortunately, he then had a remarkable turnaround, especially after meeting Salai—a young, vibrant art student. Their relationship gives each of them great synergy and has done wonders for Leonardo's health, productivity and reputation. Leonardo recently received the "Artist of the Year" award in his home country and is now drawing international attention.

Leonardo has provided the following information in relative order of importance for the negotiation.

1. Artistic Content, Design, and Integrity

Leonardo insists on being the judge of what should be included in the multi-media installation—artistic expression, components, and design. Knowing how construction plans can change and how integral the work will be to the physical setting, Leonardo also insists that III must notify him of any proposed site alteration that might affect the intended character and appearance of his work. Leonardo also wants to follow his usual pattern of researching a project and getting a sense of "place." That means visiting III itself for an extended period, but could also mean other travel to research the project. Leonardo expects that this will take place at the Institute's expense.

Leonardo thinks this approach is especially important here. It's well known that donors have tried to influence the Institute's direction, as happened in a recent dust-up between the CEO of FrontierX and the Institute's board around trying to get the Institute involved in colonizing Mars. Leonardo worries that the Institute would want to dictate elements or design choices to satisfy donors or patrons, and he'll have none of that. This factor is a deal-breaker. Leonardo would rather not go forward with the project if III isn't satisfied with his formal proposal (see below); but once the agreement is signed and work started, III shouldn't be able to withhold payment for work completed substantially in accordance with the proposal.

2. Purchase Price

Leonardo has never been one for saving, and has an expensive lifestyle. He expects a substantial amount for this commission—enough to help him prepare for retirement and provide a foundation for Salai's own emerging career. Leonardo's last three works sold for the following amounts (all figures translated to CAD):

Cerebrum	$498,000
Collegium	$350,000
Blockchain	$310,000

These works were sold through an agent who took a 50% commission; even so, the sales produced a substantial net sum (i.e., half the above prices) compared to what Leonardo received from sales of earlier works. In the discussions that have taken place so far, there has been no indication of what the Institute would be willing to pay. But given the site-specific nature of the project and the fact that its technical complexity is likely to be more than double that of *Cerebrum*, his most complex project so far, Leonardo feels that a price in the neighbourhood of CAD $1 million would be justified. Leonardo thinks the Institute should be able to afford it: he has heard that last year III reported a surplus (revenues less expenses) of nearly CAD $13.6 million. Leonardo would accept a lower purchase price if items 3 and 4 below are fully funded. But he won't take less than CAD $660,000 because he feels that it would cheapen the value of his earlier works too much.

3. Consultation, Research and Presentation

Leonardo sees this project as giving him a chance to have a sort of all-expense-paid vacation in the Institute's home city. He'd like III to pay for four trips, with a generous allowance for meals, accommodations and entertainment expenses. Leonardo wants Salai to accompany him on all these trips for "inspiration." The first trip would be to get a feel for the location of the Institute's proposed new buildings and its surrounds and to meet with the architects and Institute's director and other personnel. The second would be to continue to get a sense of "place" and to present preliminary ideas to III. The third would be to present a formal proposal, including sketches, mock-ups or other forms of presentation, making changes as needed until the Institute is satisfied. The fourth trip would be in conjunction with delivery and installation.

4. Payment Schedule

Leonard wants a third of the price before the first trip; the next third, when the Institute is satisfied with the formal proposal; the final third, after delivery and installation. Leonardo knows that the norm is half upon acceptance of the formal proposal and half upon delivery and installation, but given the context of the transaction and the research and consultation needed, he thinks the 1/3-1/3-1/3 model is appropriate. It's not a deal-breaker, but an important priority. Reimbursement should take place shortly after each visit.

5. Other Terms

Leonardo is flexible on other terms that the Institute might propose, such as copyright, moral rights or liquidated damages for non-completion. But if the Institute decides to deaccession the installation, he'd like the right to buy it back. Of course, he hopes that nothing as horrific would happen as the recent attempt by two art provocateurs who wanted to cut up a painting and use the canvas to make decorative faces for their line of designer watches.[6] In any case, you have full discretion to be creative and to deal with any items that arise, consistent with Leonardo's overall interests and priorities. His whole attitude with respect to the project would also be enhanced if the Institute could help Salai, such as providing exposure for Salai's art or assisting with Salai's professional development.

6. Additional Information

You may provide additional non-self-serving information and details consistent with the facts stated above and in the General Information for Both Parties.

Confidential Information for the Institute's Representatives
The Institute is thrilled to be building a new, futuristic headquarters to house its collections and collaborative space for its ideationists. It is the result of a multi-year fundraising campaign to pay for the building's CAD $390 million cost. The Institute has reported a surplus (revenues less expenses) in each of the last three years, as follows:

FY 2019: CAD $4.2 million.
FY 2018: CAD $13.6 million.
FY 2017: CAD $12.2 million.

The drop in last year's surplus is due primarily to a one-time charge resulting from the disposition of assets at less than their depreciated value.

[6] See Richard Orange, Danish court rules artist's work cannot be cut up to make watches (2 December 2019) *The Guardian* online: https://www.theguardian.com/world/2019/dec/02/danish-court-rules-artist-work-cannot-be-cut-up-to-make-watches-tal-r.

The negotiation to secure a multi-media installation by Leonardo results from a conditional gift of CAD $11 million by Vicki Patel to fund the construction of the wing that contains the donor's lounge and meeting rooms. Despite her controversial status as a supermodel and fashionista, the Institute plans to name the wing in her honour.

The only condition of Vicki's gift is that the Institute must secure one of Leonardo's multi-media "interventions" for the wing. Vicki loves Leonardo's work and owns some of it. The Institute was concerned that Leonardo is a bit idiosyncratic, but is willing to work with the donor's request. III looked into buying one of Leonardo's existing works, *Cerebrum*, to meet Vicki's condition. It was valued at about CAD $498,000. But the Institute envisions something even more sophisticated and complex, and Vicki thought that III needed a tailor-made work in any event. III doesn't really have much choice: it needs to commission a Leonardo work.

The Institute has provided the following information in relative order of importance for the negotiation.

1. Purchaser Satisfaction

Because of the work's prominent location, it must be of such a quality as to make it a showcase for the new wing and the building itself. The Institute therefore wants its director and board members to review and approve the project before Leonardo begins work. It also insists on being able to refuse to proceed if the work as presented in the formal proposal (see below) does not meet the Institute's subjective satisfaction. This is a deal-breaker for the Institute. But as long as the completed work objectively accords with the approved formal proposal, III has no problem with making the full and final payment (see below).

2. Illness, Death or Incapacity of the Artist

III is concerned about Leonardo's health and ability to complete the work on schedule. The staff are aware of his past depression and drug use. To the extent that artists ever "retire," Leonardo is approaching retirement age, and one never knows what might happen before the project is completed. The Institute thinks it would be reasonable for the agreement to provide that if Leonardo becomes too ill to work or is otherwise unable to complete the project by the agreed time, III would owe no additional payments to Leonardo beyond what has already been paid. In that situation, the work, to the extent completed, would be delivered to and be the property of III, and III would be free to have the work completed by another artist according to Leonardo's proposal. If Leonardo does not complete the work for any other reason, the Institute wants to be able to cancel the project, with Leonardo refunding all amounts paid to him.

3. Ownership Rights and Moral Rights

The Institute wants to be the absolute owner of all rights to the installation, including, to the extent permitted by law, a waiver of Leonardo's moral rights, if applicable. That is, despite any provision of the law, III wants to be able to destroy the work, to remove and store it, and to relocate it. Of course, it doesn't expect that anything will happen such as the recent attempt by two art provocateurs who wanted to cut up a painting and use the canvas to make faces for their designer watches.[7] If the integrity of the work is not preserved, the Institute is willing to agree that it will no longer describe the work as created by Leonardo. If it decides to deaccession the work, it would be willing to give Leonardo the right to buy it back. The rights transfers must take place by the time of receiving the final payment.

4. Purchase Price and Expenses

The Institute will pay pretty much what it takes to get Leonardo to create the work. It doesn't want to have to go back to Vicki and renegotiate her gift unless absolutely necessary. Of course, the cost should be kept as low as possible, consistent with the goals of having a showcase work. In addition to the purchase, III will pay all reasonable expenses incurred by Leonardo to research and plan the installation. In analogous circumstances, III's board has approved an overall expenditure cap—purchase price and expenses—amounting ten percent of a conditional gift. Applying such a cap in this case would translate to a total expenditure of

[7] See Richard Orange, Danish court rules artist's work cannot be cut up to make watches (2 December 2019) *The Guardian* online: https://www.theguardian.com/world/2019/dec/02/danish-court-rules-artist-work-cannot-be-cut-up-to-make-watches-tal-r.

CAD $1.1 million, but the Institute would consider paying more if it had to.

5. Payment Schedule

The Institute's usual practice for commissioned works is to pay half the purchase price at the time of making the commitment (that is, after the formal proposal has been accepted) and the other half on delivery and installation. But if Leonardo is willing to agree to the terms most important to the Institute, III will compensate him in advance for such work as is necessary to research, plan and present his proposal. Ideally, this should not exceed 25% the agreed price, on the assumption that if the Institute decides not to go forward with the proposal, Leonardo will be able to keep the advance payment without any further obligations. But this amount is negotiable. If there is an advance payment as suggested here, the balance would likely be divided into two further payments: one when the Institute is satisfied with the formal proposal; the final one, after delivery and installation.

6. Other Terms

The Institute is flexible on other terms that Leonardo might propose, such as copyright, moral rights or liquidated damages for non-completion. Leonardo's representatives have full discretion to deal with any items that arise, consistent with III's overall interests and priorities. The Institute wants Leonardo to be enthusiastic about the project.

7. Additional Information

You may provide additional non-self-serving information and details consistent with the facts stated above and in the General Information for Both Parties.

Appendix B: Judges' Scoring and Ranking Sheets[8]

CNNC Ranking Sheet (Two-Party Round)

Judge's Name: ________________ Judge's Cell #: ______________________

Room #: _________

Team #: _____	Team #: ________

Based on my personal opinion, having observed the negotiation between these teams, I rank the teams I observed as follows:

Most effective team: ______

Suggested Criteria:

- Remember to consider each team's ethical conduct in assigning rankings. Examples of unethical conduct include the following: (1) misrepresenting material facts, (2) exceeding settlement authority, or (3) inventing self-serving material facts.
- Remember that parties need not reach an agreement, and that in some situations, the best outcome might be no agreement at all. Judges should focus on each team's planning and the negotiation process itself, rather than on whether the teams reach an agreement.

A good negotiation outcome, from the perspective of a specific team being judged, is often one that:

- Is better than the best alternative to a negotiated agreement;
- Satisfies the interests of
  - the client—very well
  - the other side—acceptably (enough for them to agree and follow through)

[8] Published with permission from the Canadian National Negotiation Competition ("CNNC").

  - third parties—at least tolerably (so they won't disrupt the agreement);

- Adopts a solution that is the best of all available options;
- Is legitimate—no one feels "taken";
- Involves commitments that are clear, realistic, and operational;
- Involves communication that is efficient and well understood; and
- Results in an enhanced working relationship, so the parties and/or their lawyer can deal with future differences more easily

Please leave the ranking document in the envelope provided in the room. A member of the organizing committee will pick it up.

CNNC Scoring Sheet (Two-Party Round)

Team #: ____________________ Team #: ____________________

Please complete questions a to k while the teams are preparing for the self-analysis and questions l to o after the teams' self-analysis.

a) How skillful was the team in obtaining and using relevant information from the other team?

1 2 3 4 5 6 7 1 2 3 4 5 6 7

1 = POOR; 4 = average/neutral; 7 = EXCELLENT

b) How skillful was the team in providing information to the other team while protecting confidential or negative information?

1 2 3 4 5 6 7 1 2 3 4 5 6 7

1 = POOR; 4 = average/neutral; 7 = EXCELLENT

c) How effective was the team in using the time available for negotiation in light of the client's interests and goals?

1 2 3 4 5 6 7 1 2 3 4 5 6 7

1 = POOR; 4 = average/neutral; 7 = EXCELLENT

d) How skilled was the team in adapting its strategy, for example to new information or unforeseen moves by the other team?

1 2 3 4 5 6 7 1 2 3 4 5 6 7

1 = POOR; 4 = average/neutral; 7 = EXCELLENT

e) How well prepared was this team, judging from its performance and apparent strategy?

1 2 3 4 5 6 7 1 2 3 4 5 6 7

1 = POOR; 4 = average/neutral; 7 = EXCELLENT

f) To what extent was this team perceptive and skillful at reading the other negotiating team's cues?

1 2 3 4 5 6 7 1 2 3 4 5 6 7

1 = POOR; 4 = average/neutral; 7 = EXCELLENT

g) To what extent did this team appear to be reasonable and realistic?

1 2 3 4 5 6 7 1 2 3 4 5 6 7

1 = POOR; 4 = average/neutral; 7 = EXCELLENT

h) To what extent did this team appear to be persuasive and convincing?

1 2 3 4 5 6 7 1 2 3 4 5 6 7

1 = POOR; 4 = average/neutral; 7 = EXCELLENT

i) Did the way the team managed its relationship with the other team contribute to achieving its client's interests and maintain an appropriate level of courtesy and professionalism?

1 2 3 4 5 6 7 1 2 3 4 5 6 7

1 = POOR; 4 = average/neutral; 7 = EXCELLENT

j) How effective was the team in working together, backing each other up, and sharing responsibility?

1 2 3 4 5 6 7 1 2 3 4 5 6 7

1 = POOR; 4 = average/neutral; 7 = EXCELLENT

k) To what extent did the outcome of the session, regardless of whether agreement was reached, serve the client's goals?

1 2 3 4 5 6 7 1 2 3 4 5 6 7

1 = POOR; 4 = average/neutral; 7 = EXCELLENT

Questions to be to be completed after teams' self-analysis

Team #: ______________________ Team #: ______________________

l) How effective was the team in planning, anticipating challenges and assessing its own strategy?

1 2 3 4 5 6 7 1 2 3 4 5 6 7

1 = POOR; 4 = average/neutral; 7 = EXCELLENT

m) How accurate was the team in identifying the effectiveness of its strategy and performance?

1 2 3 4 5 6 7 1 2 3 4 5 6 7

1 = POOR; 4 = average/neutral; 7 = EXCELLENT

n) How adequately did the team learn from today's negotiation?

1 2 3 4 5 6 7 1 2 3 4 5 6 7

1 = POOR; 4 = average/neutral; 7 = EXCELLENT

NEGOTIATING ETHICS

o) Based on your observation, do you believe the negotiating teams observed or violated the ethical standards of the legal profession? For example, (1) did a team misrepresent material facts? (2) did a team exceed its settlement authority? or (3) did a team invent self-serving material facts?

Please circle one:

Team #: ______	Team #: _________
Observed ethical standards	Observed ethical standards
Violated ethical standards	Violated ethical standards

If you think a team potentially violated an ethical standard, please briefly explain the team's conduct:

CNNC Comment Sheet

Additional comments

Judge's Name: __________________ Room #: __________

Team #: _______________

STRENGTHS:

AREAS FOR IMPROVEMENT:

Team #: ______________

STRENGTHS:

AREAS FOR IMPROVEMENT:

Questions

1. Discuss the competencies that the negotiation competition has chosen to emphasize as the ingredients for an effective negotiation. Do you agree with the competencies identified? What values and beliefs underlie these competencies? How would you rewrite them if you were developing your own set for effective negotiation?
2. In law as in many other areas, communication is one of the most crucial skills for success. But what does communication mean in a negotiation context? Analyze this in terms of specific subskills that you think are needed for effective communication in negotiation. Provide an example for each subskill. Reflect on your own strategies to improve communication in negotiation and how you might improve your own, or your students', communication skills.
3. In the setting of the negotiation competition, law students compete in front of a panel of judges and receive feedback. Appendix B provides questions that judges are invited to address in giving feedback to students. How would you redraft the questions, based on your vision of effective negotiation? Using reflection and self-assessment, how would you customize those feedback questions for YOU? To draft these, you should first reflect on your own learning priorities (what do you do well as a negotiator, and what might you want to improve), and then consider how feedback from an expert could assist with those learning goals. How much would these focus on 'how you are' in the negotiation, as opposed to its outcome?

4. Reflect on a negotiation in which you took part where you didn't know your counterpart very well.

- What sorts of things might you have learned if, at the end of the negotiation, you were given a critique of your strategy by a negotiation expert who had knowledge of all parties' confidential information and settlement preferences?
- What role did other factors (e.g., culture, emotions, or bias—yours or your counterpart's) play in the negotiation process? Explain. In hindsight, is there anything you would have done differently to take these factors into account so as to improve the process, the outcome, or both?

5. The authors address their attempts to increase equity, diversity, and inclusion in the context of a negotiation competition. In your view, what can be done to advance formal and substantive equality in negotiation competitions, and mooting programs more generally? Consider the process of mooting or competing from the application process through to granting awards, from perspectives of disability, Indigeneity, race, gender and sex, or other social markers.

Glossary

Appellate and Trial Advocacy Moots:	Types of law student competitions that differ from the CNNC. Appellate moots focus on legal knowledge, theorizing, and arguing complex legal doctrine in an adversarial model. Trial advocacy moots develop skills for litigating cases before a judge or jury. These competitions do not focus on many skills necessary for the "lawyer of the future," such as interest-based problem-solving, and often suffer from a lack of connection to real clients.

BATNA:	Best Alternative to a Negotiated Agreement, a key negotiation concept students learn to assess for themselves and the other party. A party's BATNA impacts their resistance point.
Canadian National Negotiation Competition (CNNC):	A competition for law students designed to nurture competencies vital for modern legal practice through experiential negotiation. It provides opportunities for students to engage in negotiations similar to those lawyers face, receive expert feedback, and grapple with complex scenarios involving business and social policy. The educational component is paramount.
Cognitive Biases:	Factors that can impede negotiation and professional identity development, falling into categories unrelated to stereotypes (like anchoring-and-adjustment bias) and those related to stereotypes (implicit biases). Students learn to acknowledge and understand these biases through the competition and training.
Competencies:	The knowledge, skills, attitudes, judgment, and values that are vital to law students' success in legal practice. These include understanding key negotiation concepts, managing information and process, communicating and relationship-building, advocating for client interests in a problem-solving environment, managing biases, ethical decision-making, and reflective practice.
Experiential education:	An effective teaching method in law school that integrates theory and practice by combining academic inquiry with actual experience. It helps students develop competencies critical to their

	success as lawyers, such as adjusting to professional roles, becoming better problem-solvers, developing interpersonal skills, and learning how to learn from experience.
Reflective practice:	A core competency in Canadian legal education and practice that integrates theory and practice. Taught effectively through experiential education, it helps students analyze performance, think critically, generalize from experience, and develop professional judgment. The CNNC requires students to engage in reflective practice under expert guidance.
WATNA:	Worst Alternative To a Negotiated Agreement, a key negotiation concept students learn to assess for themselves and the other party. A party's WATNA impacts their resistance point.
Zone of Possible Agreement (ZOPA):	The area that lies between the parties' resistance points. CNNC problems are typically written so that each issue has a ZOPA and is capable of resolution.

Competing Interests The authors have no conflicts of interest to declare that are relevant to the content of this chapter.

References

Bora Laskin Faculty of Law. (2025). *Kawaskimhon National Moot 2025*. https://www.lakeheadu.ca/programs/departments/law/law.lakeheadu-kawaskimhon/about

Canadian Client Consultation Competition. (2025). https://www.clientconsultationcomp.ca/about/

Canadian National Negotiation Competition. (2025). https://www.canadiannationalnegotiationcompetition.com/

Casey, T. (2014). Reflective practice in legal education: The stages of reflection. *Clinical Law Review, 20*(Spring), 317–354.

Farrow, T. C. W. (2008). Representative negotiation. In Hanycz et al. (Eds.), *The theory and practice of representative negotiation* (pp. 11–39). Emond Montgomery.

Federation of Law Societies of Canada. (2024). *National Requirement.* (Approved March 12, 2024 to come into effect January 1, 2029). https://flsc.ca/what-we-do/canadian-law-school-programs/.

Fisher, R., Ury, W., & Patton, B. (2011). *Getting to yes: Negotiating agreement without giving in* (3rd ed.). Penguin Books.

Folberg, J., & Golann, D. (2016). *Lawyer negotiation: Theory, practice, and law* (3rd ed.). Wolters Kluwer.

Folberg, J., & Reynolds, J. (2022). *Lawyer negotiation: Theory, practice, and law* (4th ed.). Wolters Kluwer.

Govaerts, M. J. B. (2008). Educational competencies or education for professional competence? *Medical Education, 42*(3), 234–236.

Grossman, P. et al. (2005). *Unpacking practice: the teaching of practice in the preparation of clergy, teachers, and clinical psychologists*. Paper presented at the Annual Meeting of the American Education Research Association, Montreal, Canada, 2005.

Guthrie, C., & Orr, D. (2006). Anchoring information, expertise and negotiation: New insights from meta-analysis. *Ohio St J Disp Resol, 21*(3), 597–628.

Hanycz, C. M. (2008). Introduction to the negotiation process model. In Hanycz et al. (Eds.), *The theory and practice of representative negotiation* (pp. 41–66). Emond Montgomery.

International Negotiation Competition. (2025). https://law-competitions.com/

Keet, M. (2017). Litigation risk assessment: A tool to enhance negotiation. *Cardozo Journal of Conflict Resolution, 19*, 17–42.

Kleefeld, J., & Pohler, D. (2019). Internalizing cognitive bias: An experiential exercise for teaching and learning the anchoring effect. *Brock Education: A Journal of Educational Research and Practice, 28*(2), 33–47.

Kozinski, A. (1997). In praise of moot court—Not! *Columbia Law Review, 97*(1), 178–197.

Leering, M. (2014). Conceptualizing reflective practice for legal professionals. *Journal of Law and Social Policy, 23*, 83–106.

Lewicki, R. J. et al. (2011). Essentials of negotiation (1st Canadian edn.). McGraw-Hill Ryerson.

Macfarlane, J. (2017). *The new lawyer: How clients are transforming the practice of law* (2nd ed.). UBC Press.

Menkel-Meadow, C. (1999). Taking problem-solving pedagogy seriously: A response to the attorney general. *Journal of Legal Education, 49*, 14–21.

Morrison, M. (1995). May it please whose court? How moot court perpetuates gender bias in the 'real world' of practice. *UCLA Women's Law Journal, 6*, 49–84.

Shariff, M., Parkes, D., Heckman, G., Hilder, V., & Lugtig, S. (2016). Academic innovation committee on the Robson hall J.D. Curriculum: Consultation paper. *Manitoba Law Journal, 39*(2), 241–396.

Smyth, G. (2024). *Learning in place: A living landscape of practice* (3rd ed.). Open Library.

Stabler, R. G. (2023). All rise: Pursuing equity in oral argument evaluation. *Nebraska Law Review, 101*(2), 438–486.

Stuckey, R., et al. (2007). *Best practices for legal education.* Clinical Legal education Association.

Sullivan, W. M., Colby, A., Welch Wegner, J., Bond, L., & Shulman, L. (2007). *Educating lawyers: Preparation for the profession of law.* Jossey-Bass.

Tversky, A., & Kahneman, D. (1974). Judgment under uncertainty: Heuristics and biases. *Science, 185*(4157), 1124–1131.

University of Manitoba Faculty of Law. (2023, November 24). *National Family Law Negotiation Competition finds permanent home at UM Law.* UM Today News. https://news.umanitoba.ca/national-family-law-negotiation-competition-finds-permanent-home-at-um-law-osgoode-hall/

Wiggins, C. B., & Lowry, L. R. (2005). *Negotiation and settlement advocacy: A book of readings* (2d ed.). Thomson.

Arbitration

Natella Malazoniia

Abstract This chapter provides an overview of arbitration, a widely used method for resolving disputes outside of national courts. It details arbitration's primary characteristics, such as its flexibility, confidentiality, and the ability for disputing parties to choose expert decision-makers. The chapter also assesses its notable advantages, including quicker speed of the process and the finality of arbitral awards. Conversely, the chapter investigates potential disadvantages, such as the limited avenues for appeal or the uncertainty that can arise if an arbitration agreement is not drafted carefully. Additionally, the chapter explores the various forms of arbitration, including domestic and international arbitration, and discusses how arbitration can be effectively combined with other dispute resolution methods, such as Med-Arb (a combination of mediation and arbitration) or Arb-Med (where arbitration is followed by mediation). Moreover, the chapter delves into the complexities of the legal framework that governs the arbitration process, highlighting the importance of statutes, treaties, rules, and guidelines for the process. Finally, it underscores the critical role of the arbitration agreement, discussing its essential elements and the

N. Malazoniia (✉)
University of Manitoba, Winnipeg, MB, Canada
e-mail: natella@mswpg.ca

L. E. Reimer and R. Jochelson (eds.), *The Other Side of the Bar*,
https://doi.org/10.1007/978-981-96-9748-9_8

implications of well-drafted agreements in ensuring a fair and efficient arbitration process.

Keywords Arbitration · Autonomy · Expert arbitrators · Confidentiality · Neutral forum · Finality of the award · Enforceability

Introduction

Arbitration is a method of dispute resolution that allows the parties to create a private system of justice tailored to their specific needs. Unlike traditional court processes, arbitration is less formal but still adversarial and usually results in binding decisions. Its unique features have made it a popular choice for resolving both domestic and international disputes.

Arbitration has many attractive features compared to traditional litigation due to its inherent flexibility. It allows parties to determine the procedural structure, choose decision-makers, maintain confidentiality, and speed up the resolution process. However, it is important to recognize that both domestic and international arbitration are governed by established legislative frameworks that regulate their operation. This chapter will examine the specific characteristics of these two types of arbitration.

Domestic arbitration is predominantly utilized to resolve commercial disputes. However, in some jurisdictions, it is also applicable to additional areas, such as employment or family matters, particularly in instances concerning property division or spousal support. In contrast, international arbitration encompasses three main categories: International Commercial Arbitration, Investor-State Arbitration, and State-to-State Arbitration (Born, 2021). While a wide range of disputes can be settled through arbitration, there are specific limitations. National legal frameworks generally specify which types of disputes cannot be arbitrated and must be addressed in national courts. For the international arbitration process, for example, the non-arbitrable categories typically include family law matters, criminal issues, patent validity disputes, and bankruptcy proceedings.

Arbitration is a voluntary process that requires mutual consent from the parties unless specific statutory provisions mandate it in certain circumstances. Once this consent is established, it generally prevents the parties from seeking resolution through national courts. Usually, the consent to arbitrate will be given in the form of an arbitration agreement where parties may specify their additional preferences and choices for the process. As a result, the arbitration agreement plays a crucial role in the legal framework of arbitration, making careful drafting essential for a smooth dispute resolution. Conversely, poorly drafted provisions can lead to significant complications, causing delays and increasing costs.

This chapter aims to analyze the characteristics, advantages, and disadvantages of arbitration as a dispute resolution mechanism. It will explore the different types of arbitration and the legal framework that governs the process. Additionally, it will examine the intricacies of arbitration agreements. Through this exploration, the chapter seeks to enhance the understanding of arbitration's role in contemporary legal practice.

Arbitration: Characteristics, Benefits, and Drawbacks

Arbitration offers a unique pathway for parties to resolve their disputes outside of national courts, leading to a binding and enforceable decision. The ability of parties to tailor the process to the specific nuances of their dispute has made arbitration a highly favoured method of conflict resolution, contributing to its increasing popularity.

Arbitration provides a neutral forum, freeing parties from the constraints of a specific court and, in the case of international disputes, a particular jurisdiction. This neutrality is crucial when parties are concerned about the potential advantages afforded by the other party's home country (Born, 2021). By creating a level playing field, arbitration ensures that all sides are positioned relatively equally and can engage in an impartial process. Parties can choose any arbitral institution they wish or even opt for a process that will not be administered by any institution. This provides them with control over the neutrality of the forum where dispute resolution occurs.

Parties involved in arbitration have significant autonomy. One of the main indicators of this is that they can select the decision-makers for the process or establish criteria for their selection, as well as the method by which they are appointed. They also have control over the number of arbitrators, ensuring that the case is given comprehensive consideration and that the resulting decision is fair. Moreover, disputants can choose the rules that will govern the proceedings and determine other choices, which can significantly influence the process. For example, parties can decide whether their dispute will be administered by an arbitral institution or handled in an ad hoc manner. Importantly, parties grant jurisdiction to the arbitral tribunal and can define the scope of its authority to render decisions. The ability of parties to shape the arbitration process is largely unrestricted, limited only by the mandatory provisions of applicable arbitration statutes, which generally provide a considerable degree of freedom.

One of the primary advantages of arbitration over traditional litigation is the ability to select expert arbitrators. When a dispute arises in a specific field where technical knowledge is essential for understanding the nuances of the case, arbitration emerges as an ideal choice. This process allows parties to appoint arbitrators with expertise in that particular area, enabling them to comprehend the situation more quickly and thoroughly than if they were relying solely on expert witness reports. There is no requirement for arbitrators to have a legal background, which greatly expands the parties' choices in selecting arbitrators. However, it is generally advisable to include a lawyer among the arbitrators to ensure that the proceedings run smoothly. Lawyer arbitrators can facilitate drafting a high-quality award, aiding in enforcement while minimizing potential complications.

Confidentiality is an option that parties can choose in arbitration. It is not automatically a feature of the arbitration process. However, parties have the freedom to specify in their agreement that they want the process to be kept confidential. They do not need to justify their choice or explain their reasons for wanting confidentiality. Nonetheless, confidentiality may be compromised if the losing party does not comply with the arbitration award, as this may require the national court system to be involved in enforcement. Except for this limitation and possible jurisdictional obligations to share certain information, arbitration provides a venue for dispute resolution that allows parties to maintain confidentiality, protecting their reputations and sensitive information from being disclosed to the public.

The finality of the award is a crucial factor that enhances its appeal. This finality is guaranteed by the limited grounds on which an award can be challenged or set aside, and typically, there is no opportunity for appeal in international arbitration. Once a decision is made, it is binding, providing certainty and closure for the parties involved. In contrast, domestic arbitration may allow for more grounds to appeal an arbitral award, depending on the specific jurisdiction. Parties can address their rights to appeal in the arbitration agreement by either waiving this right entirely or specifying the process for any appeal. For example, the appeal may be directed to a national court or another arbitration tribunal.

One of the key reasons arbitration is highly effective and often the preferred choice for dispute resolution is its strong enforceability (Born, 2021). Typically, when there are no complications regarding the validity of the arbitration agreement or an award, enforcing the award poses little challenge, even if the losing party fails to comply. An arbitral award can be enforced through national courts, similar to a court decision. In the realm of international arbitration, the United Nations Convention on the Recognition and Enforcement of Foreign Arbitral Awards (United Nations, 1958) has established a pro-arbitration framework worldwide. More than 170 countries are signatories to this convention, allowing parties to enforce arbitral awards through their national court systems when necessary. In addition to this treaty, there are other conventions that can enhance the enforceability of international arbitration awards, such as the Inter-American Convention on International Commercial Arbitration (1976) and the European Convention on International Commercial Arbitration (1961). Generally, national courts have no problems recognizing arbitral awards, which promotes international commercial relationships and ensures effective mechanisms for dispute resolution.

These characteristics offer various benefits to the parties involved, including a faster process and the expertise of arbitrators, which ensures fair and reasonable awards, convenience, and relative informality in proceedings. Parties typically have the option to determine the scope of discovery and the presentation of evidence, which influences both the duration and cost of the process. Additionally, the finality of the award benefits the parties' budgets by minimizing potential appeal costs.

Sometimes, the benefits of arbitration can become drawbacks, depending on the circumstances and choices made. For instance, the cost of the arbitration process can significantly surpass that of litigation if the parties opt for a tribunal comprised of multiple arbitrators and choose an administering institution with high fees. While arbitration is typically faster than traditional litigation, its duration can vary based on the nature of the dispute and how the process is customized. This can lead to longer timelines, especially in cases where there are disputes regarding the validity of the arbitration agreement, which may result in parallel proceedings in both national courts and arbitration, further escalating costs. Moreover, the confidentiality associated with arbitration can have negative implications, as it does not create precedents and can hinder uniformity. Additionally, the voluntary nature of arbitration, which requires the consent of all parties to engage in the process, complicates the involvement of those who have not expressly consented to arbitrate the dispute.

Thus, arbitration can be an effective means of resolving disputes when approached knowledgeably. It can be an efficient, expedient, and fair process. However, it is crucial to consider all the nuances, as the potential benefits can easily turn into drawbacks.

Overview of Arbitration Types

The arbitration process can be categorized into domestic and international arbitration. Domestic arbitration occurs when the parties involved in the dispute are from the same country, the arbitration takes place within that country's borders, and the governing law is also that of that country. In contrast, international arbitration involves disputes that possess an international element. As specified in Article 1(3) of the UNCITRAL Model Law on International Commercial Arbitration (United Nations 1985), this includes scenarios where the parties conduct business in different states, the arbitration is held outside the country where the parties operate, a substantial portion of the obligations is fulfilled across different states, or the parties have explicitly agreed that the subject matter of the arbitration agreement pertains to more than one country.Furthermore, International arbitration is divided into three categories: International Commercial Arbitration, Investor-State Arbitration, and State-to-State Arbitration (Moses, 2017).

International Commercial Arbitration addresses cross-border disputes in the commercial realm, such as issues arising from the failure to deliver goods or services as specified in a contract, as well as payment disputes.

Investor-state arbitration is a mechanism for resolving conflicts between investors and the host state where the investment has been made. This process often involves specialized institutions, notably the International Center for the Settlement of Investment Disputes (ICSID, 2024).

State-to-state arbitration, typically administered by the Permanent Court of Arbitration (PCA), deals with conflicts such as boundary delineations between countries, post-war disputes, and environmental issues

(Permanent Court of Arbitration). As indicated by its title, the parties involved in these disputes are generally States or State entities.

Another way to classify arbitration is by distinguishing between Institutional Arbitration and Ad hoc Arbitration. Institutional Arbitration means that parties may choose to engage a specialized organization to oversee the administrative aspects of the arbitration process, following its established rules (Moses, 2017). While these institutions do not interfere with the substantive elements of the proceedings, some of them provide oversight on the form of the award and bring attention to substantive issues, leaving the arbitral tribunal the discretion to accept or disregard such guidance. This oversight is essential for ensuring that the arbitral award adheres to high standards of arbitration practice, which facilitates its enforcement, avoiding complications. Additionally, arbitration institutions are responsible for assisting with appointing arbitrators, maintaining their standards throughout the process, and managing fees.

Conversely, in ad hoc arbitration, the burden of administrative tasks falls entirely on the arbitral tribunal, its assistants and the parties themselves. Parties can select specific rules tailored for this type of arbitration, which may direct them to established institutions for assistance with appointing arbitrators. Frequently, parties utilize the well-regarded UNCITRAL rules (United Nations, 1985), which have stood the test of time, or they may choose to create custom rules tailored to their unique procedural requirements. Ad hoc arbitration offers considerable flexibility, allowing parties to shape the process according to their preferences. However, this also means they forgo the support of administering institutions and their expertise, which can be invaluable in situations where arbitration becomes challenging or parties intentionally undermine the process.

The arbitration process can sometimes be integrated with other methods of dispute resolution, such as med-arb or arb-med. When parties choose to utilize the med-arb process, they can include provisions in their contract to first attempt to resolve their dispute through mediation. If mediation is unsuccessful, they will then proceed to arbitration. In this scenario, if the mediator is qualified to act as an arbitrator, they can expedite the decision-making process based on the evidence and testimonies presented by the parties. Alternatively, the case may be referred to a different arbitrator. The efficacy of this approach lies in the pressure generated by the possibility of a binding decision from an arbitrator, motivating parties to strive for a mutually agreeable resolution during mediation.

Arb-med follows a similar concept, beginning with arbitration, where each party presents their case and shares relevant information. Subsequently, the arbitrator issues an award that is sealed in an envelope. The parties then enter into mediation, with the arbitrator serving as a mediator. If they are unable to reach an agreement during mediation, the previously rendered award becomes enforceable. In both processes, decisions reached through mediation can be made binding, often taking the form of a consent award that is enforceable as an arbitration award if not voluntarily executed.

A distinctive type of arbitration process is known as final offer arbitration or baseball arbitration. This method involves the parties presenting their proposed amounts for a reward. Following this, the arbitrator conducts a hearing, during which the parties can present arguments and evidence to support their offers. At the conclusion of the proceedings, the arbitrator is required to select one of the offers without making any modifications, thereby rendering a final award. This procedure encourages parties to submit reasonable offers with the hope that their proposal will be chosen by the arbitrator. The method's popularity in major US baseball leagues for determining player salaries has led to its nickname, baseball arbitration (Moses, 2017).

Arbitration encompasses various modifications of the process, providing parties with options that better align with their desires and expectations. It fosters a private quasi-judicial method of conflict resolution that effectively addresses arbitrable disputes.

Arbitral Institutions

The increasing popularity of arbitration as a means of dispute resolution has resulted in a rise in the number of institutions dedicated to administering these processes. Some of these entities focus exclusively on specific areas or types of cases, as exemplified by the London Maritime Arbitration Association (LMAA) and the International Centre for Energy Arbitration (ICEA) (Moses, 2017). Furthermore, there are institutions that manage both domestic and international disputes, sometimes implementing distinct rules for each category or exclusively addressing international matters.

The ADR Institute of Canada serves as an example of an institution capable of administering both domestic and international disputes. According to its rules: "While the Rules were crafted primarily to facilitate the resolution of domestic, commercial disputes, parties may choose to apply them to international or non-commercial disputes as well" (ADR Institute of Canada). In most instances, this option is typically reserved for parties who are both Canadians. In addition to arbitration rules and services relevant to this form of conflict resolution, the institute also provides ADRIC National Mediation Rules and ADRIC Med-Arb Rules (ADR Institute of Canada). Thus, this avenue may offer parties many choices and provide comprehensive assistance.

The London Court of International Arbitration (LCIA) is among the most esteemed international institutions globally. The LCIA Court comprises up to thirty-five members, in addition to representatives from affiliated institutions and former Presidents (LCIA). Although it includes the term "Court," it does not function as a conventional court in the typical sense. The LCIA offers efficient, flexible, and impartial administration of arbitration and other alternative dispute resolution (ADR) proceedings, irrespective of location or applicable legal system. Its dispute resolution services are accessible to all contracting parties without any membership prerequisites (LCIA). The LCIA Court serves as the ultimate authority on the proper application of its rules, with key responsibilities including appointing tribunals, addressing challenges to arbitrators, and managing costs (LCIA).

The International Court of Arbitration (ICC) is another world's leading arbitral institution. Established in 1923 to resolve disputes in international commercial and investment disputes (ICC, 2024). Although called a court in name, the ICC doesn't make formal judgments on disputed matters. Instead, it administers arbitrations by exercising judicial supervision of arbitration proceedings. As stated on their website, the purpose of this institution is to ensure proper application of the 2021 Arbitration Rules, as well as assist parties and arbitrators in overcoming procedural obstacles (ICC, 2024). These efforts are supported by the Court's Secretariat, which is made up of more than 100 lawyers and support personnel, operating through their offices in Paris, New York, Sao Paolo, Singapore, Abu Dhabi and Hong Kong (ICC, 2024).

The increasing demand for arbitration services, along with the growing reliance on this method of conflict resolution, has resulted in the establishment of various domestic and international arbitration institutions worldwide. These organizations often provide additional alternative dispute resolution options, such as med-arb or mediation (ADR Institute of Canada). It is common for multiple international arbitration institutions to operate within a single country or city, making it crucial to specify the exact name of the institution in the arbitration agreement to prevent potential confusion. The diversity of arbitral institutions offers a wide range of service quality and costs, meeting different needs and expectations. This trend highlights the effectiveness of a privately operated justice system supported by a legal framework that promotes the evolution of arbitration on a global scale.

Legal Framework Governing Arbitration

Arbitration is a structured legal process characterized by fundamental principles and limitations. It offers parties flexibility and autonomy within a multi-layered legal framework comprised of rules and regulations designed to facilitate the arbitration process.

The legal framework for arbitration begins with the parties' arbitration agreement. The consent to arbitrate a dispute is essential. Without it, other legal frameworks and regulations cannot be invoked. In addition to affirming their consent to arbitrate, the parties' agreement may also delineate significant choices regarding the process, which will have mandatory implications.

It is advisable for the arbitration agreement to specify whether the parties wish for the process to be administered by an arbitral institution or prefer ad hoc arbitration. By designating a particular arbitral institution and/or set of rules, the parties determine how the arbitration process will proceed, making the application of those rules mandatory. Often, these rules provide a default option for the process unless the parties agree to alternative arrangements. Consequently, even when selecting an established set of rules for arbitration, parties retain the freedom to customize them, provided that specific provisions are not mandatory.

The next layer of law that applies to the arbitration process is the law of the seat. It is important to specify this law in the arbitration agreement. The law of the seat governs the intervention and oversight of the arbitration process by the jurisdiction in which it is located. While this regulation is typically not overly intrusive, it is significant as it sometimes determines the validity of arbitration agreements and the grounds for challenging or setting aside arbitration awards. If assistance is needed to obtain certain evidence, the national court at the seat of arbitration will provide support. In Canada, each province has its international and domestic statutes regulating different types of arbitration. All statutes that regulate international arbitration are based on model law except for the province of Quebec, where both international and domestic arbitration processes are regulated by the Code of Civil Procedure (Quebec, 2020). Despite not adopting the UNCITRAL Model Law, the regulation aligns with the common practice of arbitration. Additionally, if at least one of the parties to the arbitration is Her Majesty in right of Canada, a departmental corporation or a Crown corporation or if its maritime or admiralty matters, the process will be regulated by the *Commercial Arbitration Act* (Canada, 1985).

Parties are generally encouraged to specify the law that governs both the arbitration agreement and the main contract. This helps simplify the tribunal's task of determining the applicable law. It is important to note that the governing law for each can be different. Although the absence of a designated law does not render the arbitration agreement invalid and does not prevent the tribunal from proceeding, it can lead to unpredictability regarding the outcome. In such cases, the tribunal will need to determine the applicable law themselves. Given the limited grounds for appealing or challenging an arbitration award, this unpredictability can have significant consequences. Therefore, the ability to choose the governing law for both the arbitration process and the main contract is a considerable advantage. However, if this choice is neglected, it can negatively impact the entire arbitration process.

In the upcoming customization of the legal framework, parties may consider various guidelines and rules. For instance, they can specify in the arbitration agreement that the evidence will be presented in accordance with the IBA Rules on the Taking of Evidence in International Arbitration (International Bar Association, 2020). By doing so, these rules become mandatory for the arbitration process. Conversely, parties might choose not to include any specific guidelines in the arbitration agreement, leaving the selection of applicable rules as an optional choice. Typically, arbitral tribunals will decide which guidelines to follow to ensure uniformity and predictability in the proceedings. Examples of such guidelines include the UNCITRAL Notes on Organizing Arbitral Proceedings 2016 (United Nations, 2016), the IBA Rules of Ethics for International Arbitrators 1987 (International Bar Association, 1987), and the IBA Guidelines on Conflicts of Interest for Arbitrators 2024 (International Bar Association, 2024), as well as the Guidelines on Party Representation 2013 (International Bar Association, 2013), among others.

The subsequent layer of legal regulation is relevant to international arbitration and concerns conventions governing the process and recognition and enforcement of arbitral awards. Several prominent conventions in this area include:

1. The Convention on the Recognition and Enforcement of Foreign Arbitral Awards (New York, 1958) (United Nations, 1958);
2. The Inter-American Convention on International Commercial Arbitration (1976) (Inter-American Convention, 1976);
3. The European Convention on International Commercial Arbitration (1961) (European Convention, 1961) (European Convention, 1961);
4. The Convention on the Settlement of Investment Disputes Between States and Nationals of Other States (ICSID Convention, 1965) (ICSID, 1965);
5. The Hague Convention for the Pacific Settlement of International Disputes (1899) (Hague Convention, 1899).

These conventions provide the foundational framework for pro-arbitration regimes globally, encouraging the use of arbitration while promoting uniformity and high standards in arbitration practices. When parties have an arbitral award that requires enforcement, they can select the convention that facilitates this process and initiate enforcement in accordance with its provisions. Certain conventions specifically address particular types of international arbitration, such as the ICSID Convention, which governs Investor-State disputes (ICSID, 1965), and The Hague Convention, which established the PCA, where State-to-State arbitrations typically occur (Hague Convention, 1899).

Collectively, these statutes, rules, and regulations allow arbitration to meet the needs of modern dispute resolution practices outside national courts. They create a flexible yet effective framework, enabling disputing parties to make decisions that influence the comprehensiveness, duration, and cost of the process. However, parties must exercise caution when drafting their agreements, as the advantages of arbitration's flexible nature can easily become drawbacks if specifications are not clearly articulated.

The Arbitration Agreement

Arbitration agreements, as previously emphasized, are essential in establishing the framework and process of arbitration. A well-crafted arbitration agreement can significantly enhance the efficiency and effectiveness of the conflict resolution process, whereas a poorly designed one may introduce additional challenges, potentially leading to disputes regarding its validity, scope, and the intent behind its language. It is important to note that there is no one-size-fits-all approach to determining the scope of arbitration clauses. In this section of the chapter, we will identify the key elements necessary for an arbitration agreement and examine the critical considerations that should be addressed before making a decision.

An arbitration agreement can take one of two forms: an arbitration clause embedded within the main contract or a standalone arbitration agreement. Typically, parties integrate an arbitration clause into the main contract to ensure that any disputes are resolved outside national courts. In cases where an arbitration clause is absent and a dispute arises, parties can enter into a separate arbitration agreement to refer the matter to arbitration. However, a significant challenge of forming an arbitration agreement after a dispute has occurred is that the disputing parties may argue over even minor details, complicating the establishment of such an agreement. Thus, it is advisable to incorporate an arbitration clause into the contract initially if arbitration is the preferred method for resolving conflicts. In this scenario, even if the main contract is found to be invalid, the doctrine of separability allows the arbitration agreement to remain in effect. This means that the parties can still initiate arbitration to address disputes, such as those concerning the existence of the contract.

The essential elements that are highly recommended for inclusion in an arbitration agreement are as follows:

- Seat of arbitration
- Institutional or ad hoc arbitration
- Scope of the arbitration clause
- Governing Law
- Appointment or number of arbitrators
- Language
- Other modifications

The seat of arbitration plays a critical role in the arbitration process, as it establishes the legal framework governing the proceedings. Domestic and international arbitrations are typically regulated by different statutes; domestic arbitration adheres to laws relevant to domestic issues, while international arbitration follows statutes applicable to cross-border disputes. The seat of arbitration refers to the legal jurisdiction in which the arbitration takes place, which may differ from the physical venue of the hearings. Additionally, the law governing the primary contract may not align with the law of the seat of arbitration. The arbitration law of the chosen seat will guide the arbitration process and address any gaps not covered by the agreed-upon rules or arbitration agreements. If parties designate a seat without specifying an arbitral institution or the method for appointing arbitrators, the courts of that jurisdiction can assist in establishing an arbitral tribunal. The law of the seat may also be used to determine the validity of arbitration agreements and to provide grounds for challenging an award. Consequently, it is advisable to select a seat recognized for its arbitration-friendly regime.

As mentioned above, parties have to decide if they prefer the dispute to be resolved ad hoc or if they want the assistance of an arbitral institution. If parties desire more control over the process and flexibility in terms of rules, or if they want to draft their own rules, they will proceed with ad hoc options. Usually, this choice is made in cases when one of the parties of the arbitration is a state (Moses, 2017). While engaging with arbitral institutions entails paying fees for their services, these organizations offer greater assurance and established standards for managing the administrative aspects of the process.

The scope of an arbitration agreement is a crucial element, as it defines the limits of the tribunal's jurisdiction. If the scope is not clearly articulated, certain issues may fall outside the coverage of the clause, resulting in those issues being resolved in national courts. This situation undermines the benefits of arbitration. It is important to understand that arbitrators only possess the authority granted to them by the parties in the arbitration agreement.

To ensure that arbitration proceeds smoothly, it is essential to clarify all fundamental expectations regarding the conflict resolution process, including the applicable law governing the arbitration agreement. If this is not adequately specified, the arbitral tribunal may need to determine it independently using various approaches. For instance, they could apply the law of the seat of the arbitration or the law governing the main contract. This applicable law will address issues related to the parties' capacity to validly enter into an arbitration agreement, the formal validity of the arbitration agreement, the interpretation of the agreement, or the non-arbitrability of disputes. Therefore, to promote certainty and predictability, it is advisable to explicitly state the law underpinning the arbitration agreement.

The appointment of arbitrators is a critical aspect of the arbitration process, as their knowledge and expertise greatly impact the quality of the final award. While this can be a significant advantage of arbitration, it should be approached with caution due to the limited grounds for challenging an award, even if it seems unjust or contains legal errors. Therefore, it is prudent to choose individuals who possess not only a deep knowledge of the relevant field but also substantial experience in arbitration and a talent for crafting clear and well-structured awards.

Moreover, consideration of the arbitrator's availability is essential, as their level of busyness can affect the efficiency of the process, including the scheduling of hearings and related activities. Parties may also specify certain preferences in their arbitration agreement, such as the arbitrator's area of expertise or language proficiency. However, it is important to remember that imposing such requirements can narrow the pool of potential candidates, so they should only be indicated when they are truly significant for the process.

The parties must determine the number of arbitrators that will constitute the tribunal, typically choosing either one or three. Since those drafting an arbitration clause may not fully foresee the nature of potential future disputes, they can create a formula stipulating that disputes below a specified monetary threshold should be resolved by a single arbitrator, while those exceeding that amount should be addressed by a panel of three arbitrators. It is also essential to clarify the mechanism for selecting and appointing arbitrators. If the parties do not establish this mechanism and refer instead to applicable rules, the appointment of arbitrators will proceed in accordance with those established rules. Furthermore, the parties may designate an appointing authority to minimize disputes regarding their selections. For instance, this authority could be assigned to an arbitral institution or a specific national court. However, it is important to consider that choosing a national court as the appointing authority may prolong the process of forming the tribunal. In situations where a tribunal of three arbitrators is favoured, the typical appointment method involves each party selecting one arbitrator, who then jointly appoints a presiding arbitrator.

Language plays a crucial role in the considerations of the parties involved, as it affects both the accessibility of the process and its associated costs and speed. If the parties are multilingual and prefer the proceedings to be conducted in two different languages, they must be mindful of the expenses related to hiring translators for hearings, as well as the requirement to translate all documents into both languages. Additionally, they should consider the time necessary for these tasks. Generally, it is advisable to select a single language for the arbitration; however, it is essential that all parties have an equal opportunity to present their case.

Modifications to the arbitration agreement can also include provisions regarding confidentiality and appeal rights. Confidentiality is one of the key advantages of arbitration, but it does not occur automatically. To ensure that the arbitration process, related documents, and outcomes remain confidential, this must be explicitly stated in the arbitration agreement. While some institutional rules or governing laws may contain confidentiality provisions, it is crucial for parties to verify that this aspect is explicitly addressed in the relevant rules or statutes, as confidentiality is not inherently guaranteed.

When considering the right to appeal in international arbitration across various jurisdictions, it is crucial to recognize that the option to appeal is typically unavailable. The only recourse for a losing party is to seek to challenge or set aside an award. However, this does not extend to challenging it on the basis of a question of law. This limitation reinforces the finality of the decision, which may, however, pose a significant disadvantage for the losing party who disagrees with the outcome. For domestic arbitration, the possibility of appeal is determined by applicable law. For instance, under provision 44(2) of the *Manitoba Arbitration Act*, parties are given the opportunity to appeal even if the arbitration agreement does not expressly include this option. The provision states: "If the arbitration agreement (other than a family arbitration agreement) does not provide that the parties may appeal an award to the court on a question of law, a party may appeal an award to the court on a question of law with leave" (Manitoba, 1997).

These elements of the arbitration agreement play a significant role in shaping the arbitration process and determining its scope, duration, costs, and overall effectiveness. By carefully considering the drafting of an arbitration agreement, parties can tailor the private system of justice to suit their specific needs, resulting in a more expedient, equitable, and streamlined process. However, it is easy to overlook the importance of each element in the agreement at the time of drafting, especially when a dispute has not yet arisen. It is often recommended to involve a lawyer with expertise in the arbitration, as they can provide insight into the complexities of the arbitration agreement and its implications once a dispute occurs.

Conclusion

Arbitration offers a unique avenue for resolving disputes by blending the benefits of both private and public justice systems. The flexibility granted to the parties allows them to customize the arbitration process to meet their specific needs while ensuring that the resulting arbitration award is binding and enforceable.

The main advantages of arbitration include access to expert decision-makers, speed, the finality of decisions, and confidentiality. However, there are also drawbacks, such as high costs, uncertainty if the arbitration agreement is poorly drafted, and limited grounds for challenging an award, even if it contains a legal error.

Arbitration can take various forms, including institutional arbitration and ad hoc arbitration. It can also be combined with other dispute resolution methods, such as mediation, resulting in processes like Med-Arb or Arb-Med. This adaptability underscores the flexible nature of arbitration, making it an excellent choice for arbitrable cases.

The legal framework surrounding arbitration consists of multiple layers of statutes, rules, and regulations, all influenced by the parties' choices. Understanding the implications of each legal choice is crucial to creating a favourable legal environment for the arbitration process. At the core of each arbitration is the arbitration agreement, which confirms the parties' consent to arbitrate and includes essential elements that shape the entire process.

To deepen our understanding of arbitration within the broader landscape of conflict transformation, the process must be situated within a framework of relational justice. This perspective reminds us that legal procedures are not merely technical mechanisms for dispute resolution, but are also human encounters marked by recognition, dignity, and the potential for healing. Arbitration, when thoughtfully designed, can serve as a space where parties are not only heard but also respected and acknowledged in their full social and relational contexts. This shifts the focus from winning or losing to fostering processes that affirm relationships, restore trust, and enable genuine resolution—outcomes that go beyond the scope of traditional adjudication.

Moreover, engaging with arbitration as a **transformative practice** and a site of **epistemic repair** challenges us to confront whose voices are amplified or marginalized in legal forums. Often, what counts as valid knowledge or testimony in arbitration reflects dominant norms, while the lived experiences and worldviews of less powerful groups are sidelined. By adopting a transformative lens, legal practitioners and students alike are encouraged to critically assess the structures underpinning arbitration and to work toward inclusive practices that honor diverse forms of knowing. This involves designing processes that do more than resolve disputes efficiently—they must also seek to shift power imbalances, open space for collaborative meaning-making, and create conditions under which all participants can participate fully and fairly.

In summary, arbitration is a distinctive dispute resolution process with unique features and characteristics. It reshapes the traditional understanding of private conflict resolution by offering increased flexibility and freedom to disputing parties, applicable to both domestic disputes and international conflicts.

Questions

1. Critically assess how arbitration can serve the interests of disputing parties better than litigation. In what circumstances might arbitration not be the preferred option?
2. Analyze the legal principles and policy considerations that govern when and how a dispute may be referred to arbitration. How might these differ across jurisdictions?
3. Discuss the legal and practical implications for parties once a valid arbitration agreement is in place. How does it impact access to courts?
4. Evaluate the essential elements required for a valid arbitration agreement. How might ambiguities in drafting affect the enforceability of an arbitration clause?

Glossary

Arbitration:	A method for resolving disputes outside of national courts. It is a private system of justice that allows parties to create a process tailored to their specific needs. Arbitration is less formal than traditional court processes but usually results in binding decisions.
Autonomy:	Parties involved in arbitration have significant autonomy, allowing them to select decision-makers, establish criteria for their selection, control the number of arbitrators, and choose the rules governing the proceedings. This ability to shape the process is largely unrestricted, limited only by mandatory provisions of applicable statutes.
Expert arbitrators:	A primary advantage of arbitration is the ability to select decision-makers with expertise in a specific field relevant to the dispute. This allows them to understand technical nuances quickly and thoroughly. Arbitrators are not required to have a legal background.
Confidentiality:	This is an option that parties can choose in arbitration. It is not automatic but can be specified in the arbitration agreement. Choosing confidentiality helps protect parties' reputations and sensitive information from public disclosure.
Neutral forum:	Arbitration provides a neutral forum, freeing parties from the constraints of a specific national court and jurisdiction, which is crucial when parties are concerned about potential advantages afforded by another party's home country. This helps create a level playing field.
Finality of the award:	Arbitral awards are final and binding. This finality is guaranteed by the limited grounds on which an award can be challenged or set

	aside, and typically there is no opportunity for appeal in international arbitration.
Enforceability:	Arbitral awards have strong enforceability. An award can be enforced through national courts, similar to a court decision. International arbitration benefits from conventions like the New York Convention, signed by over 170 countries, which facilitates enforcing awards through national court systems worldwide.

Competing Interests The author has no conflicts of interest to declare that are relevant to the content of this chapter.

References

ADR Institute of Canada. (n.d.). *ADRIC arbitration rules*. Accessed December 1, 2024. https://adric.ca/wp-content/uploads/2017/08/2016_ARBITRATION_RULES_Booklet_2016_Aug2017.pdf

Born, G. B. (2021). *International commercial arbitration* (3rd ed.). Kluwer Law International.

Canada. (1985). *Commercial Arbitration Act*. R.S.C., 1985, c. 17 (2nd Supp.). Accessed December 1, 2024. https://laws-lois.justice.gc.ca/eng/acts/c-34.6/fulltext.html

International Bar Association. (1987). *Rules of ethics for international arbitrators*. Accessed December 1, 2024. https://www.ibanet.org/document?id=Rules-of-ethics-for-international-arbitrators

International Bar Association. (2013). *IBA guidelines on party representation in international arbitration*. Adopted by resolution of the IBA Council, May 25, 2013. Accessed December 1, 2024. https://www.ibanet.org/MediaHandler?id=6F0C57D7-E7A0-43AF-B76E-714D9FE74D7F

International Bar Association. (2020). *IBA rules on the taking of evidence in international arbitration*. International Bar Association. https://www.ibanet.org/resources-for-arbitrators

International Bar Association. (2024). *IBA guidelines on conflicts of interest in international arbitration*. Approved by the IBA Council, May 25, 2024. Accessed December 1, 2024. https://www.ibanet.org/document?id=Guidelines-on-Conflicts-of-Interest-in-International-Arbitration-2024

International Centre for Settlement of Investment Disputes. (n.d.). Accessed December 1, 2024. https://icsid.worldbank.org/
LCIA. (n.d.). *Organisation*. Accessed December 1, 2024. https://www.lcia.org/LCIA/organisation.aspx
Manitoba. (1997). *The Arbitration Act*, C.C.S.M. c. A120. Manitoba: Government of Manitoba. Accessed December 1, 2024. https://web2.gov.mb.ca/laws/statutes/ccsm/a120.php
Moses, M. L. (2017). *The principles and practice of international commercial arbitration* (3rd ed.). Cambridge University Press.
Permanent Court of Arbitration. (n.d.). *Home*. Accessed December 1, 2024. https://pca-cpa.org/home/
Quebec. (2020). *Code of Civil Procedure*, CQLR c. C-25.01. Accessed December 1, 2024. https://www.legisquebec.gouv.qc.ca/en/document/cs/c-25.01
United Nations. (1958). *Convention on the recognition and enforcement of foreign arbitral awards (New York Convention)*. Accessed December 1, 2024. https://www.newyorkconvention.org/english
United Nations. (1985). *UNCITRAL model law on international commercial arbitration*. United Nations Commission on International Trade Law. Accessed December 1, 2024. https://uncitral.un.org/sites/uncitral.un.org/files/media-documents/uncitral/en/19-09955_e_ebook.pdf
United Nations. (2016). *UNCITRAL notes on organizing arbitral proceedings*. Accessed December 1, 2024. https://uncitral.un.org/en/texts/arbitration/othertexts/notes
United Nations. (n.d.). *UNCITRAL arbitration rules*. Accessed December 1, 2024. https://uncitral.un.org/en/texts/arbitration/contractualtexts/arbitration
ICC International Court of Arbitration® - ICC - International Chamber of Commerce. (2024). *ICC*. Accessed December 1, 2024. https://iccwbo.org/dispute-resolution/dispute-resolution-services/icc-international-court-of-arbitration/

Dispute Resolution in Sports

Martine Dennie and Ryan Hall

Abstract This chapter provides an overview of the dispute resolution systems in place for both the Canadian amateur sport system and professional sports leagues. Through an examination of the governance models of sports organizations, we look at the internal dispute resolution processes and when an appeal to an external body is allowed, including the Sport Dispute Resolution Centre of Canada ("SDRCC"). The SDRCC is a federal entity, which offers mediation and arbitration services for sports disputes. The federal system for dispute resolution has undergone recent developments, including the creation of the Office of the Sports Integrity Commissioner in 2021 to oversee the Universal Code of Conduct to Prevent Maltreatment in Sports. In contrast, we examine the dispute resolution processes in professional sports, which differs dramatically from the amateur system. Since professional sports leagues are unionized workplaces, the dispute resolution mechanism is collectively bargaining between the league and the players' associations. The result is

---

M. Dennie (✉)
Faculty of Law, University of Manitoba, Winnipeg, MB, Canada
e-mail: martine.dennie@umanitoba.ca

R. Hall
MLT Aikins LLP, Winnipeg, MB, Canada

L. E. Reimer and R. Jochelson (eds.), *The Other Side of the Bar*,
https://doi.org/10.1007/978-981-96-9748-9_9

a collective bargaining agreement, which outlines how disputes are to be resolved, and typically excludes recourse to judicial courts. This chapter is shaped around the ongoing safe sport crisis in Canada and the increasing number of lawsuits filed by athletes for the alleged systemic negligence of their sports organizations, which point to significant weaknesses in the sports dispute resolution systems.

Keywords Dispute resolution · Sports governance · Amateur sports · Professional sports · Safe sport · Arbitration · Collective bargaining

Introduction

Disputes occur in all areas of life, especially when individuals exist in close proximity with each other—and sports are no exception. As popularity for both amateur and professional sports increased, sports were commercialized and turned into a profitable business. Sociologists of sports have long pointed to the commercialization and commodification of sport leading to changes in the structures and goals of certain sports (Coakley & Donnelly, 2004). Indeed, legal scholars similarly argue that the commercialization of sport has led to numerous disputes related to, for instance, contracts, intellectual property, and labour (Mitten & Opie, 2012) and "invoked the need for protection of different and very often conflicting interests of the stakeholders in sport" (Kolev, 2012, p. 230). Accordingly, the commercialization and commodification of sports is equally responsible to the creation of modern dispute resolution systems in sports (Casini, 2012).

Modern sports organizations became structured hierarchically according to level of play from local and regional clubs, provincial and territorial sporting organizations ("PSOs"), and national sporting organizations ("NSOs"); all of whom oversee the entirety of the amateur sports system in Canada. There are also organizations at the international level that oversees the sport in question for international events such as the Olympic Games. Let's take the sport of ice hockey for example: The International Ice Hockey Federation ("IIHF") is responsible for international hockey, including controlling the international rulebook, determining official guidelines for international events, and running various programs on a global scale ("International Ice Hockey Federation," n.d.). Meanwhile, Hockey Canada is the national governing body for ice hockey in Canada and works on partnership with the provincial and territorial hockey organizations, the Canadian Hockey League, and U Sports to grow the game at all levels (Hockey Canada, "Mandate and Mission", n.d.).

Overseeing the entire sports system is the federal government agency Sport Canada, which is the Department of Canadian Heritage branch responsible for administering sport programs across the country. All NSOs are governed by the *Canada Not-for-profit Corporations Act* (2009) and are recently required to adopt the *Canadian Sport Governance Code* ("The Governance Code," n.d.) by April 2025 to remain eligible for federal funding to promote better governance principles ("Leadership and Governance," n.d.). The Code outlines certain requirements, such as board composition for NSOs, financial matters, transparency, and athlete representation ("The Code," n.d.). Meanwhile, professional sports leagues in Canada, such as the National Hockey League ("NHL") and the Canadian Football League ("CFL") operate independently of the amateur system as they are self-governing entities without any government oversight beyond for-profit corporate legislative requirements.

In this chapter, we will provide an overview of the complex dispute resolution system in place for handling sports-related disputes in various settings. We will describe the complaint intake procedures available to a grieving party within the Canadian amateur sport system, including the procedures for filing an external appeal to dispute resolution tribunals, including the Sport Dispute Resolution Centre of Canada ("SDRCC") and when recourse to the judicial courts is appropriate. We will also discuss the systems in place for disputes that occur in the professional sports setting to demonstrate how dispute resolution occurs in the context of unionized sports that bind parties to procedures outlined in a collective bargaining agreement ("CBA").

There are numerous pathways to dispute resolution in sports: traditional litigation, arbitration, mediation, mediation/arbitration, and collective bargaining agreements that outline detailed grievance and dispute resolution procedures. The relationship between litigation and alternative dispute resolution in sports is complex (McArdle, 2015). As such, this chapter will provide an introductory overview of these processes. Throughout this chapter, we will focus on the safe sport crisis currently ongoing in Canada to frame our discussions and to highlight the weaknesses in these existing systems.

Dispute Resolution in the Canadian Amateur Sports System

Despite governmental oversight, sports organizations are private and voluntary associations (Jodouin, 2005; Mazzuco & Findlay, 2024), meaning that they are made up of individuals, many of whom are volunteers, who work together towards a common goal or purpose (Findlay, 2022). These associations may be incorporated or not. They can be standalone organizations such as a private local golf club or they can be part of a larger hierarchical system such as a provincial association that has a contractual relationship with the national federation. As private and voluntary associations, they have the significant ability to govern themselves with relatively little oversight (Mazzuco & Findlay, 2024). As such, when disputes take place, sports organizations typically handle them internally and render their own decisions before any appeal to an external body may occur. Accordingly, the dispute resolution mechanisms in place within the Canadian amateur sport system is complex.

The rules governing any given association's authority will typically be found in their governing documents, including a constitution, by-laws, and/or policies. Associations are free to structure themselves as they see fit, including adopting their own policies and internal decision-making processes, but the SDRCC offers resources and templates for drafting such governing documents (SDRCC, "Resources", n.d.). A decision by a sporting organization at any level of play may give rise to a dispute for any given reason, whether it is related to governance, team selection, funding, doping, disciplinary sanctions, or a safe sport matter.[1] Sports organizations typically have an internal dispute resolution policy in place that will dictate how a dispute might be resolved beginning with a complaint intake process, a procedure for handling the complaint and decision-making, and any appeal processes in place (Jodouin, 2005).

Internal processes for resolving disputes are advantageous in numerous ways, including offering the parties a timely and flexible process while

[1] For an example of this hierarchical governance structure, please visit the SDRCC's "Example of Governance and Sport Policy Structure" on their website: https://www.crdsc

being more cost-effective than traditional litigation. There are, however, inherent limitations to handling disputes internally, including actual or perceived bias (Findlay, 2022). In attempt to address some of these issues related to internal dispute resolution procedures, the Canadian government sought to implement an external, independent appeal process to give sports organizations and athletes alike a way to plead their case before an impartial decision-maker. The result was the creation of the SDRCC.

A recent example demonstrates the importance of external dispute resolution services due to the inherent issue with conflicts of interests within internal appeal processes. At issue in the 2021 arbitration decision *Humphries v Bobsleigh Canada Skeleton* ("BCS") *and Hays*, Canadian Olympic Champion Kaillie Humphries appealed to the SDRCC due to concerns about BCS being able to investigate itself following her complaint of harassment by a coach [Hays] and the organization's management.

Humphries explained throughout this process that her reasons for appealing to the SDRCC were to receive procedural fairness for herself, and equally as a matter of public interest to "work towards more transparent and independent safe sport mechanisms in Canada so that athletes feel safe coming forward with complaints" (*Humphries v BCS and Hays*, July 2021, p. 6). The SDRCC ultimately determined that the internal investigation conducted by BCS had been improperly done and ordered a new investigation (*Humphries v BCS and Hays*, September 2021).

The Sport Dispute Resolution Centre of Canada

The SDRCC was created by the Canadian federal government pursuant to *The Physical Activity and Sport Act* (2003) to offer the Canadian sport community access to dispute resolution services, including arbitration and mediation, for conflicts that arise out of decisions made by sporting bodies. Parties in a sports dispute have been increasingly turning to alternative dispute processes in the last decade, particularly due to arbitration and mediation services addressing concerns around the ability of sports organizations to make decisions impartially (Findlay, 2022).

The SDRCC is funded through the Ministry of Canadian Heritage and administered by a 12-person Board of Directors appointed by the federal Minister of Sport and offers a range of arbitration and mediation services in both English and French. As such, pursuant to Article 3.3 of the *Canadian Sport Dispute Resolution Code* (the "Code") (Sport

Dispute Resolution Centre of Canada, 2021), they maintain a roster of "Dispute Resolution Professionals qualified as Mediators, Arbitrators and Med/Arb neutrals" to satisfy their mandate. Each professional added to the roster must have expertise in dispute resolution as well as "possess recognized experience in sport" (SDRCC, 2021, Article 3.3). The requirement to possess such expertise of sports is important to ensure that the unique world of sports is considered in decision-making. The importance of such industry knowledge in resolving sports disputes is noted elsewhere (Godin, 2017; Jodouin, 2005).

The Code further outlines the specific tribunals in place at the SDRCC and their respective roles: Ordinary Tribunal (SDRCC, 2021, Article 6), the Doping Tribunal (SDRCC, 2021, Article 7), the Safeguarding Tribunal (SDRCC, 2021, Article 8), and the Appeal Tribunal (SDRCC, 2021, Article 9). Only decisions by the Doping and Safeguarding Tribunals may be appealed (SDRCC, 2021, Article 9). The SDRCC will gain jurisdiction over a dispute when all internal appeal processes have been exhausted or when all parties involved in the dispute agree to waive internal procedures and appeal to the SDRCC (SDRCC, 2021, Article 3).

The scope of review at the SDRCC is to conduct a hearing de novo. In other words, the panel hearing the case will "review the facts and apply the law," which means they have the power to reverse the decision that led to the dispute and impose their own remedies deemed suitable in the circumstances (SDRCC, 2021, Article 6.11). This approach gives greater discretion to the SDRCC hearing appeals than other approaches typically adopted by administrative tribunals who tend to prefer a standard of reasonableness. When a decision-maker adopts a standard based on reasonableness, it means that they will consider the decision made by the sports organization and look to whether the decision-maker interpreted the organization's governing documents and policies fairly and has exercised their discretion in good faith and without arbitrariness (Corbett et al., 2008). While some decisions may draw on a standard of reasonableness,[2] the Code explicitly allows de novo hearings, and even requires it in some circumstances when the sports organization failed to conduct an internal appeal process or denied the claimant's right to be

[2] For example, in *Humphries v BCS and Hays* (2021), the SDRCC found that the BCS internal investigation had been "neither thorough nor reasonable" and that "the decision of the Board of BCS to accept the Report cannot stand" (p. 41).

heard (SDRCC, 2021, Article 6.11). In such cases, the panel will hear the facts and evidence of the case and render a resolution regardless of any previous internal decisions. A body of case law has since developed through the SDRCC and a database is publicly available on their website (SDRCC, "Dispute Resolution Secretariat", n.d.). Despite the SDRCC's official mission statement being "about education and prevention" and "about providing tools and guidance to help resolve minor disputes quickly and informally," (SDRCC, "About", n.d.), the ongoing safe sport crisis led the federal government to put in place yet another external dispute resolution body.

The Office of the Sport Integrity Commissioner

In 2021, the SDRCC was mandated by the Canadian government to establish an independent safe sport mechanism to address widespread maltreatment in sport (Canadian Heritage, 2021). In response, the Office of the Sport Integrity Commissioner (OSIC) was created. The OSIC is tasked to implement the Universal Code of Conduct to prevent Maltreatment in Sports ("UCCMS"). The UCCMS applies to all NSOs that receive federal funding. The OSIC advances the UCCMS by overseeing the following: (1) a complaint intake process; (2) conducting preliminary assessments and investigations; (3) maintain a database of imposed sanctions; and (4) monitoring compliance by sports organizations (UCCMS, 2022).

It is important to note that the OSIC does not have jurisdiction to oversee the adoption and imposition of sanctions, nor can they impose mediated outcomes or legal remedies for UCCMS violations. The OSIC simply has jurisdiction to administer the UCCSM in accordance with the contractual mandate from the Government of Canada and they can only oversee matters related to the UCCMS – that is, matters alleging maltreatment and discrimination (OSIC, "Authority and Jurisdiction," n.d.). Any sanction imposed on a party must be outlined in the UCCMS, which include apologies, suspensions, and permanent bans. The OSIC may also opt to launch a "Sport Environment Assessment" ("SEA") wherein they can make recommendations intended to improve the sport environment for current and future participants. A SEA is entirely voluntary, and the reports are only recommendations for implementation; OSIC cannot impose changes (OSIC, "Sport Environment Assessment," n.d.).

Dispute Resolution and the Safe Sport Crisis

The internal processes outlined in the policies of sports organizations have been criticized for being unfair and biased since most complaints involve the organization itself as a party to the complaint (Findlay, 2022; Godin, 2017). Further, there is increasing evidence that sports organizations are failing to adopt and enforce meaningful policies to not only handle complaints filed by participants, but to prevent the maltreatment from occurring in the first place (Mazzuco & Findlay, 2024). As such, scholars and athletes alike are calling for change within the sport system and the dispute resolution system with numerous advocacy groups speaking out, including Gymnasts for Change (n.d.), Fencing for Change (Fencing for Change Canada, 2023), and Scholars Against Abuse (Giannitsopoulou et al., 2023).

The Canadian sport system is in crisis as many sports organizations in Canada are "saturated in harassment, bullying, and abuse" (Ross, 2022, para 1), despite existing internal and external dispute resolution mechanisms in place. As argued by sports law scholars Marcus Mazzuco and Hilary Findlay (2024), "the sport system itself is broken and the prevalence of maltreatment is symptomatic of system-wide issues. Both historical and current incidents of maltreatment continue to come to light despite efforts to implement various remedial measures" (p. 3).

The term "Safe Sport" (which is currently being rebranded by the Canadian government as "integrity in sport" hence the Sport *Integrity* Commissioner) refers to "athletes' right to participate in sport without being bullied, neglected, discriminated against, or abused psychologically, physically or sexually" (Donnelly et al., 2022, p. 165). Safe Sport was widely recognized as an issue in sport in the 1990s, where, in 1996, Sport Canada required all NSOs to adopt harassment and complaint policies to qualify for federal funding (Cordonier, 2022). Sports organizations at all levels have thus began implementing numerous safe sport policies to protect participants due to increased allegations of abuse across numerous sports around the world (Gurgis et al., 2022). However, athletes continue to face numerous forms of harassment and abuse in sports including emotional harm, sexual violence, interpersonal violence, and racial and sexist microaggressions (Gurgis et al., 2022). Donnelly et al. (2022) specifically point to the culture of sport and the autonomy of sports organizations to self-regulate and handle disputes internally with little oversight as primary reasons for ongoing safe sport concerns.

As outlined by Donnelly et al. (2022), "[i]t was widely recognized by athletes that, not only was there widespread conflict of interest involved in sport organizations investigating themselves, but also that making a report of maltreatment could lead to punitive and possibly career ending retaliation" (p. 167). For example, a 2022 independent report was released investigating Canada Soccer's safe sport policies and their institutional response to allegations of abuse against Bob Birarda, who was the head coach of the Under-20 Women's National Team ("U-20 WNT") at the time. The investigation found that Canada Soccer mishandled the allegations against Birarda primarily due to the head coach and the U-20 WNT being allowed to operate with minimal oversight. Birarda was working with minimal to no supervision and there was "a complete lack of familiarity" with Canada Soccer's Harassment Policy (McLaren Global Solutions, 2022, p. 19). It was also found that athletes faced punishment if they complained, or they received threats of retaliation, to dissuade them from filing a complaint. Retaliation often consisted of reduced playing time and demeaning verbal treatment at team practices (McLaren Global Solutions, 2022, p. 4849). Similar experiences with retaliation for reporting maltreatment and safe sport issues were found in an independent report conducted within Gymnastics Canada (McLaren Global Solutions, 2023).

In response to the safe sport crisis, and specifically the news reports that Hockey Canada paid a settlement to a victim of sexual abuse allegedly committed by members of a World Junior hockey team[3] (Westhead, 2022), the Canadian government launched a series of safe sport hearings to work towards greater safety measures and eradicate maltreatment from sports resulting in an 182-report (Fry, 2024). Ciara McCormack, a former soccer player coached by Birarda and the known whistleblower in the Birarda case (McCormack, 2019), participated in the safe sport hearings and explained "that being silenced was worse than the abuse" and that, it was realizing that for the decade we tried to report Birarda, the silencing we faced wasn't born out of a dysfunctional system, but rather was done with a wilful precision, a system where to play sports in Canada meant and means doing so with a deliberate lack of protection from abuse,

[3] Five former junior hockey players are currently on trial facing charges of sexual assault. All five players plead not guilty. The trial began on April 22, 2025 and continues at the time of writing this chapter (Westhead, 2025).

as well as the threat of retaliation for speaking out about it. (Fry, 2024, p. 75).

Following the creation of OSIC, which has been referred to as "good, but not enough" (Ross, 2022) and the safe sport hearings, the Canadian government launched a national commission—The Future of Sport in Canada Commission ("the Commission"). The Commission is tasked with reviewing "the Canadian sport system and make recommendations on concrete and effective actions" as they relate to safe sport and, more specifically, "to policy, funding structures, governance, reporting, accountability, conflicts of interest, systems alignment, culture, and legal considerations" (Canadian Heritage, 2024). The OSIC was officially phased out by the Canadian Government on July 31, 2025, with the administration of the UCCMS transferred to the Canadian Centre for Ethics in Sports (Canadian Centre for Ethics in Sports, n.d.). Meanwhile, the Future of Sport Commission released its first preliminary report on August 28, 2025 (Future of Sport in Canada Commission, 2025). Time will tell whether the Commission will be a success in reforming the Canadian amateur sport system.

Professional Athletes and Collective Bargaining

Agreements

Professional sports are not immune from safe sport violations. Professional leagues typically operate independently of the national dispute resolution mechanism. As unionized workplaces, most major leagues have a players' association in place that bargains on behalf of athletes to enter into a contractual relationship with the league in the form of a Collective Bargaining Agreement ("CBA"). Once a CBA is in place, labour laws take over to manage the relationship between the athlete and their employer (the league and their respective team). In other words, any dispute between an athlete and their employer will be subject to the dispute resolution procedures that are collectively bargaining during CBA negotiations.

There are many instances that exemplify the need for safe sport policy and dispute resolution mechanisms in professional sports, including class action lawsuits for concussions suffered in violent sports. Scholars also note the many ways that the commercialization of professional sports and the power dynamics put the safety of participants at immense risk

(Brayton et al., 2019). A recent example involving an NHL team, the Chicago Blackhawks, is illustrative of the power imbalances in the professional sport setting. Player Kyle Beach accused Blackhawks video coach, Brad Aldrich, of sexual assault wherein Aldrich threatened Beach's professional hockey career if he did not partake in sexual acts (Cozen O'Conner, 2022), not unlike convicted hockey coach Graham James who threatened the careers of young boys if they spoke up about the sexual abuse committed against them (*R v James*, 2012).

In response to the allegations against Aldrich, the National Hockey League Players' Association ("NHLPA") subsequently solicited an independent review of the incident in light of accusations that the Blackhawks and the NHLPA failed to take the allegations seriously, and instead chose not to take action against Aldrich for fear that it would ruin the momentum the team had as they played for the 2010 Stanley Cup championship (Westhead, 2021). In 2022, following an investigation into the response to Beach's allegations of abuse, it was found that the failure to act stemmed from "a failure of communication" (Cozen O'Conner, 2022, p. 5). The fact that that the abuse occurred in 2010 and it was not until 2022 that any action was taken illustrates the importance of a clear complaint intake and dispute resolution policy in professional sports. This mirrors the issues found in amateur sports which propelled the safe sport movement. Beach was a professional athlete who was still taken advantage of, abused, and whose maltreatment was not taken seriously by the organization until many years later. This exemplifies the need for safe sport policies and programs, and more importantly their proper enforcement, not only in amateur sports but equally in professional sports.

Dispute Resolution Processes in Professional Sport

As mentioned, professional sports typically fall within the world of labour law wherein the relationship between employer (the league and teams) and employees (the athletes) is governed by a CBA. The players' association in various professional sport leagues represent the interests of their member players who are employed and participate within these leagues. An effective CBA is not only important for dispute resolution, but for all areas of ensuring a proper and fair workplace overall for professional athletes. It is important that these leagues uphold principles of good governance and cooperate as much as possible in their participation with the player associations and CBA processes. The process to adequately handle disputes as they arise vary depending on the type of dispute. In general, dispute in sport can be categorized in three summarized types: (1) commercial disputes, (2) disputes between sport organizations and their members, and (3) dispute of discipline from wrongdoing (Fang, 2018). For the purposes of this chapter, we will focus on disputes between professional leagues and their athletes.

The most common method of dispute resolution in professional sports is arbitration. The processes for arbitration are outlined in each respective CBA. For example, the NHL CBA allows the NHL or NHLPA to initiate a grievance where a dispute arises involving the interpretation or compliance with any provision of the CBA and must be resolved exclusively using the procedures set out within the CBA (NHLPA, 2013, Article 17.1–17.2). The CBA stipulates that a "Grievance Committee" will hear the matter and provide a decision, which is binding on the parties (NHLPA, 2013, Article 17.4). Article 18 of the CBA sets out processes for the league Commissioner to discipline a player for off-ice conduct, including the power to expel or suspend a player, cancel a player contract, or impose a fine (NHLPA, 2013, Article 18-A.2–18-A.3). The Commissioner may also launch an investigation to determine the facts of the incident and to determine appropriate discipline. Should the player choose to appeal the Commissioner's decision, the CBA stipulates that an independent arbitrator will hear the matter (NHLPA, 2013, Article18-A.4).

While mediation is not currently widely used in resolving professional sports disputes, it is noted that it could be viable as an informal way to assist in dispute resolution (Godin, 2017). Disputes related to player contracts are common in professional sports, which occurs when a league and player cannot agree to the terms of the contract. For example, when the terms of an NHL contract are in dispute, the NHL CBA stipulates that any grievance will be heard by an impartial or system arbitrator (NHLPA, 2013, Article 11.2). The CBA also outlines an arbitration mechanism for salary dispute resolution, similar to that of other professional leagues. The CBA will outline certain elements, including when players are eligible for salary arbitration wherein an independent salary arbitrator determines fair compensation for that player. The decision of an arbitrator in such cases is binding on both the team and the player (NHLPA, 2013, Article 12). The CBA equally outlines measures in place to ensure fairness and when a party may choose not to sign a contract at all (NHLPA, 2013, Article 12.10).

Salary arbitration is only one example of a dispute arising out of professional contract negotiation, but it exemplifies the importance of having clear dispute resolution policy embedded within the CBA. Since unionized workplaces are subject to labour laws, which stipulate that all disputes between unions and employers about the interpretation and application of CBAs be resolved by labour arbitrators rather than judges. For instance, numerous court cases involving unionized athletes demonstrate the courts' unwillingness to interfere with binding contracts and their dispute resolution processes. In *Bruce v Cohon*, a 2016 lawsuit filed by a Canadian Football League player for concussions suffered by the player while playing football, the BC court determined that it lacked jurisdiction to hear the case. Rather, "the disputes raised by Mr. Bruce arise from the 2014 Collective Agreement and can only be resolved through the grievance and arbitration process" (para 93). In other words, the matter is to be settled pursuant to the terms of the CBA, or the player may grieve the matter via the appropriate labour relations board.

We can also point to the safe sport crisis as it unfolds in professional sports for further illustration of dispute resolution processes in this setting and identify gaps in this setting. Professional teams and leagues have governance models that handle these disputes internally or levy additional disciplinary measures outside of judicial courts (Cordonier, 2022) or the SDRCC which does not have jurisdiction in professional sports (SDRCC, 2024). For most professional leagues, the ability of a league or team to take action against a participant for a safe sport violation, such as abuse, harassment, or discrimination against another player, falls under the language typically found in the player contract which binds the player to league and team policies (for example, see paragraphs 4 and 18 of the NHL Standard Players' Contract in Exhibit A of the CBA). Professional leagues have adopted various policies that outline their powers to discipline players for conduct, such as the NFL's Person Conduct Policy (NFL, 2022), which may give rise to a dispute. The policies form part of the CBA pursuant to the player contracts and must consequently follow the grievance procedures in the CBA.

Litigation or Alternative Dispute Resolution in Sports?

While external bodies like the SDRCC are intended to keep sports disputes out of the judicial courts, the latter maintains an important role in the adjudication of sports-related matters (Jodouin, 2005). Courts are often hesitant to interfere in sports disputes, particularly in professional labour disputes where a CBA is in place, but sports organizations cannot eliminate the courts' jurisdiction "through the terms of a private parties' contract, no matter how tightly drafted those terms may be" (McArdle, 2015, p. 35). Litigation is thus not impossible. There must, however, be a valid cause of action to necessitate judicial intervention. For example, both NFL and NHL players have launched lawsuits against their respective leagues for head trauma suffered as a result of playing these contact sports.

In the 2015 lawsuit against the NFL (NFL Concussion Litigation, 2015), the plaintiffs faced the issue that workers cannot sue their employer if it requires the interpretation or application of terms of the CBA. Accordingly, the players argued their case under "medical monitoring," claiming that the league failed to inform them of the risks associated with contact sports and concussions. If the league knew the risks and failed to inform the players, it would fall outside the scope of the CBA's injury prevention stipulations. Similarly, in the lawsuit against the NHL (NHL Concussion Litigation, 2018), the players argued that despite growing scientific evidence on concussions, the NHL either took no steps to protect them or took insufficient steps to make them aware of the real risks of playing in the NHL, which would have protected players from unnecessary long-term brain damage. Creative legal strategies were, however, needed to ensure that courts had jurisdiction over these matters (Heard, 2013; Telis, 2014). Both cases settled without the leagues admitting legal responsibility.

Meanwhile, the Canadian amateur sport system is experiencing a dramatic surge in lawsuits suggesting that dispute resolution efforts thus far – from the SDRCC and the OSIC to independent investigations and governmental interventions – are not sufficient to address the ongoing safe sport crisis, which demonstrates significant weaknesses in the existing system. In fact, athletes are increasingly seeking redress from harms suffered as sports participants by turning to the law. Mazzuco and Findlay (2024) argue that lawsuits grounded in systemic negligence are likely more effective than the traditional cause of action grounded in vicarious liability that argues the organization failed to prevent or control the harm.

In contrast, a lawsuit in systemic negligence allows plaintiffs to recognize the broader cultural issues and the direct role the organization plays in causing harms. Systemic negligence thus provides an alternate legal basis for recognizing the direct role of the organization in creating and promoting a culture in which abuse becomes part of the organizational ethos and is allowed to persist unabated, often as a normalized part of organizational operations. This organizational culture describes the commonly held values and norms, social practices, expectations, and assumptions that characterize and epitomize a particular institution, and defines what is encouraged, discouraged, accepted, or rejected within a group. The culture of an organization can have a profound effect on the decision-making of members of the organization and their resultant actions. (Mazzuco & Findlay, 2024, p. 39).

Several ongoing lawsuits grounded in systemic negligence allege numerous concerning behaviours that point to systemic issues and highlight the power imbalances between organizational leadership and individual athletes. The power and influence yielded by administrators, coaches, trainers, and other team personnel is paramount. For instance, former gymnast Amelia Cline is the representative plaintiff in a proposed class action lawsuit against Gymnastics Canada and 11 Provincial and Territorial Member Associations (PMOs) for systemic negligence, breach of fiduciary duty, and vicarious liability. In the first paragraph of the statement of claim (2022), the plaintiffs claim:

> Globally, the sport of gymnastics has come under scrutiny for its culture of cruelty. Factors such as a 'win-at-all-costs' approach, young and mostly female gymnasts, and inherent power imbalances, along with a culture of control and an overarching tolerance of abusive behaviour have all led to the creation of an environment where abuse and mistreatment of athletes are commonplace and the physical and psychological health of gymnasts is consistently subordinated to performance. The plaintiffs further claim that they faced retaliation for reporting abuse, such as being ignored in practice, being excluded from activities and tournaments, and having their Olympic careers threatened. (*Cline v Gymnastics Canada*, 2022, para 85)

The defendants in this lawsuit are the governing bodies for gymnastics across Canada. Since these organizations are responsible for setting their own policies and enforcing them, the plaintiffs claim that, as the NSO overseeing the entire sport, Gymnastics Canada have a duty to supervise and control the PMOs and all "registered participants," including coaches, and to ensure they developed, implemented, and enforced "reasonable policies, practices and standards" (*Cline v Gymnastics Canada*, 2022, para 35).

Similarly, the plaintiffs claim that PMOs have a duty to supervise and control all local and municipal member clubs, including their coaches (*Cline v Gymnastics Canada*, 2022, para 40). Ultimately, the plaintiffs claim that the defendants are responsible for abusing the athletes, including various forms of sexual, physical, and psychological abuse, by failing to discharge their duties and by tolerating and/or condoning the abuse done by coaches, and at times by "staff, administrators, physiotherapists and other employees, agents or servants of Gymnastics Canada, PMOs, and/or Member Clubs under the jurisdiction and oversight of Gymnastics Canada and its PMOs" (*Cline v Gymnastics Canada*, 2022, para 81).

Another example comes from former Canadian Hockey League ("CHL") players in a lawsuit alleging abusive hazing practices against the CHL, its three regional affiliates, and all teams in the CHL. The players claim that the CHL is plagued by a "toxic culture" that allowed various forms of abuse to persist, including "racist, sexual, sexualized, homophobic and/or otherwise discriminatory" abuse (*Carcillo v Canadian Hockey League*, 2020, para 88). Plaintiffs further claimed that they were subject to "negative repercussions for reporting or even refusing to submit to the Abuse," which included reduced ice time, being traded to another team, increased levels of abuse, and seeing their chances of being drafted into the NHL impacted negatively (*Carcillo v Canadian Hockey League*, 2020, para 95). An independent review panel later found that the CHL has allowed abusive practices to become a cultural norm and that players "fear of retribution or punishment, power imbalances, and loyalty" (Thériault et al., 2020, p. 15). The Ontario Superior Court has refused to certify the *Carcillo* lawsuit as a class action in 2023 (*Carcillo v Canadian Hockey League*, 2023). The parties are scheduled to appear at the Court of Appeal in 2025 (Koskie Minsky LLP, 2024).

Other lawsuits for systemic negligence are currently moving their way through the courts, including a lawsuit against Water Polo alleging sexual harassment, discrimination, and abuse (Jones, 2022). Athletes are also pursuing a proposed class action lawsuit against Artistic Swimming alleging psychological abuse, neglect, and harassment (Tyr Class Actions, n.d.). Despite internal policies and appeal processes, federal interventions, existing dispute resolution mechanisms, there remains significant weaknesses in how amateur and professional sports are governed and controlled.

Conclusion

As argued by McKee (2022), "real harm can come from powerful institutions acting permissively or insubstantially in the face of abuse". The safe sport crisis has highlighted the weaknesses in the complex dispute resolution system currently in place in Canada. The Canadian amateur sport system, which includes local clubs all the way to national associations with oversight by the federal government, typically have internal procedures for handling disputes. In Canada, parties to a dispute may appeal to an external body – the SDRCC – for mediation and arbitration services once the internal process is exhausted.

While the SDRCC was intended to the final appeal mechanism, it does not limit a party's right to file a lawsuit in the judicial court system. In contrast, the professional sport system is shaped by labour law and the provisions of a collectively negotiated agreement that outline the agreed-upon procedures for filing a complaint and appealing a decision. Despite these differing systems between the amateur and professional sports models, similar issues arise with athletes increasingly turning to the law to address broader cultural issues, from power imbalances in the governance structures to the normalization of abusive practices across all levels of sports. It remains to be seen how the turn to the law will affect the way that sports are controlled and governed internally and how external forces, including governmental oversight and independent dispute resolution bodies will tackle ongoing disputes and safe sport concerns across Canada.

Questions

1. How does the structure of dispute resolution systems in amateur sports differ from those in professional sports, and what are the implications for athletes' rights and protections?
2. To what extent can independent bodies like the SDRCC and OSIC address systemic issues of maltreatment and bias within the Canadian amateur sport system?

3. Should professional sports leagues adopt external, independent dispute resolution mechanisms similar to those in amateur sports, and what would those look like? Or, is the current system of collective bargaining sufficient? Why or why not?
4. Given the rise in lawsuits alleging systemic negligence in sports organizations, what reforms to internal governance and dispute resolution processes might better protect athletes from harm?

Glossary

Alternative Dispute Resolution (ADR) A range of dispute resolution methods outside traditional court proceedings, including arbitration and mediation, commonly used in sport to resolve conflicts efficiently and privately.

Arbitration A formal process where a neutral third party (arbitrator) hears evidence and arguments from the disputing parties and renders a binding decision. In Canadian sport, this is often done through the Sport Dispute Resolution Centre of Canada (SDRCC).

Appeal A request to review and potentially overturn a decision made by a sports organization or previous arbitrator. Many sport organizations have internal appeal procedures.

Athlete Agreement A contract between an athlete and a national sport organization (NSO) outlining expectations, obligations, and dispute resolution processes.

Canadian Sport Dispute Resolution Code A binding set of rules governing dispute resolution through the SDRCC, including procedures for mediation, arbitration, and appeal.

Code of Conduct	A set of standards outlining expected behavior for athletes, coaches, and officials. Breaches can lead to disciplinary actions and disputes.
Discipline Panel	A body within a sport organization that hears and decides on disciplinary issues such as rule infractions, harassment, or doping violations.
Early Resolution Facilitation (ERF)	A voluntary, confidential process offered by the SDRCC to help parties resolve issues quickly before formal procedures.
Mediation	A voluntary, non-binding process where a neutral third party helps disputing parties reach a mutually agreeable resolution.
National Sport Organization (NSO)	A governing body for a sport at the national level responsible for managing athlete development and competition. Often a party in disputes.
Procedural Fairness (Natural Justice)	The requirement that processes be unbiased and allow each party a fair opportunity to present their case. Central to all sport dispute resolutions.
SDRCC (Sport Dispute Resolution Centre of Canada)	An independent body funded by the Government of Canada that provides dispute resolution services for sport-related issues

Competing Interests The authors have no conflicts of interest to declare that are relevant to the content of this chapter.

References

Canadian Heritage. (2021). *Minister Guilbeault announces new independent safe sport mechanism.* https://www.canada.ca/en/canadian-heritage/news/2021/07/minister

Canadian Heritage. (2024). *Terms of reference—The future of sport in Canada commission*. https://www.canada.ca/en/canadian-heritage/campaigns/future-sport/terms-reference.html

Canadian Centre for Ethics in Sports. (n.d.). https://cces.ca/report-safe-sport

Casini, L. (2012). The making of a lex sportiva by the Court of Arbitration for Sport. In R. C. R. Siekmann & J. Soek (Eds.), *Lex sportiva: What is sports law?* (pp. 149–171). T.M.C. Asser Press.

Coakley, J., & Donnelly, P. (2004). *Sports in society: Issues and controversies* (1st Canadian ed.). McGraw-Hill Ryerson.

Corbett, R., Findlay, H., & Lech, D. (2008). *Legal issues in sport: Tools and techniques for the sport manager*. Emond Montgomery Publications.

Cordonnier, E. (2022). *Safe sport in Canada: An overview of litigating and resolving safe sport disputes*. https://wt.ca/safe-sport-in-canada-an-overview-of-litigating-and-resolving-safe-sport-disputes/

Cozen O'Connor. (2022). *Report to the National Hockey League Players' Association regarding the union's response to reports by Kyle Beach and others concerning sexual misconduct by a former employee of a National Hockey League club*. https://www.nhlpa.com/news/1-22297/nhlpa-releases-results-from-independent-review

Dispute Resolution Secretariat. (n.d.). *Sport Dispute Resolution Centre of Canada*. https://www.crdsc-sdrcc.ca/eng/dispute-resource-databases-jurisprudence

Donnelly, P., Kerr, G., & Kidd, B. (2022). Contesting the autonomy of sport to realize the right to safe sport: A Canadian case study. *The International Sports Law Journal, 22*(2), 165–170. https://doi.org/10.1007/s40318-022-00234-w

Fang, Q. (2018). Dispute resolution in professional sports. *PM World Journal, 7*(5), 1–11.

Fencing for Change Canada. (2023). *Open letter from Fencing for Change Canada*. https://www.globalathlete.org/our-word/fencers-join-thousands-of-canadian-athletes-calling-for-a-national-judicial-inquiry

Findlay, H. (2022). *Legal aspects of sport and recreation*. Emond.

Fry, H. (2024). *Safe sport in Canada: Report of the Standing Committee on Canadian Heritage*. House of Commons. https://www.ourcommons.ca/Content/Committee/441/CHPC/Reports/RP13203713/chpcrp12/chpcrp12-e.pdf

Future of Sport in Canada Commission. (2025). Preliminary Report. https://www.canada.ca/en/canadian-heritage/campaigns/future-sport/participate/interim-report.html

Giannitsopoulou, S., Ross, M., Dennie, M., & O'Byrne, N. (2023). How transformative justice can address abuse in Canadian sport. *The Conversation*. https://theconversation.com/how-transformative-justice-can-address-abuse-in-canadian-sport-198122

Godin, P. D. (2017). Sport mediation: Mediating high-performance sports disputes. *Negotiation Journal, 33*(1), 25–52.

Gurgis, J. J., Kerr, G., & Darnell, S. (2022). 'Safe sport is not for everyone': Equity-deserving athletes' perspectives of, experiences and recommendations for safe sport. *Frontiers in Psychology, 13*, 1–13.

Gymnasts for Change Canada. (n.d.). *In relentless pursuit for change in Canadian sport*. https://www.gymnasts4changecanada.com/

Heard, K. A. (2013). The impact of pre-emption in the NFL concussion litigation. *University of Miami Law Review, 68*(1), 221–250.

Hockey Canada. (n.d.). *Mandate and mission*. https://www.hockeycanada.ca/en-ca/corporate/about/mandate-mission

International Ice Hockey Federation. (n.d.). *Member national organizations*. https://www.iihf.com/

Jodouin, A. L. (2005). The Sport Dispute Resolution Centre of Canada: An innovation development in Canadian amateur sport. *Journal of Legal Aspects of Sport, 15*(2), 295–316.

Jones, A. M. (2022). Former members of Canada's national water polo team have filed a $5.5M lawsuit against the federation, alleging abuse. *CTV News*. https://www.ctvnews.ca/canada/article/former-members-of-canadas-national-water-polo-team-have-filed-a-55m-lawsuit-against-the-federation-all eging-abuse/

Kolev, B. (2012). Lex sportiva and lex mercatoria. In R. C. R. Siekmann & J. Soek (Eds.), *Lex sportiva: What is sports law?* (pp. 223–233). T.M.C. Asser Press.

Koskie Minsky LLP. (2023, December 7). *CHL hockey abuse class action—Latest developments*. https://kmlaw.ca/cases/chl-hockey-abuse-class-action/

Koskie Minsky LLP. (2024). *Carcillo v Canadian Hockey League*. https://kmlaw.ca/cases/chl-hockey-abuse-class-action/

Mazzuco, M., & Findlay, H. (2024). Finding a way forward: Addressing organizational factors contributing to systemic maltreatment in Canadian sport. *Manitoba Law Journal, 47*(8), 1–30.

McArdle, D. (2015). *Dispute resolution in sport: Athletes, law and arbitration*. Routledge.

McCormack, C. (2019). *A horrific Canadian soccer story—The story no one wants to listen to, but everyone needs to hear*. https://ciaramccormack.com/2019/02/25/a-horrific

McKee, T. (2022). Fixing the problems at Hockey Canada will be diGicult without leadership changes. *The Conversation*. https://theconversation.com/fixing-the-problems-at-hockey-canada-will-be-diGicult-without-leadership-cha nges-187751

McLaren Global Sport Solutions. (2022, July 28). *McLaren Independent Canada Soccer Review*. https://www.mclarenglobalsportsolutions.com/pdf/CanadaSoccerReview_MGSSFinalReport_July28_2022.pdf

McLaren Global Sport Solutions. (2023, January 25). *A framework for change: How to achieve a culture shift for gymnastics in Canada*. https://www.mclarenglobalsportsolutions.com/pdf/Gymnastics-Report-Jan-22-2023.pdf

Mitten, M. J., & Opie, H. (2012). '"Sports law"': Implications for the development of international, comparative, and national law and global dispute resolution. In R. C. R. Siekmann & J. Soek (Eds.), *Lex sportiva: What is sports law?* (pp. 173–222). T.M.C. Asser Press.

National Football League. (2022). *Personal conduct policy*. https://nflpaweb.blob.core.windows.net/website/Departments/Salary-Cap-Agent-Admin/2022-NFL-Personal-Conduct-Policy.pdf

National Hockey League Players' Association. (2013). *Collective bargaining agreement between National Hockey League and National Hockey League Players' Association*. https://www.nhlpa.com/the-pa/cba

Office of the Sport Integrity Commissioner. (n.d.). *Authority and jurisdiction*. https://sportintegritycommissioner.ca/jurisdiction

Office of the Sport Integrity Commissioner. (n.d.). *Sport environment assessment*. https://sportintegritycommissioner.ca/sport-environment-assessment

Ross, M. (2022). Addressing athlete abuse in Canadian sport requires internal change and external investigators. *The Conversation*. https://theconversation.com/addressing-athlete-abuse-in-canadian-sport-requires-internal-change-and-external-investigators-188783

Sport Dispute Resolution Centre of Canada. (2021). *Canadian sport dispute resolution code*. https://www.crdsc-sdrcc.ca/eng/dispute-resolution-code

Sport Dispute Resolution Centre of Canada. (n.d.). *About*. https://www.crdsc-sdrcc.ca/eng/about-mission

Sport Dispute Resolution Centre of Canada. (n.d.). *Resources*. https://www.crdsc-sdrcc.ca/eng/dispute-resource-contract-templates

Sport Information Resources Centre of Canada. (n.d.). *Leadership and governance*. https://sirc.ca/leadership-governance/

Telis, M. (2014). Playing through the haze: The NFL concussion litigation and Section 301 pre-emption. *Georgetown Law Journal, 102*(6), 1841–1884.

The Governance Code. (n.d.). *Canadian sport governance code*. https://nso.olympic.ca/wp-content/uploads/2021/10/Canadian_Sports_Governance_Code.pdf

Thériault, C., Kennedy, S., & Sauvageau, D. (2020, October 31). *Independent review panel report*. Canadian Hockey League. https://cdn.chl.ca/uploads/chl/2022/01/21095713/PlayerWellbeingUpdate_FINAL.pdf

Tyr Class Actions. (n.d.). *Artistic swimming class action*. https://class-actions.tyrllp.com/artistic-swimming-class-action.html

Universal Code of Conduct to Prevent and Address Maltreatment in Sport. (2022). *Obice of the Sport Integrity Commissioner*. https://sportintegritycommissioner.ca/files/UCCMS-v6.0-20220531.pdf

Westhead, R. (2021, October 27). Kyle Beach speaks with Rick Westhead about his lawsuit against the Chicago Blackhawks organization. *YouTube*. https://www.youtube.com/watch?v=OBpRpaNR2tg

Westhead, R. (2022, July 20). Hockey Canada will no longer use investment fund to settle alleged sexual assault claims. *TSN*. https://www.tsn.ca/westhead-hockey-canada-will-no-longer-use-investment-fund-to-settle-alleged-sexual-assault-claim-1.1827598

Westhead, R. (2025, May 9). Marathon cross-examination of E.M. continues at London hockey trial. TSN. https://www.tsn.ca/hockey-canada/marathon-cross-examination-of-e-m-continues-at-london-hockey-trial-1.2303223

Access to Justice and Dispute Resolution Skills

Natasha L. Brown

Abstract Access to justice is a pressing issue in Canada. Currently there is a trend within the justice system to decrease both court delays and costs in order to increase access to justice. Dispute resolution, when used effectively, has these benefits while also benefiting a less-discussed area of access to justice: relationships. This chapter critically examines the positive impact that alternative dispute resolution (ADR) has on access to justice within Canada. ADR increases access to justice by decreasing both the cost and time it takes to resolve disputes. Education regarding ADR expands access to justice by both increasing the public's knowledge and increasing lawyers' effectiveness at using ADR. Most significantly, ADR improves relationships between the parties involved in the dispute and within the communities in which ADR is utilized. If strategies such as diversity-based practice and lawyer competencies are integrated into ADR, there is significant capacity to improve relationships between the legal profession and marginalized communities. This chapter aims to encourage the use of ADR in Canada and to demonstrate how marginalized communities can be better served through the use of ADR.

N. L. Brown (✉)
Faculty of Law, University of Manitoba, Winnipeg, Canada
e-mail: natasha.brown@umanitoba.ca

L. E. Reimer and R. Jochelson (eds.), *The Other Side of the Bar*,
https://doi.org/10.1007/978-981-96-9748-9_10

Keywords Access to justice · Alternative dispute resolution · Mediation · Disputes · Diversity · Justice · Relationships · Restorative justice · Legal education

Introduction

Access to justice is a pressing issue in Canada. Currently there is a trend within the justice system to decrease both court delays and costs in order to increase access to justice. Dispute resolution, when used effectively, has these benefits while also benefiting a less-discussed area of access to justice: relationships. This chapter critically examines the positive impact that dispute resolution—in particular, alternative dispute resolution (ADR)—has on access to justice within Canada. ADR increases access to justice by decreasing both the cost and time it takes to resolve disputes. Education regarding ADR expands access to justice by both increasing the public's knowledge and increasing lawyers' effectiveness at using ADR. Most significantly, ADR improves relationships between the parties involved in the dispute and within the communities in which ADR is utilized. If strategies such as diversity-based practice and lawyer competencies are integrated into ADR, there is significant capacity to improve relationships between the legal profession and marginalized communities. This chapter aims to encourage the use of ADR in Canada and to demonstrate how marginalized communities can be better served through the use of ADR.

Barriers to Access to Justice

The Canadian justice system is intended to ensure that all people are treated fairly and equitably under the law. Access to justice means everyone should have the knowledge, resources, and services to seek an effective resolution when they have experienced unjust or unlawful treatment or have a conflict with another party (Fenske & Froese, 2017). This is achieved through fair processes and fair outcomes, which results from a person having the opportunity to be heard in a meaningful way (Fenske & Froese, 2017).

Unfortunately, for many Canadians, access to justice is unattainable due to an abundance of barriers. Some of these barriers may include any or all of the following:

- Cost (including the legal fees, court filing fees, expert fees, transcript fees, etc.)
- Communication barriers
- Time (including the many days/months/years it may take to reach a solution and the office hours of lawyers, courts, government services)
- Inaccessible legal information
- Complex legal processes
- Misapprehensions and misconceptions about how the legal system works and what kinds of remedies and outcomes are achievable
- Geographical inaccessibility of needed supports and services
- Physical inaccessibility of legal services
- Prior or ongoing negative experiences with lawyers
- A colonial legal system that disadvantages those who are members of historically disadvantaged groups
- A feeling of disconnectedness to the litigation process and/or its outcome

In 2016, it was reported that almost one-half of all adult Canadians will experience a serious legal problem over the course of a three-year period (Farrow et al., 2016), with many of those reporting one serious legal problem will experience multiple legal problems (Currie, 2016). Knowing this, it is imperative that the legal system shift away from its traditional model which has embedded within it many of the above-noted barriers.

In *A Roadmap for Change*, the Canadian National Action Committee on Access to Justice in Civil and Family Matters recommended a number of changes to increase access to justice, including increasing early management of legal issues through negotiation and informal dispute resolution services (Action Committee on Access to Justice in Civil and Family Matters, 2013b). By offering alternative dispute resolution processes as alternatives to the traditional court-based model for resolving disputes, economic, social and cultural access to justice barriers can be lessened.

Mediation and Access to Justice

As outlined in the chapter on Mediation by Jennifer L. Schulz, mediation is a prime example of how dispute resolution contributes to overcoming access to justice barriers. As a form of dispute resolution, it may offer an alternative path to justice that is more accessible, faster, less costly, and often more satisfying for the parties involved, making it an important tool for improving access to justice for a broader range of individuals. People without legal representation, or those who may feel intimidated by formal court settings, can feel more comfortable in mediation sessions. This can make justice more accessible to those who might otherwise avoid pursuing a claim due to complexity or fear of the court system.

The reduced adversarial nature of mediation is particularly beneficial in family law disputes, especially when children are involved. Lawyers bear a responsibility to advise their clients on the broader implications of their choices, and in family law this includes that which may affect their children's well-being. By fostering collaboration, mediation reduces hostility and creates opportunities for fair settlements, which is then more likely to result in enduring resolutions for families. Mediation encourages a constructive and cooperative approach, helping parents focus on long-term co-parenting relationships.

Indigenous law and culture place a "primary emphasis on the ideals of restorative justice" (*R. v. Gladue*, para 70; emphasis in original). Due to the less adversarial nature of mediation, it is particularly advantageous in supporting restorative ideals. Mediation provides a culturally relevant avenue for addressing disputes, with a process that centers on human interrelatedness and healing, offering meaningful engagement for all parties involved (Chartrand & Horn, 2016, p. 4). With mediation, a restorative approach is not meant to restore relationships to where they were before a conflict, but rather to bring individuals to a position where they can promote mutual understanding and accountability, aiming to rebuild trust and foster healthier interpersonal dynamics moving forward (Chartrand & Horn, 2016, p. 4).

Defining Mediation for Access to Justice

In its simplest definition, mediation is a negotiation between disputing parties, assisted or facilitated by a neutral. This neutral party, the mediator, is not empowered to impose a settlement; however, their presence alters the dynamics of the negotiations which often helps shape the final settlement (Government of Canada, "Dispute Resolution"). Mediation is a flexible and adaptable process that focuses on achieving a mutually agreeable resolution for both sides. Unlike the traditional litigation system which may delay settlement discussions until later in the process, mediation typically occurs early in the legal process (Keet & Salamone, 2001, p. 65). This early intervention potentially saves time and resources for all involved.

Effective Legal Skills

Effective dispute resolution requires lawyers to develop skills that go beyond those required for traditional legal advocacy; however, advocacy skills from traditional litigation are often easily transferrable to mediation, with some necessary alteration.

Interest-based negotiation skills are vital as counsel must recognize the value of participants' voices. Counsel must shift away from addressing strictly legal issues; instead acknowledging broader human interests and concerns. This focus may differ from traditional litigation approaches where there is a common desire among litigators to identify facts and translate them into a legal remedy, an approach which becomes misplaced in mediation settings (Keet & Salamone, 2001, p. 65). Lawyers must also manage client expectations effectively and employ flexibility and a willingness to explore settlement alternatives that may not have previously been considered.

The types of discussions that take place between a lawyer and their client within a mediation setting may also look different than those in traditional litigation. An emphasis on collaboration, understanding, and creativity allows lawyers to navigate dispute resolution processes in a way that serves their clients' best interests while working towards long-term, constructive outcomes. Doing so requires input from the client which goes well beyond the usual giving of instructions for legal negotiations (i.e. in mediations the client must communicate much more than just the "bottom line") (Macfarlane, 2001, p. 207). Familiarity with various dispute resolution options is important so that an appropriate ADR mechanism can be chosen. "Soft-skills" are also vital to the process of mediation, as the other side may walk away for reasons such as counsel taking an inappropriate (aggressive) tone (Macfarlane, 2001, p. 207). Therefore, the ability of a lawyer to build rapport with the client on the other side is an asset that is beneficial to mediation (Macfarlane, 2001, p. 207).

Managing Dispute Resolution in a Mediation Setting

Mediation often involves issues that carry high levels of emotion that must be sorted between the parties, particularly when the issue concerns a contentious relationship. Engaging in dispute resolution prior to and during mediation is vital for this reason and can knock down some of the barriers to justice described above. Lawyers play an important role in guiding clients to identify and articulate their goals, while addressing attitudes and emotions that may impact the process (Keet & Salamone, 2001, p. 78). This includes recognizing that emotions, such as anger or frustration, may initially prevent clients from participating effectively. In such cases, lawyers should work with their clients to determine whether the cause of resistance can be addressed or whether it is appropriate to reconsider the timing of the negotiations (Keet & Salamone, 2001, p. 81). Lawyers must also consider the mediation setting itself, ensuring that participants feel comfortable and that the physical environment supports effective communication (Keet & Salamone, 2001, p. 84).

Throughout the mediation, lawyers should balance providing emotional support to their clients with facilitating control over the session. While a lawyer should explain that some expression of emotion is acceptable, they must also explain that attacks or otherwise unproductive language is not appropriate (Keet & Salamone, 2001, p. 84). Lawyers need not prevent their clients from expressing anger but should stay alert to its effects on the opposing parties. Reframing and redirecting techniques can be particularly effective in managing emotional outbursts and promoting constructive dialogue (Keet & Salamone, 2001, pp. 92–93). For instance, negative or confrontational statements can be re-worded to communicate concerns in a way that facilitates productive discussion.

In supporting clients, lawyers should resist making assumptions about motivations and instead ask questions that demonstrate curiosity and encourage cooperation (Keet & Salamone, 2001, p. 92). Taking an active and strategic approach ensures that the energy surrounding a conflict is redirected toward productive discussion, fostering an environment that is conducive to resolution (Keet & Salamone, 2001, pp. 78–79). When asking follow-up questions to the opposing client, a lawyer should ensure this is done in a way that demonstrates curiosity rather than mimicking a cross-examination. Asking questions for clarity and to confirm assumptions is an important step in the mediation process but should not be done in a way that discourages co-operation (Keet & Salamone, 2001, p. 92). Finally, when considering who should attend the mediation, the lawyer should consider the comfort of both parties and the promotion of effective communication (Keet & Salamone, 2001, p. 84).

The Broad Benefits of Mediation for Access to Justice

In cases which are appropriate for mediation, the process can present significant advantages. As mediation can occur early in the litigation process, it helps to reduce delays and the legal costs associated with resolving disputes (Keet & Salamone, 2001, p. 65; Otis & Boulanger-Bonnelly, 2022, p. 54).

As a flexible alternative to court procedures, mediation has the capacity to accommodate a broader range of interests and perspectives than traditional litigation (Otis & Boulanger-Bonnelly, 2022, p. 54). By encouraging open dialogue and prioritizing the voices of those involved, mediation broadens the scope of dispute resolution to address underlying human concerns and interests (Keet & Salamone, 2001, p. 65). This adaptability often leads to creative and customized solutions that are tailored to the specific needs of the parties, which may look different than the legal remedies available according to the facts of a file when using a traditional approach.

Mediation's focus on reconciliation supports collaborative problem-solving and can contribute to stronger relationships and improved co-operation after a conflict (Charkoudian et al., 2017, p. 38). Reconciliation is simply finding a dignified road forward that everyone can support, in which each party feels respected and that, as time goes by, the principles guiding reconciliation are evident in action. Mediation also allows participants to engage actively in resolving their disputes. This often supports the pedagogical function of fostering practical dispute resolution skills that clients can then employ in future interactions (Otis & Boulanger-Bonnelly, 2022, p. 54).

Mediation recognizes the value of participants' voices and addresses human interests that lay beyond strictly legal issues (Keet & Salamone, 2001, p. 65). This helps create a more restorative focus within dispute resolution, which positively impacts all mediation participants. This is particularly significant for Indigenous participants as it directly connects to the restorative focus in Indigenous cultures and laws (see *R. v. Gladue*).

Mediation is also often able to accelerate the negotiation process while giving clients ownership over the resolution of their conflict (Vasey, 2006).

It is well-reported that Canadians do not have adequate access to justice within the traditional family law legal system (Family Justice Working Group of the Action Committee on Access to Justice in Civil and Family Matters, 2013a). Approximately 38% of all Canadian marriages end in divorce, which results in approximately 70,000 divorce orders annually. It is presumed that more people are impacted by family law disputes than by any other single area of the law, especially when considering the many individuals who are potentially impacted by a single-family separation (Family Justice Working Group of the Action Committee on Access to Justice in Civil and Family Matters, 2013a). Family law court processes are often complex, unaffordable and inaccessible. In order to increase access to justice in family law, emphasis must be placed on offering alternatives to the traditional litigation model.

Mediation in family law offers significant benefits in this regard, particularly due to its less adversarial nature. This approach is especially valuable in disputes where parties must maintain an ongoing relationship after settlement, as is often the case when children are involved. Mediation positively impacts relationships between parties by fostering communication and collaboration (see the section called 'The Impacts of Dispute Resolution on Long-Term Relationships' later in this chapter).

Many individuals within the Canadian family law legal system face barriers to accessing family law legal services, often due to cost or the difficulty of representing themselves effectively without legal counsel (Goldberg, 2021, p. 3). As a result, Canadian provinces are now examining, and in certain jurisdictions requiring mediation services or other ADR models, as a required first step when seeking to resolve a family law dispute. For example, in Manitoba, in the vast majority of cases, parties must attempt to resolve their family law matters through an out-of-court dispute resolution process before turning to traditional litigation (*The Family Law Act,* s.5). Manitobans can choose to retain a mediator of their choice or can utilize the services of Manitoba Justice's Family Resolution Services in order to obtain no-cost mediation services. These types of services employ a collaborative, holistic, and interdisciplinary approach to dispute resolution, offering families meaningful support throughout the process (Goldberg, 2021, p. 3) and meet the following eight guiding principles on family law innovation set out by the Canadian National Action Committee on Access to Justice in Civil and Family Matters (Family Justice Working Group of the Action Committee on Access to Justice in Civil and Family Matters, 2013a, p. 20):

(1) Collaboration
(2) Client-Centred
(3) Empowered Families
(4) Integrated Multidisciplinary Services
(5) Early Resolution
(6) Voice, Fairness & Safety
(7) Accessible
(8) Proportional

For mediation to effectively contribute to access to justice, it must be both available and actively encouraged as an option. Parties should also be made aware of its benefits such as self-determination and consensual decision-making, in addition to cost-savings (Acharya, 2023, p. 725). Broader education has expanded the use of mediation in law, responding to the barriers posed by traditional litigation and increasing demand for alternative dispute resolution initiatives (Acton, 1999, p. 257).

Many Canadians report that an adversarial justice system does not adequately meet their needs. There has been a resulting increase in demand for mediation due to the barriers that litigation provides. When coupled with broader education on ADR options, this has led to more ADR initiatives becoming available (Acton, 1999, p. 257).

Education in law schools plays a critical role in equipping future lawyers with the skills necessary for effective dispute resolution, thereby enhancing access to justice. By teaching law students about less adversarial options such as mediation, they are better equipped to navigate and overcome cultural barriers, particularly those related to Indigenous peoples and cultures, as highlighted in the *Gladue* principles (see *R. v. Gladue*). Additionally, law students and their future clients benefit from students receiving education which addresses economic barriers in accessing legal services (see Otis & Boulanger-Bonnelly, 2022, p. 54).

Recently, Canadian law schools are revising their law school curriculums to respond to Canada's Truth and Reconciliation Commission's

Calls to Action, specifically, Call to Action #28. In Manitoba, for example, The University of Manitoba, Faculty of Law expanded its curriculum to include skills-based training in intercultural competency, dispute resolution, human rights, and anti-racism (Lugtig, 2016, p. 19; Truth and Reconciliation Commission of Canada). This comprehensive educational framework aims to prepare law students with the necessary knowledge and skills base to work effectively with clients. It includes a significant amount of instruction on current and future challenges facing the legal profession and justice system, with special attention paid to access to justice issues (Lugtig, 2016, p. 19). Placing a stronger emphasis on the psychological and emotional dimensions of conflict within the law school curriculum is practically relevant to students' future roles as dispute resolvers (Macfarlane, 2001, p. 197). Doing so necessitates a blending of doctrinal and problem-solving approaches to reflect the realities of conflicts (Macfarlane, 2001, p. 197).

In order to proceed with mediation, clients must be willing to engage in such a process. While public awareness and support for ADR is growing, more public education is necessary. Increasing public education on ADR would allow parties to a conflict make informed choices about whether to pursue mediation. Such resources could be disseminated through written guides, online information sessions, or even in-person sessions, with some arguing that such information sessions should be mandated (Acharya, 2023, p. 736). The public would benefit from becoming more aware of the nature of the process, including its facets of self-determination, consensual decision-making, cooperative problem solving, and opportunities to exchange empathetic understanding (Acharya, 2023, p. 721). The more understanding there is about the process, the more the public gains a true choice of process (Acharya, 2023, p. 736).

Facilitating Access to Justice in Practice

Mediation, and dispute resolution generally, are having a positive impact on access to justice across Canada. Given the success of mediation and other ADR methods, these methods should be promoted and encouraged in legal practices in order to increase access to justice. Dispute resolution and its impact on specific areas of practice are outlined below.

Civil and Family Law

Statistics on mediation programs across Canada have demonstrated the benefits of mediation for access to justice. In a Saskatchewan study, 65–75% of mediation sessions were successful with only 5% being reported as unproductive (Keet & Salamone, 2001, p. 66). In an Ontario pilot project, more than 2000 cases over a three-year period were diverted to mediation, 60% of which settled in whole or in part (Keet & Salamone, 2001, p. 66).

In a Québec mediation program, it was reported that while settlement rates were similar between "mediated" and "non-mediated" cases, mediation offered a significant advantage concerning the length of time taken to reach a settlement. The average time between a statement of claim and a judgement or out of court settlement was 19.5 months and 15.5 months, respectively. In comparison, a mediated agreement was reached in 8.6 months on average (Keet & Salamone, 2001, p. 67).

Consistently shorter resolution times were also reported in Saskatchewan, with the average time to reach a mediated agreement being reduced by 44%. Regarding client satisfaction, the Saskatchewan study found that mediation helped clients understand how to proceed with the case and improved their understanding the issues of the case (Keet & Salamone, 2001, pp. 67–68). Similar findings in relation to overall satisfaction were reported from the Ontario and Québec studies (Keet & Salamone, 2001, p. 68).

The University of Windsor Mediation Services is an example of a community-based mediation program that was the first clinical mediation program to be established at a Canadian law school. The for-credit, experiential learning program provides free client-centred dispute resolution services and engages in community outreach with at-risk youth, young offenders, high school students, and numerous not-for-profit agencies (Vasey, 2006, p. 1). The program's outreach helps to expand the reach of its services, which thereby increases the impact of mediation and subsequently improves access to justice. The service provides dispute resolution, negotiation, and mediation training to student and community groups such as high school classes, peer mediation groups, young offenders, and on-campus organizations (Elman, 2009, p. 14). Law students in the program mediate conflicts such as those related to residential tendencies, small businesses, and neighbourhood disputes (Elman, 2009, p. 14). The program not only helps the immediate community, but also assists with public education surrounding dispute resolution and educating future law students about mediation (see the section Dispute Resolution Skills and Education in this chapter).

Similarly, the Osgoode Mediation Clinic at York University empowers individuals to play a critical role in the outcome of their conflicts. The clinic offers free mediation services in the areas of youth conflicts, housing disagreements, family disputes, campus related issues and personal and professional conflicts and reports that many of its clients "feel better as a result of having had the opportunity to have their experiences heard and validated" (St. Stephen's Community House and Winkler Institute for Dispute Resolution—Community Mediation Research Report, 2020).

Programs such as the University of Windsor Mediation Services and the Osgoode Mediation Clinic are instrumental in the pursuit of access to justice as they raise awareness about mediation amongst members of the public as a viable option (Vasey, 2006, p. 1). Mediation has been identified by some as the single most significant tool that can be used to make the legal system more accessible (Vasey, 2006, p. 1).

Operating as part of the British Columbia public justice system, the Civil Resolution Tribunal (CRT) is Canada's first online tribunal. The CRT operates under the authority of the *Civil Resolution Tribunal Act* as an independent, quasi-judicial tribunal. CRT offers an accessible and affordable way to resolve many types of civil law disputes without the need for a lawyer or to attend court. While participants are permitted to have legal representation, the CRT provides detailed legal information and self-help tools to help people reach agreement through a collaborative, problem-solving approach. Timeliness, flexibility, accessibility, affordability and efficiency are all guiding principles of the CRT dispute resolution services. When participants are unable to resolve a dispute, a tribunal member (independent legal expert) can make a decision about it, and these decisions can be enforced like court orders.

In the 2023–24 fiscal year, the CRT closed 6126 disputes, the majority of which consisted of small claims (Annual Report, p. 19). The average time to reach a resolution varies according to the type of claim, but the overall net time to resolution was 153 days in 2023–24 (Annual Report, p. 33). In anonymous surveys of CRT participants, including applicants, respondents, and representatives, 83% indicated that they felt the CRT treated them fairly throughout the process, 85% indicated that the CRT provided information that prepared them for dispute resolution, and 82% indicated that they would recommend the CRT to others (Annual Report,

p. 36). Additionally, 22% of survey respondents reported using a smartphone to access CRT services, highlighting its accessibility for those who may not own ordinary computers or have home internet. Participants often acknowledge the online process not requiring travel or parking and contentment that they were provided with the opportunity to explain their side of the dispute (Annual Report, p. 40).

While access to justice often addresses people's ability to enter the legal system, it is equally important that people are provided with opportunities to get out of the system affordably (Vasey, 2006, p. 1).

Criminal Law

(a) The *Young Offenders Act*, the *Youth Criminal Justice Act*, and Dispute Resolution

Criminal Justice for Youth in Canada is increasingly utilizing dispute resolution to help youth reduce youth recidivism. According to Jackson (1992), the *Young Offenders Act* (YOA) recognizes the importance of community-based corrections and pre-trial diversion (64). The YOA has since been replaced with the *Youth Criminal Justice Act* (YCJA), which places more of an emphasis on extrajudicial measures and has been more successful in keeping Canadian youth out of jail (Government of Canada, "Youth Criminal Justice Act"). A key objective of the YCJA is to increase the use of non-court responses to less serious offences by youth. These extrajudicial measures improve early intervention with youth and play a role in the development of community-based responses to youth crime (Government of Canada, "Youth Criminal Justice Act").

Programs such as victim-offender reconciliation groups continue to develop both outside the criminal justice system and as an aspect of diversions (Jackson, 1992, p. 64). Reconciliation requires extensive dispute resolution, including the reintegration of the offender into society and holistic restoration of the victim, offender, and community (Jackson, 1992, p. 67). For reconciliation to be effective, there must be practical mechanisms that support peaceful, continuing community relationships to reduce the sources of conflict. There must also be an opportunity for participants to learn dispute resolution skills so that they can be applied to other instances of conflict within the community (Jackson, 1992, p. 80). Extrajudicial measures outlined by the YCJA include police referrals, which allow police to refer youth to community programs, including recreation programs and counselling services. This is intended to help youth avoid committing offences (Government of Canada, "Youth Criminal Justice Act").

Under the YCJA, a "Conference" is defined as "a group of people brought together to give advice to a police officer, judge, justice of the peace, prosecutor, provincial director or youth worker who is required to make a decision under the YCJA" (Government of Canada, "Youth Criminal Justice Act"). Conferences can give advice on decisions such as extrajudicial measures and the reintegration of the young person into their community following custody (Government of Canada, "Youth Criminal Justice Act"). A Conference can include the parents of the youth, the victim, people familiar with the youth, and community agencies or professionals whose knowledge may help with the decision (Government of Canada, "Youth Criminal Justice Act"). Conferences can be understood as a restorative mechanism that focuses on developing proposals for repairing the harm done to the victim of the young person's offence (Government of Canada, "Youth Criminal Justice Act").

(b) Winnipeg's Out-Of-Custody Youth Intake Court

Winnipeg, Manitoba's new Out-Of-Custody Youth Intake Court creates an environment for youth that allows for early intervention, personal discussions and second chances. It also decreases delays and the number of youths who are set to go to trial. Approximately twice per month, the new Out-Of-Custody Youth Intake Court brings together a judge, Crown attorney, defence lawyer, and young people accused of crimes to sort out issues "quickly from the very beginning" (Gowriluk, 2024). This court deals with cases that do not require severe punishments (Gowriluk, 2024). Within this framework, lawyers and judges collaborate to address challenges as they arise, employing approaches ranging from empathetic discussions with youth to offering opportunities for them to learn from their mistakes (Gowriluk, 2024). By intervening early, the court holds the potential to divert youth from a trajectory of continued criminal involvement. After its first year of operation, the Out-of-Custody Youth Intake Court has already demonstrated success in reducing the number of youth going to trial (Gowriluk, 2024).

Access to Justice: Building and Sustaining Collaborative Relationships

An empirical study on lawyer competencies for access to justice revealed that a significant distrust of lawyers exists within marginalized communities (Marsden & Buhler, 2017, pp. 193–194). This distrust was often attributed to: lawyers' association with the justice system; their lack of personal relationships with clients; and, the perception that the law and legal professionals primarily serve the wealthy and powerful (Marsden & Buhler, 2017, pp. 194–195). Participants further identified lawyers' detachment from the community, manifested through physical absence in addition to class and racial divides, as a notable concern (Marsden & Buhler, 2017, p. 194). Lawyers were frequently perceived as part of institutional structures, authorities, or social services that have historically inflicted harm upon these communities. Personal experiences within such contexts were found to reinforce distrust among marginalized groups (Marsden & Buhler, 2017, pp. 194–195). To more effectively increase access to justice, trust must be built between marginalized communities and the legal profession.

Lawyer Competency Skills and Trust-Building

Establishing trust between the legal profession and marginalized communities requires a relational approach that prioritizes empathy, respect, and cultural understanding. This trust is necessary in order to increase access to justice for those individuals who are members of historically disadvantaged groups. Diversity-based ADR requires lawyers to build meaningful relationships with their clients, which involves understanding their cultures, recognizing systemic barriers, and demonstrating humility and compassion. Research highlights that when lawyers (or law students) show empathy and possess even a basic understanding of their clients' backgrounds, clients are more likely to trust them, share critical information, attend appointments, and collaborate on case strategies (Marsden & Buhler, 2017, pp. 187–188). Effective communication skills, including active listening and sensitivity to cultural contexts, are also essential for fostering trust and ensuring clients feel valued and heard (Marsden & Buhler, 2017, p. 187).

When working with marginalized communities, the necessary lawyer competencies extend beyond individual interactions and into those which concern systemic and community-focused practice. Relational competencies such as community presence, hospitality, and relationship building serve a dual purpose by building trust through reputation and connection while also increasing lawyers' knowledge of resources, networks, and connections in the community that clients can access (Marsden & Buhler, 2017, pp. 187–188). For this to be effective, lawyers must take a systemic and holistic approach to their work with clients, which can be done through establishing peer and mentorship relationships and participating in activism on behalf of communities. Lawyers must have the ability to establish and maintain respectful, long-term relationships in adversarial contexts and in contexts in which colonial relations are present (Marsden & Buhler, 2017, p. 205). It is also important that lawyers understand the history of the community they are working with and the multigenerational impacts of colonization (Marsden & Buhler, 2017, p. 205).

Building such relationships does not happen instantaneously. An attitude of humility, respect, self-reflection, compassion, and empathy is required, with the lawyer understanding that they should present themselves as being on the same level as their clients (Marsden & Buhler, 2017, p. 198). In communication with clients, lawyers should maintain boundaries in order to respect a person's agency while also being cognizant of giving feedback that is not judgmental or paternalistic (Marsden & Buhler, 2017, p. 201). This can be done by asking questions in a way that conveys openness, listening, and understanding, while avoiding interrogation-style questioning (Marsden & Buhler, 2017, pp. 201–202). Lawyers can only competently represent their client's interests if there is a trust relationship. In a study, participants gave examples of building relationships such as bringing food, having a physical presence in a community, and getting to know people over longer periods of time and in situations beyond specific legal issues, as effective ways to build trust (Marsden & Buhler, 2017, p. 205).

Working to understand the client's emotional side of their situation is important, and showing empathy is one way that lawyers can create a feeling of safety between themselves and their client (Marsden & Buhler, 2017, pp. 198, 202). Employing such attitudes contributes to the understanding of one's own cultural and related biases, which is essential to engaging in intercultural and anti-racist lawyering (Marsden & Buhler, 2017, pp. 200–201). It is important for lawyers to have cultural humility and to be cognizant of the limits of their knowledge towards clients and communities (Marsden & Buhler, 2017, p. 207). In addition to cultural knowledge, understanding systemic issues such as the history and impact of colonialism and its connections to the legal system is important. Further to this, a lawyer should understand how the legal system creates hardship in connection with other systems (e.g. poverty, homelessness, addictions, mental health issues, social exclusion) (Marsden & Buhler, 2017, p. 196).

A lawyer should also utilize context-informed listening and communication skills. Understanding the client's whole story, including context and details about their current situation can aid in communication and support an ability to provide explanations that demonstrate that the lawyer cares about their client (Marsden & Buhler, 2017, pp. 198–199). Diversity-based ADR must emphasize a nuanced understanding of communication skills and how it relates to equality and access to justice (Marsden & Buhler, 2017, pp. 205–206). Studying how advocates are failing or succeeding in communication can enable the necessary communication skills (as discussed, above) to be taught and used (Marsden & Buhler, 2017, p. 206).

Lawyers must be trained in critical self-reflection, which includes recognizing implicit bias, understanding dominant lawyering culture and its roots in traditional Western values, analyzing power in interactions, and being aware of the relevance of lived context (Marsden & Buhler, 2017, p. 206). The use of shared knowledge and experience, and importance of exposure to new perspectives through direct experience should be incorporated into law schools (Marsden & Buhler, 2017, p. 206).

To improve access to justice, lawyers serving marginalized communities must have the trust and support of the communities they represent, as meaningful advocacy requires strong relationships and mutual understanding (Marsden & Buhler, 2017, p. 207). The community clinic model is suggested as the most effective form of legal aid, offering a framework that facilitates engagement and connection with diverse populations (Marsden & Buhler, 2017, p. 207). To further develop the necessary competencies, broader empirical studies are needed in Canada to explore the skills and approaches that best support marginalized communities (Marsden & Buhler, 2017, p. 207). Law schools and law societies are also encouraged to promote diverse admissions and incorporate practitioners' lived experiences into training, enhancing lawyers' ability to understand context, build relationships, and engage meaningfully with diverse communities (Marsden & Buhler, 2017, p. 207).

Diversity-Based Practice

Key Point: The use of diversity-based practice in ADR allows for minority voices to be heard by incorporating culture into the ADR process, making efforts to increase minority participation, and embracing the principle of equity as opposed to equality. Establishing relationships through ADR or similar processes in a culturally sensitive way helps build bridges between diverse communities.

> "Steps to encourage a diversity-based process:
>
> 1) using an equity-based approach; that is, not assuming that all parties are equal, but simultaneously rejecting that marginalized groups have no power,
> 2) easing participation by marginalized groups; this can include funds, closer location, childcare, respect for religious and cultural holidays,
> 3) capitalizing on existing skills of participants and putting less emphasis on experts and education,
> 4) privileging difference and diversity,
> 5) including as many participants as possible, and making the process as accessible as possible,
> 6) re-examining the use of accepted ADR tenets such as 'expert', 'neutral', and so on,
> 7) ensure parties design their own process, especially in agenda formulation,
> 8) avoiding traditional categorizations, thereby allowing sub-groups to have a voice." (Smyth, 2005, pp. 42–43)

Diversity-based practice is defined as an approach that emphasizes diversity as a positive and healthy force while acknowledging the social realities of difference, including the marginalization of certain individuals and groups based on economic, social, physical, or psychological factors (Smyth, 2005, pp. 30–31). This practice rejects equality-based frameworks, which treat all individuals uniformly, and instead adopts equity-based principles that address systemic inequalities and the unequal distribution of resources (Smyth, 2005, p. 31). Within the legal profession and access to justice, diversity-based practice requires proactive efforts to support the expression of diverse opinions and needs while ensuring spaces are free from hegemonic power structures (Smyth, 2005, p. 31). Practitioners must remain aware of the structural disadvantages that impact marginalized communities, grounding reforms in the actual concerns of these groups through deliberative and consultative decision-making processes (Smyth, 2005, p. 31). Furthermore, diversity-based practice challenges traditional Western norms, including dispute resolution methods, by encouraging practitioners to continuously re-evaluate internal biases and accepted practices in order to advance equity and inclusion (Smyth, 2005, p. 30).

Incorporating diversity-based practices into ADR requires an intentional focus on inclusivity and equity, particularly for marginalized communities. ADR should not aim to eliminate cultural influences but rather embrace them, ensuring that marginalized groups have a voice and are substantively and procedurally included in the process (Smyth, 2005, p. 29). As Smyth (2005) notes, ADR processes have the potential to educate and transform relationships, practices, and policies without eradicating disputants' cultural foundations. Practitioners must facilitate co-produced meanings in a manner that respects and incorporates cultural differences (p. 29). To achieve this, the mediator should either belong to the marginalized group or possess significant knowledge of their culture, language, and customs to address historical distrust in institutional consultations (Smyth, 2005, p. 32).

Diversity-based ADR emphasizes the involvement of those directly affected within the decision-making process, ensuring their issues are properly understood and their voices meaningfully heard (Smyth, 2005, p. 33). Recognizing and leveraging the knowledge and skills of participants as 'expert' resources can significantly enhance the quality of discussions and decision-making (Smyth, 2005, p. 34). Storytelling can also serve as a key tool for marginalized groups to convey the impact of policies on their daily lives (Smyth, 2005, p. 39). Additionally, facilitators should engage participants in identifying topics for discussion to ensure relevance and responsiveness to their needs (Smyth, 2005, p. 37).

To increase participation in ADR, efforts should be made to ensure all interested individuals can contribute. This might involve adjusting the location of meetings for remote participants or using technology to connect participants across regions (Simmons & Thompson, 2017, pp. 230–231; Smyth, 2005, p. 35). In recognizing that collectivist cultures often include a broader array of affected individuals such as elders, family members, or community leaders, facilitators must avoid unilaterally selecting participants and instead support inclusive participation (Smyth, 2005, p. 33). Smaller workshops, role-plays, and working groups can also foster participation, broaden perspectives, and nurture informal relationships among participants (Smyth, 2005, p. 37).

Embracing equity within ADR involves re-examining traditional procedural norms, such as the common practice of giving equal time to each party, and requires the facilitator to critically assess power dynamics between parties (Smyth, 2005, p. 40). Facilitators must also recognize that ignoring diversity and treating everyone identically denies justice to already marginalized participants (Smyth, 2005, p. 40).

The Impact of Effective Dispute Resolution on Long-Term Relationships

Dispute resolution and ADR provide several benefits for long-term relationships between parties involved in a dispute, especially within family law. For the benefits of ADR for marginalized communities, see the section Building and Sustaining Collaborative Relationships in this chapter. Facilitative mediation is particularly useful when parties want to continue their relationship following the resolution of a dispute. Being aware of the long-term benefits may motivate parties to work towards creative problem-solving and utilizing more collaborative approaches (Kidner, 2011, p. 180). When solutions are reached through mediation, the likelihood of satisfaction with the outcome of a dispute is often higher, in part due to the resolution being suggested and developed by the parties themselves (Kidner, 2011, p. 181). In the long term, those who participate in ADR are more likely to report improved relationships and attitudes towards the other party, and overall satisfaction with the outcome and justice system as a whole (Charkoudian et al., 2017, p. 38).

In a study by Charkoudian et al. (2017), participants in ADR were more likely to have an improved relationship with the other party 3–6 months after the engagement regardless of whether they settled, which confirms that ADR can have important long-term relational benefits (p. 41). Many participants who reported enhanced relationships also report avoiding further disputes or being equipped to resolve them more easily due to an improved understanding dispute resolution, and increased trust in the other party after engaging in ADR. Therefore, it is evident that mediation has potential to improve long-term relationships beyond the relationship that is the focus of the mediation itself. In a study concerning Environmental Dispute Resolution by the US Institute for Environmental Conflict Resolution, 60% of participants indicated that they felt able to meet with other participants to discuss issues of concern, 61% found it easier to discuss controversial issues, and 64% found it easier to work productively with other participants with whom they have disagreements after engaging in ADR.

When individuals engage in ADR, it is less likely that they will return to court for an enforcement action than in all other legal cases, including those where the parties settled on their own, with a court verdict, or not at all (Charkoudian et al., 2017, p. 9). Successfully reaching an agreement through ADR decreases the probability of returning to court by 21%, and not returning to court can positively impact relationships by preventing them from becoming more adversarial (Charkoudian et al., 2017, p. 41).

Overall, the process of mediation can help improve long-term relationships through its less adversarial approach. ADR participants are more likely to indicate an ability to express their thoughts and concerns, identify all underlying issues, resolve issues completely rather than just partially, and acknowledge responsibility for the situation than those who proceed through standard court processes (Charkoudian et al., 2017, p. 38). Evidently, this finding applies to all ADR participants, regardless of whether the parties settled (Charkoudian et al., 2017, p. 38).

As previously mentioned, ADR has especially notable benefits for family disputes specifically in its efficacy in maintaining family relationships (Bernstein, 1998). In family disputes involving children, relationships between the parties typically continue. Co-parenting relationships must therefore survive dispute resolution processes, and ADR stands out as an appropriate process in such cases due to its less adversarial nature which supports the preservation of long-term relationships, not only between co-parents but also between parents and their children (Ontario, 1996, p. 76). Animosity in parental relationships can have negative effects on children, so it is beneficial for lawyers to take a less adversarial approach when engaging in family dispute resolution.

Questions

1. What legal organizations are you familiar with that use alternative dispute resolution or dispute resolution strategies? In a small group, research some of these organizations. How are they using ADR strategies to increase access to justice in the community? How could the organization's efforts be improved upon?

2. Imagine that you are tasked with representing a marginalized community in a mediation process. What steps would you take to build a trustworthy relationship between you and the community? What requests would you make to the mediator to ensure that the process is fair and equitable for the community?
3. Are there concerns about power imbalances between parties in mediation, and how can mediators address this to ensure fairness?
4. How can the legal profession balance the promotion of mediation with the need to preserve the role of courts in ensuring justice?

Glossary

Access To Justice:	Everyone should have the knowledge, resources, and services to seek an effective resolution when they have experienced unjust or unlawful treatment or have a conflict with another party. This is achieved through fair processes and fair outcomes, which result from a person having the opportunity to be heard in a meaningful way. It is also important that people are provided with opportunities to get out of the legal system affordably.
Alternative Dispute Resolution (ADR):	ADR is a process used effectively to decrease both court delays and costs, thereby increasing access to justice. It also improves relationships between the parties involved in the dispute and within the communities where it is used. ADR processes can lessen economic, social, and cultural barriers to access to justice. ADR participants are also more likely to report improved relationships and attitudes towards the other party and overall satisfaction with the outcome and justice system.

Barriers to Access to Justice: An additional and critical part of active or reflective listening. They are the listener's demonstrated behaviors of respect and attention that reflect the meaning and content of the speaker's experience back to the speaker. Reflection can include repeating content, feelings, meaning, or a summarization by paraphrasing. For the speaker, these practices assure that the message they are communicating is more accurately understood.

Civil Resolution Tribunal (CRT): Operating as part of the British Columbia (Canadian province) public justice system, the CRT is Canada's first online tribunal. It offers an accessible and affordable way to resolve many types of civil law disputes without needing a lawyer or attending court. Timeliness, flexibility, accessibility, affordability, and efficiency are guiding principles of the CRT. When parties cannot resolve a dispute, a tribunal member can make a decision that can be enforced like court orders.

Conferences (Youth Criminal Justice Act): Under the YCJA, a "Conference" is a group of people brought together to advise police officers, judges, prosecutors, provincial directors, or youth workers making decisions under the YCJA. Conferences can provide advice on decisions such as extrajudicial measures and the reintegration of young people into their communities following custody. They can include parents, victims, people familiar with the youth, and community agencies or professionals. Conferences can be understood as a restorative mechanism focused on developing proposals for repairing harm done to the victim.

Diversity-Based Practice: This is an approach that emphasizes diversity as a positive force while acknowledging social realities of difference, including the marginalization of certain individuals and groups. It rejects equality-based frameworks that treat everyone uniformly and adopts equity-based principles that address systemic inequalities. In ADR, it means embracing cultural influences and ensuring marginalized groups have a voice and are substantively and procedurally included.

Dispute Resolution: Effective dispute resolution requires lawyers to develop skills beyond traditional legal advocacy, though some advocacy skills are transferable with alteration. Engaging in dispute resolution prior to and during mediation is vital, especially when issues carry high levels of emotion. Dispute resolution, and mediation specifically, are having a positive impact on access to justice across Canada.

Equity vs. Equality (Diversity-Based Practice): Diversity-based practice rejects equality-based frameworks, which treat all individuals uniformly. Instead, it adopts equity-based principles that address systemic inequalities and the unequal distribution of resources. An equity-based approach does not assume all parties are equal but also rejects that marginalized groups have no power. Embracing equity within ADR involves re-examining traditional procedural norms, such as giving equal time to each party, and requires critically assessing power dynamics. Ignoring diversity and treating everyone identically denies justice to already marginalized participants.

Extrajudicial Measures (Youth Criminal Justice Act): A key objective of the YCJA is to increase the use of non-court responses to less serious offences by youth. These measures improve early intervention and play a role in developing community-based responses to youth crime. They include police referrals to community programs like recreation programs and counselling services, intended to help youth avoid committing offences.

Lawyer Competencies for Access to Justice: An empirical study revealed significant distrust of lawyers within marginalized communities, often attributed to their association with the justice system, lack of personal relationships with clients, and the perception that law primarily serves the wealthy. Building trust between the legal profession and marginalized communities requires a relational approach prioritizing empathy, respect, and cultural understanding. Lawyers need skills such as cultural humility, understanding systemic issues like colonialism and its connection to the legal system, and context-informed listening and communication. Critical self-reflection, recognizing implicit bias, and understanding dominant lawyering culture are also needed. For effective dispute resolution, lawyers need interest-based negotiation skills, the ability to manage client expectations, flexibility, and familiarity with

	various ADR options. "Soft-skills" and the ability to build rapport are also vital in mediation. Lawyers play an important role in guiding clients, addressing emotions, and balancing emotional support with facilitating control over the session.
Mediation:	In its simplest definition, mediation is a negotiation between disputing parties assisted or facilitated by a neutral party (the mediator) who is not empowered to impose a settlement. Mediation typically occurs early in the legal process, potentially saving time and resources. Please see the chapter on Mediation.
Mediation Clinics (University of Windsor, Osgoode):	Community-based mediation programs like the University of Windsor Mediation Services and the Osgoode Mediation Clinic provide free client-centred dispute resolution services and engage in community outreach.
Restorative Justice:	Indigenous law and culture place a primary emphasis on the ideals of restorative justice. The less adversarial nature of mediation supports restorative ideals. Reconciliation in criminal justice requires extensive dispute resolution and involves the reintegration of the offender into society and holistic restoration of the victim, offender, and community. Please see the chapter on Restorative Justice.
Truth and Reconciliation Commission's Calls to Action:	Call to Action #28 specifically encourages Canadian law schools to revise curriculums. This framework aims to prepare students with the knowledge and skills to work effectively with

	clients, including focusing on access to justice issues.
Winnipeg's Out-Of-Custody Youth Intake Court:	:This court creates an environment for youth that allows for early intervention, personal discussions, and second chances. It decreases delays and the number of youths set to go to trial. It brings together judges, Crown attorneys, defence lawyers, and accused youth to sort out issues quickly. Early intervention holds the potential to divert youth from continued criminal involvement.
Young Offenders Act (YOA) and Youth Criminal Justice Act (YCJA)	The YOA recognized the importance of community-based corrections and pre-trial diversion. The YCJA replaced the YOA and places more emphasis on extrajudicial measures, being more successful at keeping Canadian youth out of jail. A key YCJA objective is to increase the use of non-court responses to less serious offences by youth.

Competing Interests The author has no conflicts of interest to declare that are relevant to the content of this chapter.

References

Acharya, N. (2023). Exploring the role of mandatory mediation in civil justice. *Alberta Law Review, 60*(3), 719–750.

Action Committee on Access to Justice in Civil and Family Matters. (2013a). *Meaningful change for family justice: Beyond wise words* [Final report].

Action Committee on Access to Justice in Civil and Family Matters. (2013b). *Access to civil and family justice: A roadmap for change*. Canadian Forum on Civil Justice.

Acton, K. W. (1999). The impact of mediation on legal education and on the profession. *Windsor Yearbook of Access to Justice, 17*, 256–280.

BC Civil Resolution Tribunal. (2024). *Annual report, 2023–2024*. https://civilresolutionbc.ca/wp-content/uploads/CRT-Annual-Report-2023-2024.pdf

Bernstein, M. M. (1998). Using mediation as an effective technique to achieve success in open adoptions. *Canadian Family Law Quarterly, 16*, 1–25.

Charkoudian, L., Eisenberg, D. T., & Walter, J. L. (2017). What difference does ADR make: Comparison of ADR and trial outcomes in small claims court. *Conflict Resolution Quarterly, 35*(1), 7–30.

Chartrand, L., & Horn, K. (2016). *A report on the relationship between restorative justice and Indigenous legal traditions in Canada*. Government of Canada.

Currie, A. (2016). *Nudging the paradigm shift: Everyday legal problems in Canada*. Canadian Forum on Civil Justice.

Elman, B. P. (2009). Creating a culture of professional responsibility and ethics: A leadership role for law schools. *Windsor Review of Legal and Social Issues, 27*, 93–115.

Farrow, T. C. W., Currie, A., Aylwin, N., Jacobs, L., Northrup, D., & Moore, L. (2016). *Everyday legal problems and the cost of justice in Canada: Overview report*. Osgoode Legal Studies Research Paper Series.

Fenske, A., & Froese, B. (2017). *Justice starts here: A one-stop shop approach for achieving greater justice in Manitoba*. Canadian Centre for Policy Alternatives.

Goldberg, S. (2021). Triaging and mediating to meet the needs of families under The Family Dispute Resolution (Pilot Project) Act of Manitoba. *Manitoba Law Journal, 44*(3), 62–85.

Government of Canada. (2021, July 7). *The Youth Criminal Justice Act: Summary and background*. https://justice.gc.ca/eng/cj-jp/yj-jj/tools-outils/back-hist.html

Government of Canada. (2022, August 25). *Dispute resolution reference guide: Mediation*. https://justice.gc.ca/eng/rp-pr/csj-sjc/dprs-sprd/res/drrg-mrrc/04.html

Gowriluk, C. (2024, April 24). This Winnipeg court is trying to fix how it handles its youngest offenders—One kid at a time. *CBC News*. https://www.cbc.ca/news/canada/manitoba/new-youth-intake-court-winnipeg-1.7177358

Jackson, M. (1992). Aboriginal justice in search of the pathways to justice: Alternative dispute resolution in Aboriginal communities. *University of British Columbia Law Review (Special Edition)*, 147–175.

Keet, M., & Salamone, T. B. (2001). From litigation to mediation: Using advocacy skills for success in mandatory or court-connected mediation. *Saskatchewan Law Review, 64*, 57–80.

Kidner, J. (2011). The limits of mediator "labels": False debate between "facilitative" versus "evaluator" mediator styles. *Windsor Review of Legal and Social Issues, 20*, 167–190.

Lugtig, S. (2016). A vision for experiential education at Robson Hall: Supporting students' transition to practice. *Manitoba Law Journal, 39*(2), 397–418.

Macfarlane, J. (2001). What does the changing culture of legal practice mean for legal education? *Windsor Yearbook of Access to Justice, 20*, 191–210.

Marsden, S., & Buhler, S. (2017). Lawyer competencies for access to justice: Two empirical studies. *Windsor Yearbook of Access to Justice, 34*, 186–210.

Ontario Court of Justice & Ministry of the Attorney General. (1996). *Civil justice review: Supplemental and final report*. Publications Ontario.

Otis, L., & Boulanger-Bonnelly, J. (2022). Shelters of justice in displaced persons settlements: A proposal for Rohingya camps. *University of New Brunswick Law Journal, 73*, 42–67.

St. Stephen's Community House & Winkler Institute for Dispute Resolution. (2020). *Community mediation research report*. https://www.osgoode.yorku.ca/wp-content/uploads/2021/01/Report-on-Community-Mediation.pdf

Simmons, M. E., & Thompson, D. (2017). The Internet as a site of legal education and collaboration across continents and time zones: Using online dispute resolution as a tool for student learning. *Windsor Yearbook of Access to Justice, 34*, 222–243.

Smyth, G. (2005). Considering democracy and ADR: Diversity-based practice in public collaborative processes. *Windsor Review of Legal and Social Issues, 19*, 13–34.

Susskind, L., McKearnan, S., & Thomas-Larmer, J. (1999). *The consensus building handbook: A comprehensive guide to reaching agreement*. Sage.

Truth and Reconciliation Commission of Canada. (2015). *Truth and Reconciliation Commission of Canada: Calls to action*. Truth and Reconciliation Commission of Canada.

U.S. Institute for Environmental Conflict Resolution. (2004). *Preliminary report on ECR performance: A multi-agency evaluation study*. U.S. Institute for Environmental Conflict Resolution.

Vasey, A. (2006, February). Mediation services celebrates 10th birthday. *Windsor Law Now*. https://uwindsor.ca/law/sites/uwindsor.ca.law/files/windsor%20law%20now%20v%202%20n1.pdf

Legal Research as ADR: The Three Keys Method

Matthew Renaud

Abstract This chapter will highlight a simplified approach to legal research. I have dubbed this approach, "The Three Keys Method" and it boils legal research down to engagement with three integral strategies: (1) the use of secondary sources to develop a better understanding of a legal issue, (2) finding effective primary sources of law (especially legislation and case law) for use with said legal issue, and (3) Noting up those primary sources of law (sometimes referred to as "Shepardizing" or "updating") to determine their validity. Repeated use of this straightforward strategy will lead to better outcomes for the researcher, and it is my hope that the Three Keys Method will encourage more legal professionals, regardless of discipline or experience, to engage with legal research more substantively in their practice. The analysis and suggestions offered in this chapter are based on my own experiences teaching legal research as an instructor and law librarian at the University of Manitoba, in Winnipeg, Canada.

Keywords Legal research · Information literacy · Information Seeking · Online Research · Resource Types · Access Points · Law Library

M. Renaud (✉)
University of Manitoba, Winnipeg, MB, Canada
e-mail: matthew.renaud@umanitoba.ca

L. E. Reimer and R. Jochelson (eds.), *The Other Side of the Bar*,
https://doi.org/10.1007/978-981-96-9748-9_11

Introduction

This chapter aims to highlight a simplified approach to legal research titled, "The Three Keys Method". Based upon findings uncovered in academic legal instruction, the Three Keys Method boils legal research down to engagement with three integral strategies: (1) the use of secondary sources to develop a better understanding of a legal issue, (2) finding effective primary sources of law (especially legislation and case law) for use with said legal issue, and (3) Noting up those primary sources of law (sometimes referred to as "Shepardizing" or "updating") to determine validity. Repeated use of this straightforward strategy (in the order offered above) will lead to better outcomes for researchers and save them substantial time in the process. Importantly, the 3 Keys Methods can be incorporated by any legal professional, regardless of discipline, experience or practice.

Research Key #1: Begin by Consulting Secondary Sources

As a legal research tool, secondary sources fulfill two important functions: (1) they explain or summarize the law for the researcher, and 92) they direct them to relevant primary sources, namely case law and legislation. This makes them an excellent starting point for any legal research project, namely those where the researcher is unfamiliar with the topic at hand. As such, Key #1 in the Three Keys Method is to begin your legal research project by consulting secondary sources.

Given the huge quantity of legal commentary now available (especially online), some way of distinguishing between the various kinds of secondary sources becomes useful. One way to do this is to classify secondary sources within two primary categories: Traditional Secondary Sources and Non-Traditional Secondary Sources.

Traditional Secondary Sources

Traditional secondary sources are resources published in common formats that largely pre-date the internet: books, academic periodicals, case comments, etc. These formats are long-established in the legal profession and must undergo a comprehensive period of vetting and review before they are published. This makes them highly authoritative, although the long timeline between editing and publication means a traditional secondary source can go years (and sometimes decades) without being updated.

Another challenge attached to traditional secondary sources is that many of them are not easily accessible online. Instead, they are often hidden behind paywalls, unsearchable in Google, or only retrievable via an expensive database subscription. To complicate matters further, traditional secondary sources are often tied exclusively to a specific legal publisher who dictates how a researcher can gain access to the resource. These publishers have little incentive to make their publications available for free, and rising costs have forced many researchers and legal professionals to lose access entirely.

Types of Traditional Secondary Sources:

1. **Legal Encyclopedias**: A legal encyclopedia stands as an excellent starting point for any legal research project. They provide a general overview of a given legal topic as well as footnotes that refer to applicable case law and legislation. In Canada, there are two legal encyclopedias available to researchers: The *Canadian Encyclopedic Digest (CED)* and *Halsbury's Laws of Canada*. Both are available in print or via Westlaw (CED) and Lexis (Halsbury's), respectively. In the United States, there are two popular legal encyclopedias, also available in print and online, *Corpus Juris Secundum (CJS)* and *American Jurisprudence, 2d (Am. Jur. 2d). Wex*, a free-to-use service from Cornell Law School's Legal Information Institute, is also available as an online encyclopedia.

   Strengths and Weaknesses: The primary strength of a legal encyclopedia is that it provides the researcher with (a) a basic understanding of the law, and (b) references to primary sources that are related to that area of law (this means that leading case law on a topic can be identified using a legal encyclopedia). Legal encyclopedias will also sometimes include additional content such as a table of cases, table of statutes, and a glossary of defined terms.

   Researchers should be aware that a legal encyclopedia is not to be considered a replacement for reading legislation and case law. Instead, it should be used as a starting point for a research project, prior to engagement with primary sources. Another weakness is that it may not include relevant entries for new or emerging areas of the law, since like most traditional secondary sources, legal encyclopedias undergo a time-consuming publication process.

2. **Books**: Like legal encyclopedias, a well-written book can be an excellent starting point for any legal research project. Books provide in-depth analysis on a particular area of law and are often written by scholarly experts. There are many types of books available to a legal researcher, all of which vary in breadth and depth of content. It is therefore important to choose the correct type of book depending on the type of legal issue being explored.

   a. *Legal Treatises*—A treatise is a book covering a legal topic in a comprehensive way. It provides analysis, legal rules, and references to primary sources. A treatise can also be single or multi-volume and usually sticks to covering a general topic (ex: Constitutional or Criminal Law). Treatises also have tables of contents and indexes that a researcher can use to find specific issues or sub-topics relevant to their legal issue.
   b. *Monographs*—A monograph is a singular volume that presents a more specific, or specialized overview of a legal topic. Like treatises, most monographs have a table of contents and an index to help the researcher.
   c. *Textbooks*—Textbooks are targeted more towards law students or those outside the legal profession. These provide a comprehensive introduction to the law but are less authoritative than a legal treatise or monograph.
   d. *Casebooks*—Casebooks are more of a finding tool and are comprised mainly of case law excerpts. They can be quite useful for a researcher looking for leading cases on a given subject.

Strengths and Weaknesses: A key strength is that many books are considered authoritative in their field of research. This makes them the de facto leader on a particular subject, and persuasive in court. A researcher who overlooks a major book title will be opening themselves up to potential blind spots, as it relates to their legal issue.

It is important to remember though that books can be somewhat limiting when researching new or emerging areas of the law. This is because compiling a new edition (or even new chapter) is a time-consuming process that often takes over a year to complete. If the topic is more specific, a researcher may have better luck relying on other secondary sources, such as legal periodicals or blogposts.

3. **Legal Periodicals**: Traditionally, legal periodicals have been published one issue at a time, with multiple issues falling within an assigned volume number. The issue/volume distinction is still used by most publications, even those that are made available exclusively online. The numbering is also still used in legal citation, meaning it is important for the researcher to locate the issue and volume number in order to correctly cite the source they are working with.

   Legal periodicals generally fall into two categories: 1) typical periodicals that publish on topics dealing with all aspects of the law, and 2) subject-specific periodicals that publish exclusively on a given legal subject. Like books, legal periodicals are also published in a wide variety of types, each with their own strengths and weaknesses.

   a. *Law Journals and Reviews:* These provide the researcher with a rich source of scholarly writing. Specialized or niche topics that are considered too narrow for publication in a book can be published in law journals. Many emanate from law schools (although some are published commercially) and often cover a broad range of subjects. Law journals often incorporate stringent publication measures, including peer review, editing, and proofreading. They are usually footnoted and can be incredibly valuable when trying to identify other relevant sources in the same area of research.
   b. *Case Comments:* Case comments are often published within other periodicals, including law journals, and provide commentary on court decisions. They can be quite useful as a secondary source, because they provide the researcher with context, analysis, and commentary on case law (something that is not always provided in the written decision itself).
   c. *Magazine Articles:* Less scholarly than a journal article, these tend to be geared more towards legal professionals. Magazine articles can be useful for commentary on recent developments in the law, but tend to be briefer, less formal and include fewer references than an academic source.
   d. *Newsletters:* Usually published by professional associations, newsletters tend to focus on specific areas of the law and most

of their articles are written by experts in that field. A lot of valuable information can be extracted from a newsletter, and it stands as a good entry-level resource for any research project.

Strengths and Weaknesses: Due to their shorter publication cycle, legal periodicals tend to contain more current information than books do. They also tend to have a more specific focus to their content, making them quite useful for research on an emerging area of the law. And many legal periodicals are now available for free online, including via popular services like Google Scholar and the Canadian Legal Information Institute (CanLII.org).

A researcher should be aware that unlike books, periodicals have a much wider variation of rigor when it comes to the publication process. Certain resources, such as law journals and case comments, undergo an extensive vetting process prior to being published. Other sources, however, including newsletters and magazine articles, are not vetted with nearly the same amount of precision.

Non-traditional Secondary Sources

These are secondary sources that can be easily accessed online and come in a variety of internet-friendly formats: blogs, web posts, podcasts, social media, etc. Non-traditional secondary sources are easy to locate, and their content is often updated on a regular basis. This makes them a good source of information for new developments in the law such as a groundbreaking court decision or changes to legislation.

Since non-traditional secondary sources usually have no prepublication vetting however, they lack the strict editorial oversight associated with their traditional alternatives. As such, this means the quality, reliability and accuracy of non-traditional sources remains an issue and is something a researcher must consider when choosing to engage with them.

Types of Non-Traditional Secondary Sources:

1. Blogs: A good resource to use for posts and entries on specific legal matters. Blogs are often an early source of information on a breaking news topic, a recent court decision, or a change in the law. They are also relatively easy to locate because Google and other search

engines index blogs effectively, and many organizations use strategies to raise their blog's profile (and ranking) in a search results list.

Blogs share many of the same weaknesses of other non-traditional secondary sources, however. Very few are rigorously fact-checked, and authorship can be challenging to determine, at times. Some blogs may not even have individual authors associated with posts, making it difficult to determine the reliability and expertise underlying the information provided.

2. Podcasts: Arguably the world's most popular source of information these days, podcasts are audio programs that are released in episodic format and can be downloaded or streamed online. Legal podcasts are sometimes published by an organization (a law firm, for example) but can also be published by an individual.

   The warnings about non-traditional secondary sources apply here. Researchers must use caution, investigate the source, and critically assess before moving forward with a podcast as a source.
3. Social media: Social media platforms like X (formerly Twitter), Facebook, LinkedIn, Instagram, and TikTok are now being used by legal professionals to spread information and promote expertise on a given topic. They can also be useful for obtaining information about breaking news related to changes in the law.

   As a source for legal commentary, social media has some limited uses. While it is unlikely that a researcher would cite a social media post in their legal writing, social media platforms have become important hubs for legal information. Finding those communities and identifying the experts within them can be a useful strategy to pair with more traditional secondary sources, such as book or journal articles. Experts may even provide hyperlinks to other resources that are relevant or add context to their posts.

Research Key #2: Engagement with Primary Sources of Law

Primary sources play a pivotal role in the overall legal research process. Authoritative and often binding, they are the most credible source of information that a researcher can use in their work. Key #2 in the Three Keys Method is to engage with primary sources of law.

Researchers will want to focus on using two types of primary sources to assist them with their legal problem: legislation and case law. Both represent the law itself, but the rules and principles that underpin these resources can be drastically different. As such it helps to have a basic understanding of both sources, and where to locate them.

Legislative Research

Legislation can be defined as a catch-all term for statutes and other lawmaking instruments (regulations, bylaws, etc.). As a primary source, it is incredibly important to legal problem solving. In addition to legislation in force, researchers may also need to consider legislation that is still in progress towards enactment (bills).

Unfortunately for many, looking at legislation is often perceived as an afterthought, with case law receiving far more attention during the overall research process. But if there is legislation that governs the legal issue at hand, it may provide all the information that is needed in terms of what the law permits. This means legislation should typically be referenced by the researcher before they focus too heavily on case law.

**Note* Before beginning any legislative research in earnest, it is important to have at least a basic understanding of the legislative process governing the jurisdiction being researched. There are many excellent government databases, texts, and online resources that can explain this process clearly and in detail.

Tools for Finding Legislation

Once the researcher has confirmed that there is legislation governing their legal issue, and has identified that legislation, they will then need to retrieve it and understand how it has been applied in relation to their research problem. Thankfully, there are many specialized legislative research tools available for this, with most being available online.

1. ***Legislative Databases***: Government databases are often the best initial access point for online legislative research. These resources offer the official and most up-to-date versions of legislation (which is important, since legislation is always changing because of amendments) and largely make them available free of charge. Notable

examples include Justice Laws Canada, which publishes official versions of Canadian federal statutes and regulations, and Gov.info, which is the federal equivalent in the United States.

Lexis and Westlaw can also be used for legislative research, with the caveat being that they do not include official copies of legislation. Their search functionality is superior to the government databases however, so they do represent an attractive alternative.

2. ***Annotated Statutes***: An annotated statute includes the full text of one or more statutes, in addition to commentary, history, and references to case law that has commented on or interpreted the act. They are usually published in book format, and both Lexis and Westlaw provide access to many of these titles online.

   In the online environment, this means that most annotated statutes are not fully visible because the full text is either hidden behind a paywall or only available in print. Annotated statutes can also be difficult to identify through an online search, namely because certain texts do not include the word annotated in their title.
3. ***Legislative Concordances***: Sometimes, a legal researcher will need to compare similar legislative provisions across multiple jurisdictions, or a single provision across time within one jurisdiction. Legislative concordances are resources designed with this in mind. For example, a concordance may help a researcher find Ontario's equivalent legislative provision to Manitoba's *Highway Traffic Act* or identify that section as it existed in a previous version of the statute.

   Unfortunately, legislative concordances can be tricky to locate online, primarily because they are often published as part of a larger publication. The researcher should check to see if their law library maintains a list of concordances, or directions on where to find them. Lexis and Westlaw should also be consulted as they provide access to a handful of concordances linked from their homepage.

Researching Bills

Bills do not have the full force of law, however they may be a valuable resource due to their potential to change the scope of a researcher's legal issue. As such, it is important to maintain awareness of any bills that have been introduced by government that may impact the researcher's practice area.

In order to find bills online, the researcher will need to retrieve a key piece of information, the bill number. In Canada, federal bills are identified with a letter (C for House of Commons, S for Senate) and a number indicating its place within a specific legislative session. Bill numbering restarts at 1 in every parliamentary session, so there may be several bills categorized with the same number. This means that to effectively search bills online, the researcher must therefore have additional information, including the bill's date and the name of the member who introduced it.

Monitoring Legislation

It is essential to monitor legislation in order to remain abreast of key developments in the law. By doing so, the researcher maintains current awareness and will be given advance notice of upcoming changes that may impact their work.

The quickest way to monitor legislative changes is to engage with non-traditional secondary sources. Often, blogs, newsletters and social media feeds will make note of any changes, including the introduction of new bills or statutes that have recently been amended. Law firm websites may also provide a more targeted perspective on new legislation or amendments as it relates to their area of practice.

For more detailed monitoring, there are several legislative tracking services that provide updates on bills as they progress through the various stages of government. For example, the Government of Canada's federal legislative database, LEGISinfo, allows the use of an RSS feed that provides alerts whenever new bills are introduced.

Researching Case Law

In jurisdictions based on common law, the law on a given topic is found not only in legislation but also in case law. This means that as a primary source, case law will usually have a role to play in a legal research topic, even when that topic is heavily centred around legislation. Finding cases that are useful for analysis, however, namely cases that are authoritative and on point, can be challenging and time consuming. This is especially the case today, where there exists an extremely large volume of case law available online.

Prior to the advent of the internet, case law reporters could be used to assist in easily finding court decisions. An editorial team would choose cases for publication based on the significance of the decision. This could include cases that dealt with an emerging trend in the law, a unique subject matter, or an unresolved point of law. Cases not chosen for inclusion, referred to as "unreported" or "unpublished", were not considered as significant.

The online research environment has changed the way legal professionals engage with case law however, and reporters are no longer the go-to resource they once were. Instead, most case law now gets dumped into a database or legal research service, often with little to no selection process or editorial vetting. This means the range of cases now available is much broader and less organized than it once was. With such a large volume of results, it is essential to have a good understanding of the tools available for case law retrieval, how they work and where to find them. Awareness of these tools is the first step a researcher can take in developing a strategy that is most likely to result in a list of cases that is relevant to their legal problem.

Tools for Finding Case Law

There are three tools that form the foundation of a good case law research strategy: a case digest, a case citator, and a case-law database. This is as true in the world of online research as it was in the print environment.

> ***1. Case Digests***: A case digest provides a short summary of a court decision, along with references to where the full case can be found. They are structured hierarchically, with broad subject classifications (like "contracts") further broken down into more specific legal topics. Both Lexis and Westlaw have digest services, but it should be noted that their classification systems do not align. In some cases, a classification for an area of law exists in one service, but not in the other. This means there may be differences in how information is organized among both services.
>
> ***2. Case Citators***: Case citators are indexes of cases and the primary tool used in noting up case law. Specifically, a citator will assess the strength of the researcher's case by identifying cases that have cited it, relied on its reasoning, as well as the depth of that reasoning. It can also find more cases that have been decided on the same legal issue.

Both Lexis and Westlaw have citator tools which are constantly updated with new cases. It should be noted though that both services contain a slight different body of case law, so the results pulled from the citator may be different.

3. Full-Text Case Law Databases: A full-text case law database is probably the most familiar type of online case law retrieval tool. It is designed to allow the researcher to search and retrieve the full text of any decision indexed within that database. And these cases often come bundled with other important value-added features, such as explanatory or summary headnotes, relevant keywords related to the decision, and other research tools and related secondary sources.

Special Mention—Secondary Sources: Reliable and authoritative secondary sources will point the researcher to relevant case law, without forcing them to do any further searching. This is both a time and cost-efficient strategy, because if the author of the source is an acknowledged expert, the researcher can rely on their expertise rather than spending time searching for case law on their own.

The type of secondary source used to retrieve case law (traditional or non-traditional) will depend upon the nature of the legal issue being researched. Legal encyclopedias, treatises, journal articles, and blogs, are just a few examples of sources that can provide relevant case law. Starting a legal research project with a reliable secondary source can make a big difference in giving the researcher a useful starting point and early advantage when needing to search for case law.

Monitoring Case Law

Staying up to date with case law can be achieved via a variety of methods, but the approach involved will depend on the researcher's goal. Are they needing to monitor a specific case? Decisions involving a specific area of the law? Or decisions that involve a specific keyword or phrase? Or perhaps a combination of all three?

The current awareness tools found in many legal research services can also be useful for keeping up to date with case law developments in a specific area of law. Lexis' NetLetters service, for example, provide weekly summaries of case law by practice area. And finding a prominent lawyer, law firm, or other expert can be another efficient way of retrieving information on a particular legal topic.

Research Key #3: Validating Primary Sources of Law (Noting Up)

Noting up (sometimes referred to as "Shepardizing" or "updating") is a technique used in legal research to validate primary sources of law. Researchers can note up both case law and legislation (statutes and regulations) to determine their relevance and current status, thereby ensuring they are still considered "good law". This involves checking for amendments, repeals, or subsequent judicial treatment that might impact validity. Furthermore, noting up is the fastest process available for compiling a list of cases that have cited the primary source being used in the research question. Because of this, it represents Key #3 in the Three Keys Method of simplifying legal research.

Noting Up Legislation

After it is enacted, a statute does not remain a static instrument. At any time, a new bill may be introduced that, if enacted, would add, change or repeal sections of that act. An amending statute might amend just one act, or it could start out as an omnibus bill that, once enacted, would amend many acts at the same time. This means that the researcher cannot rely on what a statute looks like at one point in time, because it is always susceptible to amendment or repeal by future acts. In other words, legislation is a moving target, and this makes noting it up such an essential research skill.

Noting up legislation has two distinctive parts: (1) Finding currency—where the researcher finds the most up-to-date version of the law (and whether it is still in force), and (2) Judicial Consideration—discovering how the courts have dealt with the legislation in questions (how has it been interpreted or applied, and have the courts commented on its constitutionality).

Noting Up Legislation Part 1: Finding Currency

In the first part of a legislative note up, the research wants to ensure that their statute (or statute provision) is in force and that they are looking at the most current version. This process can be done most easily using a legislative database for the relevant jurisdiction.

To find a statute's currency date, navigate to the current consolidated (up-to-date) version of the statute. The posted currency date can be found at the top of the page of the current statute or regulation and will give the exact date of the last consolidation.

Typically, the currency date will be a few days to a few weeks in the past, but a bill that amends a statute could be enacted into law at any time. Therefore, even a week's gap between the posted currency date and the date of the researcher's project could pose a risk that the statute or statute provision has been amended, but the changes are not yet visible. As a result, the researcher may need to enhance their currency date.

To enhance a currency date, the researcher should check to see that no amending provisions have been enacted during the gap in time. The quickest way to do this is to examine bills that have been passed into law during the time span between a statute's posted currency date and the date of the researcher's project. This can be done by searching the website of government in that jurisdiction.

Noting Up Legislation Part 2: Judicial Treatment

In part two of the note up process, the researcher wants to find case law that has dealt with the statute or provision in order to understand how courts have interpreted or applied it. This process is called "judicial treatment", and it can also be used to see how the courts have defined certain legislative terms, or whether they have commented on the constitutionality of a statute's provision.

The relevant research tool for this process is a case citator, which provides the researcher with a list of cases that have cited the section of the statute they are interested in. Note that since courts tend to deal with legislation one or more sections at a time in their analysis, it is much more efficient to look up the judicial treatment for a single provision of a statute than looking at treatment of the act as a whole.

Thankfully, this process can be easily accomplished using a few online tools. Both Lexis and Westlaw offer the use of citator tools, and the researcher simply has to navigate to the desired statute or provision, and then click on the link that provides access to the citator. This usually appears as either a tab at the top of the document, or next to each section of the statute.

It is important to note that no single citator is entirely comprehensive. There may be substantial overlap between sources, but each will include unique cases as well. As best practice, a researcher should be cross-checking their results across multiple databases (if able to) in order to fully compare note up results.

Also, there may be statutes that contain an overwhelming number of note up results attached to them. If possible, seek judicial treatment only for relevant provisions from that statute, and aim to retrieve cases that discuss those specific provisions, not the entire statute. The use of search filters can also help in refining results by level of court and date.

Noting Up Case Law

Noting up case law is a mandatory step in the legal research process and must be done whenever a researcher engages with court decisions. Thankfully, the online research environment makes this process easy to accomplish, and note up results are now returned in seconds (and are often updated in near real time).

In common law jurisdictions, noting up considers two factors that potentially impact the validity and utility of the case being used by the researcher. The first step involves verifying the complete history of the case. Lower court or tribunal decisions are susceptible to being overturned or reversed on appeal to higher-level courts. Researchers must determine whether this is true of their target case so as to confirm that the legal principles articulated in the target case are still "good law" and have not been overruled by a higher court. In the second step, the subsequent judicial treatment of the case in question is considered. This demonstrates how widely, and in what way the reasoning in the case has been considered by other courts.

Noting up case law online is convenient and can be done easily in both Lexis and Westlaw using their respective citator tools. Both have also integrated value-added features that offer researchers additional information on the history and subsequent judicial treatment of their case.

Noting Up Case Law Part 1: Case History

The history of a case may be complex and sometimes a researcher needs to consider more than merely "was my case appealed?". For example, if the case being used in their legal problem is an appeal from a lower court, was it subsequently appealed to a higher court? Was the lower court's decision affirmed? Reversed? Varied? If the decision is from the Supreme

Court, what were the outcomes in the lower court decisions? Have their been other Supreme Court decisions on this same topic? Thankfully, this information is easily accessible using a citator tool.

For this step, begin by accessing the full text decision and look for "History". Both Lexis and Westlaw provide this information, with Westlaw offering a graphical representation of a case's history and Lexis including descriptors ("Reversing", "Affirmed", etc.) that indicate the nature of the relationship. Regardless of citator used, the researcher will be able to determine how their case progressed through the court system.

When considering a case's history, it's important not to conflate the case's history with its recency. No matter how old a case is, if it has not been overturned on appeal, then it may still be considered good law. Do not discard a case merely because it is not a recent decision.

Noting Up Case Law Part 2: Judicial Treatment

The second step in the note up process involves uncovering the judicial treatment of the decision being considered by the researcher. In other words, finding other cases that have cited the decision and seeing how they have treated it. Have those courts followed the reasoning in the case? Have they distinguished it? Considered it? Etc.

Be advised that the principle of *stare decisis* is important here. In a common law jurisdiction, cases decided on the same legal issue (or similar issue) should have similar outcomes. However, courts may not entirely agree with the legal reasoning found in an earlier case involving the same laws. A decision not to follow the earlier case is traditionally justified through the assertion by the court that the facts of the two cases are different enough to warrant a different application of the law.

Searching for cases that have cited the original case being considered will also yield references to similar decisions as well as those that provide some understanding of how the law is developing. This may lead to the researcher discovering that the argument they have proposed is based on reasoning that has been weakened by recent jurisprudence. The citators will characterize the subsequent judicial treatment of the original case using a system of "treatment indicators," which provide information on the depth of treatment received by the original case. Treatment indicators help in determining the overall strength of the original case, and whether subsequent courts have uniformly accepted or rejected the reasoning in it, or whether there was mixed treatment.

Treatment indicators vary substantially in various services, not only in terms of the word used to identify a form of treatment but also in the symbols or icons that represent those words. Treatment indicators include words such as applied, considered, mentioned, disapproved, distinguished, referred to, not followed, or overruled. A single case may receive different treatment indicators depending on the service, which in other words, there is sometimes little similarity in the way the services characterize the judicial treatment of a case. This means that treatment indicators, although a highly useful research tool, are no substitute for reading the case in full.

Noting Up: Final Considerations

It is important for researchers to be aware of the fact that there exists substantial variation in note up results between legal research services. This can include discrepancies in the citing cases identified, as well as in the nature and accuracy of the judicial treatment offered. Legal editors will make different choices based on their own expertise. This means that some citators may designate a case as "citing" a statutory provision or court decision, even if it makes only the merest mention of it. Similarly, one service may decide that a citing case only "mentions" the original decision, while another may label it as "following" it.

There are two strategies to be aware of that can mitigate this potential conflict. First, a researcher should get into the habit of reading through the note up results for themselves. This will help determine the accuracy of the information provided, and whether their case or legislative provision is being correctly treated by the citator. Second, the researcher should always consider noting up their case/legislative provision in another service. The discrepancies between the two may be enough to warrant a further refining of the original search.

When to Stop Your Research

The Three Keys Method is designed to simplify the legal research process and provide an easy-to-follow roadmap for any researcher to follow. But it is also important to know when to conclude one's research and move on to the next stage of the legal problem in question. Thankfully, there are some important benchmarks that researchers can use to ensure they know when to stop researching. These should be kept in mind in order to keep searches focused and to avoid wasting time looking for resources that have little to no value.

A. *Use a research checklist*. The use of a checklist will help the researcher stay on track and inform them when they have already covered certain ground.
B. *Usesecondary sources* of all types to develop an iron-clad understanding of the law. Secondary sources will also point the researcher in the direction of relevant primary sources.
C. *Rely on traditionalsecondary sources* like books and journal articles for expert analysis.
D. Be sure to *understand the hierarchy* of primary sources of law as it relates to the research topic.

    a. This normally means looking for legislation before case law. If there is a piece of legislation that governs the legal issue in question, then case law can be used as an add-on
    b. When it is time to move on to case law, try to stick to decision from within the jurisdiction being researched. Choose cases that are binding and authoritative.
    c. Move next to persuasive case law. For example, decisions from courts outside the jurisdiction being researched. Case law from a foreign jurisdiction can also be persuasive.

If a researcher follows this progression, then they will have covered every possible relevant resource in the most efficient way possible. Further, once they have moved all the way from point A to the end of point B, then they will have reached their stopping point.

Conclusion

The Three Keys Method offers more than a technical approach to legal research; it opens a pathway toward relational justice by centering the research process as a space for meaningful engagement, not just instrumental output. By encouraging students to explore secondary sources deeply, it fosters recognition of the broader social, historical, and human context in which legal issues arise. This invites law students into a more relational practice, where legal inquiry is not just about finding answers but about understanding the lived realities behind disputes. Such an approach aligns with the commitment to processes that serve as sites of recognition, repair, and respect—an essential orientation for those seeking to transform conflict, not just resolve it.

Moreover, the method's emphasis on validating and contextualizing primary sources calls attention to the often-unseen biases and exclusions in legal systems. This serves as a tool of epistemic repair, allowing students to critically question whose voices are represented in law and whose are systematically omitted. By guiding learners to move beyond surface-level efficiency and into intentional, reflective research practices, the Three Keys Method supports truly transformative legal practice. It prepares students not only to be competent researchers but also to be practitioners who can help reshape legal processes into more inclusive, equitable, and human-centered forms of conflict transformation.

Questions

1. Identify the individual steps (in order) of the Three Keys Method. Explain each step in detail and highlight their importance.
2. When engaging with primary sources of law, why should a researcher begin by consulting legislation before they look at case law?
3. Why are secondary sources considered a valuable resource for legal research?

Glossary

Legal Research	The process of identifying and retrieving information necessary to support legal decision-making.
ADR (Alternative Dispute Resolution)	A range of dispute resolution processes that serve as alternatives to litigation, including mediation, arbitration, and negotiation.
The Three Keys Method	A simplified approach to legal research involving three main strategies: 1. Using secondary sources to understand a legal issue, 2. Finding relevant primary sources (legislation and case law), 3. Noting up those sources to check for validity and relevance.

Secondary Sources:	Commentary or analysis on the law, including textbooks, legal encyclopedias, and journal articles used to gain an overview of a legal issue.
Primary Sources of Law:	Original legal documents such as statutes, regulations, and case law that have binding authority.
Legislation:	Laws enacted by a legislative body, such as statutes or acts.
Case Law::	Judicial decisions from courts that interpret and apply the law in specific cases.
Noting Up:	The process of checking the history and treatment of a legal case or statute to ensure it remains valid and relevant.
Shepardizing:	A term originating from Shepard's Citations, referring to the practice of tracking how a legal decision has been cited by later cases to verify its continuing authority.
Validity (in Legal Research):	The status of a legal source as still being good law—i.e., not overruled, repealed, or otherwise invalidated.

Competing Interests The author has no competing interests to declare that are relevant to the content of this chapter.

Intelligence Augmentation in Alternative Dispute Resolution

Illia Roskoshnyi

Abstract This chapter establishes the conceptual foundations of AI, exploring both its technical aspects and philosophical underpinnings to understand what it is and is not, and how these perspectives shape expectations in legal settings. This is followed by a critical look at significant normative concerns surrounding AI deployment, such as privacy, transparency, and bias, discussing how AI tools can potentially amplify systemic inequalities and identifying necessary safeguards. The discussion then transitions to the practical applications of AI within ADR, detailing current tools used for legal prediction, document automation, contract analysis, and case management, and evaluating their integration and effectiveness through examples like CoCounsel and the BC Civil Resolution Tribunal. The exploration is further enhanced with case studies and hypothetical scenarios to illustrate AI's potential role in mediation or arbitration and the resulting ethical, practical, and legal challenges presented by non-human involvement in decisions. Looking ahead, the material addresses future developments and challenges, considering anticipated AI trajectories, regulatory issues, algorithmic accountability, access to justice,

I. Roskoshnyi (✉)
University of Manitoba, Winnipeg, MB, Canada
e-mail: illia.roskoshnyi@gmail.com

L. E. Reimer and R. Jochelson (eds.), *The Other Side of the Bar*,
https://doi.org/10.1007/978-981-96-9748-9_12

and the design of ADR systems that balance efficiency with human considerations. Finally, it concludes by revisiting core principles like relational justice, epistemic repair, and transformative practice, emphasizing their importance in guiding decisions about the adoption of AI, including the underlying motivations. By the end of this chapter, readers will have a critical framework for understanding AI's transformative—and potentially disruptive—role in ADR.

Keywords Artificial intelligence · Alternative dispute resolution · Privacy · Transparency · Bias · Intelligence augmentation · Legal prediction · Legal research · Legal automation

Introduction

In an era increasingly shaped by digital systems, artificial intelligence (AI) presents both an unprecedented challenge and a profound opportunity for legal practice. Nowhere is this duality more evident than in the field of alternative dispute resolution (ADR), where questions of fairness, process integrity, and human judgment intersect with algorithmic tools promising efficiency, insight, and predictive power. For legal professionals, educators, and scholars, the pressing question is no longer whether AI will impact ADR—but how, and with what consequences. At stake are not only procedural reforms but the fundamental ethos of dispute resolution: relationships, recognition, dialogue, and justice.

This chapter critically examines the integration of AI into ADR processes through the lens of this book's guiding themes: relational justice, epistemic repair, and transformative practice. These theoretical frameworks remind us that conflict is never only about interests or outcomes, but also about the ways in which people are seen, heard, and engaged—and that justice is not simply procedural but relational and contextual. As the promises of AI-driven tools are considered—faster case management, enhanced legal prediction, or even automated negotiation—how these tools reshape the very conditions for ethical engagement between parties must remain in focus. AI does not merely supplement human judgment; it intervenes in the social fabric of dispute resolution.

At the same time, the growth of AI challenges us to confront long-standing barriers in the legal system: unequal access, institutional opacity, systemic bias, and the burdens of cost and delay. In many respects, AI holds the potential to *augment* human capabilities in ways that democratize justice—enabling self-represented parties to better understand their rights, streamlining simple claims to reduce court backlogs, and supporting mediators or facilitators in managing complexity. Yet every promise is shadowed by risks: overreliance on opaque algorithms, erosion of procedural safeguards, reproduction of historical injustices through biased data, and the loss of human-centred judgment in cases that demand moral discernment and emotional intelligence.

This chapter is situated at the crossroads of these tensions. It does not offer easy solutions, nor does it take a wholly optimistic or pessimistic stance. Instead, it charts a careful and critical path through the emerging terrain of intelligence augmentation in ADR. Readers are invited to think expansively but skeptically, to imagine what is possible without losing sight of what is essential.

Artificial Intelligence in legal systems, particularly in alternative dispute resolution, is examined in this section of the chapter across six distinct parts. Establishing the conceptual foundations of AI, exploring both its technical aspects and philosophical underpinnings to understand what it is and is not, and how these perspectives shape expectations in legal settings opens the section. This is followed by a critical look at significant normative concerns surrounding AI deployment, such as privacy, transparency, and bias, discussing how AI tools can potentially amplify systemic inequalities and identifying necessary safeguards. The discussion then transitions to the practical applications of AI within ADR, detailing current tools used for legal prediction, document automation, contract analysis, and case management, and evaluating their integration and effectiveness through examples like CoCounsel and the BC Civil Resolution Tribunal. The exploration is further enhanced with case studies and hypothetical scenarios to illustrate AI's potential role in mediation or arbitration and the resulting ethical, practical, and legal challenges presented by non-human involvement in decisions. Looking ahead, the material addresses future developments and challenges, considering anticipated AI trajectories, regulatory issues, algorithmic accountability, access to justice, and the design of ADR systems that balance efficiency with human considerations. Finally, it concludes by revisiting core principles like relational justice, epistemic repair, and transformative practice, emphasizing their importance in guiding decisions about the adoption of AI, including the underlying motivations.

By the end of this chapter, readers will have a critical framework for understanding AI's transformative—and potentially disruptive—role in ADR. They will also be invited to consider how legal professionals might approach this transformation with integrity, responsibility, and care.

Conceptual Foundations of Artificial Intelligence

To understand how artificial intelligence (AI) may transform alternative dispute resolution (ADR), it is essential to begin with clarity about what AI is—and how it is variously conceived across disciplines. AI is not a monolithic concept but a constellation of definitions, aspirations, and technical architectures. In the legal context, where precision and interpretive nuance matter deeply, conceptual ambiguity can lead to misapplication, inflated expectations, or misplaced fear. In this section, two dominant frameworks for understanding AI are unpacked: AI as a subject and AI as an intelligent system (Roskoshnyi, 2024). Each framework shapes AI's role in legal decision-making, including its promise and limits can be imagined.

AI as a Subject: Intelligence, Imitation, and Consciousness

The question famously posed by Alan Turing in 1950—"Can machines think?"—inaugurated one of the most enduring philosophical and scientific debates of the twentieth century. Turing proposed what came to be known as the Turing Test, suggesting that if a human interlocutor could not distinguish between a machine and a person through textual conversation, the machine could be considered intelligent (Turing, 1950). This conceptual move reframed the question of intelligence away from metaphysical speculation toward behavioral imitation—a radical shift that continues to influence how AI is measured and understood today.

Under this view, intelligence is not tied to biological consciousness but to functional outputs: reasoning, problem-solving, language use. Marvin Minsky (1968), a pioneer in AI, similarly described the field as "the science of making machines do things that would require intelligence if done by humans." From this perspective, the boundaries between human and machine capabilities are not absolute but relative—machines may come to perform functions once thought to be exclusively human.

However, this framing has not gone unchallenged. Critics argue that imitation does not constitute understanding. The philosopher John Searle's (1980) "Chinese Room" thought experiment, for instance, demonstrated that a machine could manipulate symbols according to rules (syntax) without any grasp of meaning (semantics). This distinction matters in law, where interpretation, empathy, and contextual judgment play foundational roles. As Kristen Thomasen (2023) has noted, the work of lawyers and dispute resolution professionals is not simply about processing inputs and delivering outputs, but about managing relationships, emotions, and human complexity—domains where AI remains limited.

These concerns have only intensified in the age of large language models like ChatGPT. While these systems can generate sophisticated legal text and mimic reasoning patterns, they do not "understand" in any human sense. They are probabilistic machines, generating language based on statistical correlations "learned" or calculated from vast datasets. This can be useful in intelligence augmentation in ADR, such as summarizing documents or drafting routine clauses, but it also carries risks: "hallucinations," bias reproduction, and a lack of explainability.

Thus, when considering whether AI can replace or replicate lawyers or mediators, the questions must ask not only whether machines can think and act, but *what kind of thinking and acting matters in law*. If law is as much about narrative, persuasion, and judgment as it is about logic, then the bar for "intelligent" participation remains high.

AI as an Intelligent System: Tool, Automation, and Optimization

The second conceptual framework views AI less as a philosophical question and more as a set of engineered systems—designed to simulate or support cognitive tasks in the form of a computational program. From this standpoint, AI includes everything from rule-based expert systems and predictive analytics to natural language processing and machine learning. The emphasis is not on consciousness or equivalency to humans but on economic functionality: what tasks can machines perform, and how well these machines augment humans.

This pragmatic definition emerged out of efforts like the 1955 Dartmouth Summer Research Project on Artificial Intelligence, where pioneers like John McCarthy and Claude Shannon described the "AI problem" as that of making a machine behave in ways that would be called intelligent if a human were so behaving (McCarthy et al., 1955). Over time, AI systems have evolved through multiple generations—from early rule-based systems to today's "neural networks," which computationally simulate or imitate human behavior patterns through layers of weighted "nodes" and dynamic feedback loops.

Contemporary AI tools used in legal contexts—such as CoCounsel, Lexis+ AI, or Smartsettle—fall under this category. These systems do not "think" in the philosophical sense, but they perform or augment cognitive-like tasks: identifying legal issues in documents, predicting case outcomes, suggesting negotiation ranges. In many cases, their statistical capacity far exceeds human limits. For instance, Katz et al. (2017) used machine learning to predict U.S. Supreme Court decisions with over 70% accuracy—outperforming legal experts on consistency.

The implications for ADR are significant. If AI can help identify patterns across thousands of past settlements, or suggest likely outcomes based on similar fact scenarios, then it can serve as a powerful tool for negotiation and mediation. However, the risk of over-reliance remains. As Zerilli et al. (2020) emphasize, algorithms trained on past outcomes may encode historical biases, and without interpretability, their recommendations may go unchallenged. In a mediation setting, this could mean privileging "typical" settlements over contextually just ones.

Moreover, the line between task automation and augmentation is blurry. AI can assist with routine tasks—like scheduling, document review, or initial triage—but when it begins to shape substantive choices, such as determining what counts as a fair offer, the system crosses into normative territory. As Pamela McCorduck (2004) observed, people often stop calling something "AI" once it becomes part of their everyday life. Yet its effects on legal culture remain profound.

Synthesis: A Dual Lens for Legal Integration

Both conceptual framings—AI as a subject and AI as an intelligent system—are essential for understanding its role in ADR. The former reminds us of the philosophical and ethical stakes: machines are not human, and their capacities for interpretation, empathy, and moral reasoning are limited. The latter foregrounds the practical tools that are already reshaping legal work and offers a framework for integration grounded in capacity, not consciousness.

A dual lens is adopted. The cognitive limits of current AI are seriously considered, while recognizing its practical utility. The concern is not whether AI will replace human mediators, but how it will augment or constrain them—and under what conditions that augmentation is ethically defensible. As relational justice scholars argue, processes matter as much as outcomes. An AI tool that improves efficiency but undermines recognition, dignity, or transparency may solve one problem only to create another.

With these foundations in place, the chapter turns to the risks that attend AI adoption, particularly those concerning privacy, transparency, and bias—the subject of the next section.

Privacy, Transparency, and Bias

As artificial intelligence (AI) becomes embedded in alternative dispute resolution (ADR), questions of privacy, transparency, and bias become more than technical concerns—they become central to the ethical and relational integrity of legal processes. The deployment of machine learning in legal contexts not only introduces powerful tools but also amplifies longstanding vulnerabilities in how law processes knowledge, adjudicates claims, and safeguards dignity. This section examines how AI systems in ADR interact with personal data, reveal (or obscure) their decision-making logic, and risk replicating or exacerbating social inequities through embedded bias. Drawing on law-and-society scholarship, real-world case studies, and critical theory, this section demonstrates that the legitimacy of AI-enhanced ADR hinges not only on its effectiveness but on its fairness, accountability, and openness to scrutiny.

Privacy in the Age of Digital Dispute Resolution

Privacy is foundational to the legitimacy of ADR. Whether in mediation, arbitration, or facilitated dialogue, parties often share sensitive personal, financial, or relational information with the expectation that it will remain confidential. The introduction of AI systems into these processes complicates this expectation in several ways.

First, AI tools often require significant amounts of training data to function effectively—which may include previous case files, user profiles, communication logs, and legal records. Even anonymized data sets carry the risk of reidentification, especially when cross-referenced with publicly available information (Zerilli et al., 2020). Furthermore, many AI systems are cloud-based and built by private vendors, meaning user data may be stored, analyzed, or even sold outside the control of the legal professionals using them.

Second, some AI systems function as black boxes, in which users interact with interfaces that obscure what data is collected, how it is stored, and for what purposes it is used. Richard Posner (2008) famously argued that privacy can conflict with transparency and that a balance must be struck. However, in the context of AI-driven ADR, the risk is that the balance tips too far toward data collection and away from user control. Parties may unknowingly share data with systems that reprocess it for unrelated purposes, undermining the principle of informed consent.

A concrete example illustrates this risk. Consider a family mediation conducted via an AI-enhanced online platform. The system may log emotional tone, word choices, or response times in order to provide "insight" to the mediator—but such tracking, if undisclosed or poorly understood, may violate the spirit of privacy that ADR promises. Worse still, if the same data is later used by developers to "improve" the product, it may circulate in ways that participants never anticipated.

To protect privacy, several measures are necessary: robust data governance, clear disclosures, the use of closed-loop systems that do not export or sell user data and adjusting privacy settings. Moreover, practitioners must be trained to understand how AI tools function behind the scenes, so they can communicate effectively with clients and maintain ethical standards. Where AI becomes part of the mediation or arbitration process, parties must retain the right to opt out of data collection features—a core component of maintaining trust.

The Opacity of Algorithmic Decision-Making

Transparency—or its absence—is another major concern in AI-enhanced ADR. While many human-led dispute resolution processes operate through open dialogue and reason-giving, legal AI systems often produce outputs without explaining how they arrived at their conclusions. This lack of explainability has significant implications for due process, procedural fairness, and accountability.

The concept of "black box" algorithms is now well known: systems that provide outputs (such as legal predictions or settlement recommendations) without revealing the rules, weights, or data pathways used to generate them. Even the designers of these systems may not fully understand how deep learning networks produce specific outcomes, due to the complexity and nonlinearity of their internal architectures (Zerilli et al., 2020).

This becomes especially problematic in ADR, where decisions about fairness, equity, and remedy require interpretive reasoning. If an AI tool recommends a settlement amount in a wage theft mediation, but cannot articulate the rationale behind its number, how can the parties meaningfully evaluate it? If an arbitrator relies on an AI assistant that flags "relevant precedents" but cannot trace its path of reasoning, what happens when one party wants to challenge that logic?

The issue is compounded when proprietary systems are involved. Many AI tools used in legal tech are developed by private companies that claim intellectual property protections over their code and datasets. This creates a transparency paradox: the systems most likely to be trusted (because they are widely used) are often the least open to public scrutiny.

To mitigate this, some scholars advocate for algorithmic auditing, whereby third-party experts evaluate AI tools for fairness, bias, and logic before they are deployed in public or semi-public systems. Others suggest that explainable AI (XAI) techniques—such as rule extraction, saliency mapping, or surrogate models—should be required for all tools used in legal settings. In either case, transparency is not just a technical feature but a normative requirement: parties in ADR deserve to know how decisions are being shaped, even when technology is involved.

Bias and the Reproduction of Inequality

Perhaps the most urgent concern in AI-enhanced ADR is the risk of bias—not only in the outputs of the system but in the data on which it is trained, the assumptions it encodes, and the social contexts it reflects. As Toffler (1980) and North (2005) both emphasize, technologies are never neutral; they emerge from, and reinforce, existing institutional environments.

A landmark case that underscores this problem is the use of the COMPAS algorithm in the U.S. criminal justice system. An investigation by ProPublica revealed that the algorithm disproportionately flagged Black defendants as high risk compared to White defendants, even when controlling for recidivism (Larson et al., 2016). Though COMPAS was not used in ADR settings, the lesson is clear: if the data used to train an

AI tool reflects systemic racism, class stratification, or gendered norms, those biases will likely be perpetuated in the system's outputs.

In the context of ADR, this might manifest in an AI tool that recommends lower settlements for women in employment disputes (based on historical patterns), or one that assumes Indigenous parties are less likely to pursue enforcement (due to jurisdictional complexities). Unless carefully audited, such systems could quietly entrench injustice under the guise of neutrality.

Moreover, bias is not always quantitative. It can be epistemic—shaping what is recognized as knowledge, what counts as relevant evidence, and whose voice is heard. As Gacek and Jochelson (2024) argue, systemic ignorance is often structured and maintained through institutional practices. If AI tools are trained primarily on case law from dominant groups, or on settlements that excluded marginalized parties, they may fail to capture the full spectrum of legal reasoning and lived experience.

To address this, ADR practitioners must become critical users of AI, not passive recipients. They must ask not only whether a system "works," but for whom, under what conditions, and with what assumptions. Bias mitigation strategies—such as counterfactual testing, representational parity, and inclusive training datasets—are a start, but they must be complemented by a broader commitment to epistemic justice. This includes centering Indigenous legal traditions, valuing community-based knowledge, and questioning the default authority of algorithmic tools.

A Call for Caution and Competence

Privacy, transparency, and bias are not peripheral issues in AI-driven ADR—they are central. If ADR is to remain a space of dignity, recognition, and ethical dialogue, then the tools it adopts must be evaluated with the same care afforded to our processes. This requires not only technical literacy but critical engagement, ethical foresight, and structural awareness.

These concerns must be carried forward when considering the practical applications of AI in ADR. The next section explores how AI is currently being used to support—and sometimes replace—tasks in negotiation, mediation, and arbitration. But at each stage the following questions are asked: what is gained, what is lost, and who gets to decide?

Practical Applications of AI in Alternative Dispute Resolution

While much of the debate about artificial intelligence (AI) in law centers on theoretical risks and speculative futures, AI is already reshaping the day-to-day practices of legal professionals, including those in the field of alternative dispute resolution (ADR). Tools that support legal research, contract analysis, document automation, and outcome prediction are now widely available and increasingly sophisticated. This section examines how these tools are being integrated into ADR workflows. Not only what tasks they perform or augment is at question, but how they alter the nature of dispute resolution, the roles of practitioners, and the experience of parties.

Although some of these applications are still emerging, others are in regular use. What unites them is their function: they do not adjudicate disputes on their own (yet), but they augment human decision-making by automating, accelerating, or patterning parts of the process. At each point, questions arise: how do these tools impact fairness, participation, and judgment? What kinds of disputes are best suited to automation, and which demand human discernment? And critically, who has access to these tools—and who is left behind?

Legal Prediction and Risk Assessment

One of the most developed areas of AI application in ADR is legal prediction—the use of algorithms to forecast likely outcomes in a dispute based on prior data. For parties considering settlement, such tools can offer important clarity: what might a court decide? What are similar disputes typically resolved for? How risky is a given claim?

These tools are especially useful in mediation, where parties must assess whether to settle or pursue further litigation. Platforms like Lex Machina and Blue J Legal offer predictive analytics that can simulate possible outcomes based on jurisdiction, issue, and fact patterns. In one study, Almuslim and Inkpen (2022) found that an AI model could predict Canadian appellate decisions with an accuracy rate of 93.46%—far exceeding human averages.

In practice, this might look like a mediator inputting case details into a legal analytics platform and receiving a probabilistic range of outcomes—for example, that a wrongful dismissal claim has a 75% likelihood of success and an estimated damages range between $35,000 and $50,000.

The mediator could then share this with the parties as one data point to inform their negotiation.

However, this raises ethical and epistemic questions. If parties overly rely on algorithmic predictions, might they feel pressured to settle rather than assert claims that fall outside the statistical norm? What if the model fails to account for key cultural, contextual, or personal factors that would influence a human judge's decision? Legal prediction can assist, but it must not dictate. As Cardozo reminded us, law is not prophecy alone—it is often about indeterminate and evolving standards (Dimock, 2001).

Document Automation and Drafting Assistance

Another major area of AI application in ADR is document automation—the generation of legal forms, contracts, or agreements using guided software. Tools like Contract Express, Juro, and Spellbook now allow legal professionals to quickly produce customized documents by answering a series of prompts. These tools reduce clerical workload and increase consistency across cases.

This functionality is particularly valuable in ADR, where outcomes often culminate in written agreements (e.g., mediated settlement agreements, arbitration awards). A mediator using Spellbook, for instance, could generate a draft settlement agreement within minutes of the parties reaching consensus. The system might flag inconsistent clauses, suggest additional provisions, or even highlight unenforceable terms based on jurisdictional filters.

This capacity is especially useful in high-volume or low-stakes cases, such as landlord-tenant disputes or small claims. It also benefits self-represented parties by providing accessible, guided drafting without requiring deep legal expertise. In turn, it may promote access to justice, especially in underserved or rural areas.

Yet concerns remain. Document automation depends on template logic—it excels at standard forms but struggles with complexity, nuance, or ambiguity. Moreover, parties may mistake speed for thoroughness: just because a contract can be generated quickly does not mean it has been reviewed carefully. Legal professionals must ensure that automated documents reflect the spirit, not just the structure, of the agreement reached.

Legal Research and Strategic Planning

AI tools are increasingly used to support legal research, both for substantive law and for procedural planning. Tools like CoCounsel and CaseMine allow users to input natural language queries and receive curated case law, statute references, or strategic insights.

In ADR, this function can be harnessed to help mediators or arbitrators determine relevant legal standards, identify precedent language for awards, or prepare parties for hearings. For instance, a facilitator dealing with a cross-border contract dispute might use CoCounsel to rapidly review applicable choice-of-law provisions or enforcement standards.

These tools also have pedagogical potential. They allow junior lawyers, students, or community advocates to access high-quality legal resources without needing institutional subscriptions or senior mentorship. In turn, this may democratize legal knowledge—a core value of access to justice.

Still, these tools depend on the quality of their datasets and the clarity of the user's query. As Toffler (1980) noted, asking the right question is often more important than obtaining the correct answer to the wrong question. Users must learn to frame questions precisely, understand the limits of the system's domain, and verify results through traditional means.

AI-Enhanced Negotiation and Mediation Interfaces

More novel—and perhaps more transformative—are systems that directly mediate between parties using AI. One example is Smartsettle, a platform that facilitates blind bidding and decision optimization. Parties input their preferences and constraints, and the system suggests settlements based on overlapping zones of agreement.

In one case, Smartsettle's "robot mediator" resolved a three-month commercial dispute in under an hour (Hilborne, 2019). The system encouraged parties to adjust expectations through iterative flag placement, and it proposed a final figure without disclosing each party's private bids. The result was accepted, and the dispute was closed.

Similarly, platforms like Pactum AI are used by corporations such as Walmart to automate supplier negotiations. The AI bot proposes terms, responds to pushback, and finalizes contracts—all without human intervention (Van Hoek & Lacity, 2023).

While these examples may seem distant from traditional ADR, they signal a shift in what counts as "negotiation." If machines can identify fair terms faster than humans, and if parties accept their proposals, then what remains of the human role? Is it judgment, empathy, narrative-building? Or are these too being formalized into code?

Practitioners must grapple with these questions. AI-assisted negotiation can increase efficiency, but it may also depersonalize conflict, mask power imbalances, or reduce opportunities for storytelling and relationship repair. These losses are not trivial—they go to the heart of what makes ADR distinct from litigation.

Pre-Trial Dispute Resolution and Public Interfaces

Finally, AI is playing an increasing role in pre-trial triage and early dispute resolution, especially through online dispute resolution (ODR) platforms. The British Columbia Civil Resolution Tribunal (CRT) is a leading Canadian example. It uses expert systems to guide users through claim intake, negotiation, and facilitated resolution. If needed, an adjudicator intervenes—but the majority of cases settle beforehand.

This model reflects a broader trend toward hybrid AI-human systems, where machines structure the process and humans provide the final decision. The efficiency gains are clear: lower costs, reduced court backlogs, increased accessibility. But again, caution is needed. Systems like the CRT are highly structured—they may not allow the flexibility or responsiveness that complex cases require.

Moreover, users must be digitally literate to access these systems. Those with language barriers, cognitive disabilities, or unstable internet access may be excluded—replicating the very access issues these tools aim to solve.

Case Studies and Hypotheticals

Having explored the tools and functions of artificial intelligence (AI) within alternative dispute resolution (ADR), the chapter turns to concrete case studies and illustrative hypotheticals. This section invites readers to apply a critical lens to real-world and imagined scenarios, analyzing how AI reconfigures power, process, and participation. Rather than treating AI as a neutral assistant, the chapter examines how it shapes the epistemological and relational terrain of conflict. These examples illuminate both opportunities and limitations—and challenge readers to think about AI not only as a technical development, but as a socio-legal actor.

Case Study 1: Smartsettle in a Commercial Dispute
In 2019, Smartsettle, a Canadian-based AI negotiation platform, was used to resolve a prolonged dispute between a logistics company and a shipping contractor. The conflict involved a $50,000 disagreement over delayed delivery penalties. After three months of email exchanges and unsuccessful phone calls, the parties agreed to use Smartsettle.

Each party inputs their financial range, interests, and constraints into the system, which then facilitates a blind bidding process using flag placement and optimization algorithms. Within 45 minutes, the platform proposed a settlement amount that both parties accepted. The process was confidential, asynchronous, and fully automated. No human mediator was involved (Hilborne, 2019).

While this case showcases AI's capacity for rapid resolution, it also raises several questions. What role did narrative and recognition play in this process? Did the parties feel heard—or simply processed? How might power asymmetries (e.g., legal sophistication, platform fluency) affect input accuracy and outcomes? What if one party had declined to use the system? The efficiency is notable, but the absence of human facilitation may limit relational repair—a key component of ADR in many contexts.

Hypothetical 1: AI-Augmented Family Mediation
Consider a mediated family dispute involving co-parents navigating a post-divorce custody schedule. The parties opt into an AI-assisted mediation platform that uses sentiment analysis to monitor tone, a legal analytics engine to flag typical custody arrangements in the jurisdiction, and a chatbot to suggest draft parenting plans.

As the parties speak via video call, the system displays suggestions: "In similar cases, shared custody alternating weekly is common." It also flags that one party is exhibiting elevated emotional stress and recommends a pause. After two hours, the chatbot produces a proposed parenting plan, which the mediator reviews and refines with the parties.

This scenario demonstrates how AI might support emotional intelligence and legal precision simultaneously. But it also invites critique. How does algorithmic "suggestion" shape the parties' sense of agency? What happens if the AI's recommendations reflect systemic bias (e.g., gender norms about parenting)? Does the mediator retain control—or become a translator of the machine?

Furthermore, the use of sentiment analysis and tone monitoring introduces privacy concerns. Should the emotional state of a party be inferred by software and displayed to the other side? Might that perception be weaponized? These are not merely technical issues—they go to the core of what it means to mediate fairly and respectfully.

Hypothetical 2: Language, Power, and ODR

A tenant in a rural area speaks limited English and has a dispute with her landlord over the heat and mould conditions in her unit. She is directed to an online dispute resolution (ODR) platform run by the provincial government. The system requires uploading photos, filling out a complaint form, and negotiating with the landlord through a chat interface.

The tenant uses a mobile phone with limited data. The platform translates her complaint automatically using AI but mistranslates key terms: "black mould" becomes "dark dust," and "no heat" becomes "low temperature." The landlord rejects the complaint, citing the unclear language and insufficient evidence. The tenant exits the process without resolution.

Here, the promise of access to justice is undermined by linguistic and technological limitations. AI translation tools, while helpful, cannot yet capture the nuance of urgent housing issues—especially when combined with infrastructure gaps. Without a human facilitator to intervene, the platform amplifies rather than resolves structural exclusion.

This hypothetical echoes Fricker's (2007) concept of hermeneutical injustice: when a person's experience cannot be properly understood or expressed within prevailing epistemic frameworks. In ADR, this may manifest not in overt bias, but in the failure of systems to accommodate the full range of participant realities.

Hypothetical 3: Predictive Algorithms in Arbitration

Two software developers enter into a contract dispute over licensing terms. They agree to binding arbitration and consent to the use of an AI assistant that predicts likely outcomes based on a proprietary database of tech-sector disputes.

The arbitrator inputs the key facts and legal issues, and the system generates a probability model: "Developer A has a 68% likelihood of prevailing, with damages estimated at $72,000–$95,000." The arbitrator incorporates this into her reasoning and ultimately renders an award of $85,000.

Post-decision, Developer B challenges the award, arguing that the arbitrator relied too heavily on a non-transparent algorithm whose data and logic are protected by trade secrecy. The court upholds the award, stating that the arbitrator exercised independent judgment and that the use of analytic tools is permissible under the parties' agreement.

This scenario illustrates the integration of AI into high-stakes legal determinations. While the tool may improve consistency and efficiency, it also raises profound concerns about opacity, epistemic authority, and delegation of judgment. If parties cannot interrogate the tools used to decide their fate, what becomes of procedural fairness?

Moreover, the use of industry-specific data may introduce sectoral bias—normalizing certain outcomes as "fair" even if they are exploitative. Who curates the training data? Who validates the model's logic? Without accountability structures, these tools risk institutionalizing a narrow vision of justice.

Future Challenges and Opportunities

As artificial intelligence (AI) becomes increasingly integrated into legal practice and alternative dispute resolution (ADR), the field stands at a crossroads. On the one hand, the potential benefits of AI in ADR are immense: greater efficiency, broader access, tailored dispute management, and even enhanced procedural consistency. On the other hand, these innovations raise profound ethical, regulatory, and philosophical questions about what it means to resolve disputes fairly, relationally, and humanely. This section explores both the promises and perils of AI's evolving role in ADR—with a particular focus on future developments, governance dilemmas, and the moral obligations of practitioners.

Expanding the Reach of Justice

One of the most frequently cited promises of AI in ADR is its capacity to expand access to justice, particularly in low-resource, remote, or self-represented contexts. Online dispute resolution (ODR) systems, such as British Columbia's Civil Resolution Tribunal (CRT), demonstrate how digital interfaces can reduce procedural complexity, streamline communication, and resolve claims without the need for costly legal representation or travel.

In the coming years, these models may evolve to include more dynamic AI capabilities: natural language interfaces for non-native speakers, adaptive platforms for users with cognitive disabilities, and integrated predictive tools to help parties evaluate risks and trade-offs in real time. For example, an AI-enhanced mobile app could guide users through employment disputes by simulating possible settlement scenarios based on jurisdiction, past case data, and user input—reducing fear, confusion, and informational asymmetry.

Such innovations could help close the "justice gap," particularly for those who have traditionally been excluded from formal legal processes. Yet this expansion must be designed with equity in mind. As this volume has suggested earlier, epistemic repair requires not only access but meaningful participation—systems that recognize and validate the experiences of marginalized users. A platform that offers legal advice in fluent English but fails to understand Indigenous knowledge systems or racialized community dynamics is not just incomplete—it may actively reproduce injustice.

Redefining the Role of Practitioners

As AI takes on more procedural and analytical tasks, the role of the human ADR practitioner will inevitably shift. Mediators, arbitrators, and facilitators may become interpreters, navigators, or curators of AI-enhanced processes—helping parties understand, evaluate, and sometimes challenge the suggestions produced by automated tools.

This raises both practical and philosophical challenges. Practitioners will need new forms of technological literacy, including the ability to explain algorithms, identify bias, and assess data quality. But they will also need to reassert their distinct professional value: the capacity to build trust, manage emotion, read context, and support dignity—tasks for which AI remains limited.

Some scholars argue that we are entering an age not of full automation but of intelligence augmentation, where AI functions as a "cognitive partner" rather than a replacement (Alarie et al., 2018). Under this model, the human-AI relationship becomes collaborative: the machine provides speed and scale, while the human supplies insight, empathy, and normative judgment. Yet such collaboration must be critically managed. If practitioners become over-reliant on AI outputs or defer too quickly to data-driven recommendations, their role as moral agents may be diluted.

Anticipating Regulatory and Governance Gaps

Another looming issue is the lack of clear regulatory frameworks governing AI in ADR. While legal ethics codes and procedural rules have begun to acknowledge digital tools, most do not yet account for the complexity of machine learning systems, proprietary algorithms, or cross-border data flows.

For example, should parties have the right to know whether an advanced AI tool was used in reaching a settlement or decision? Should vendors be required to disclose the data sources and training methods behind their systems? If an AI-assisted negotiation leads to a discriminatory outcome, who is liable—the developer, the practitioner, or the platform?

Some jurisdictions have begun to respond. The European Union's proposed AI Act includes classifications for high-risk AI systems and mandatory transparency for certain applications. In Canada, the Artificial Intelligence and Data Act (AIDA) promises similar oversight, though its implementation remains uncertain. But in most ADR settings—especially in private mediation or arbitration—these tools remain largely unregulated.

This regulatory vacuum creates space for experimentation but also risk. Without clear standards, poorly tested or biased systems may proliferate, especially in low-cost platforms aimed at vulnerable users. To guard against this, law societies, dispute resolution organizations, and civil society actors must work collaboratively to establish principles of trustworthy AI in ADR—emphasizing transparency, auditability, fairness, and human accountability.

The Risk of AI Drift and Process Substitution

Beyond formal regulation, there is a subtler challenge: the drift of process norms under the influence of AI. As AI systems optimize for efficiency, consistency, or precedent, they may reshape the ethos of ADR itself—moving it away from dialogue and transformation and toward quantification and closure.

For example, predictive algorithms may lead parties to select outcomes that reflect statistical averages, rather than those that address their specific needs, relationships, or histories. A mediation platform that emphasizes fast resolution may devalue the slower, narrative-based work of mutual understanding or relational repair. Over time, parties may come to see conflict as a technical problem to be solved by machines, rather than a human encounter to be navigated with care.

This is not a hypothetical concern. As Susskind (2023) argues, the future of law is being shaped not only by what technology can do, but by how it is allowed to reshape our professional practices. If AI systems become default gatekeepers, they may harden rather than soften structural inequalities—particularly if their design privileges certain legal cultures, knowledge forms, or communication styles.

To counteract this drift, ADR practitioners must engage in normative design: shaping AI tools that reflect, rather than undermine, the values of relational justice. This includes ensuring that AI systems allow space for story, disagreement, apology, cultural difference, and non-legal resolution pathways. In short, technologies that support just processes, not just efficient outcomes must be built.

Opportunities for Ethical Innovation

Despite these challenges, there are reasons for optimism. AI systems can be leveraged not only for speed or scale but for ethically meaningful innovation. For instance, AI could help identify patterns of systemic harm across similar disputes, informing structural reforms or policy interventions. It could assist in identifying underreported grievances or flagging patterns of exclusion in outcomes by race, gender, or geography.

AI could also support new forms of participant empowerment. Imagine a platform that not only recommends likely outcomes, but walks a party through their values, priorities, and emotional goals—helping them clarify what they actually want from a dispute resolution process. Or a system that helps design community-based agreements incorporating Indigenous legal traditions, rather than defaulting to Western legal norms.

Such tools would require a radically different design logic: one that centres *care*, *participation*, and *pluralism*, rather than just prediction, efficiency and control. But they are possible—if the choice is made to invest in them. As Llewellyn (2011) writes, relational justice is about creating the conditions for people to live together in just relations. AI, like any tool, can either erode or enhance those conditions.

Conclusion

The integration of artificial intelligence (AI) into alternative dispute resolution (ADR) is not a matter of distant speculation—it is a live, unfolding transformation that demands critical attention from scholars, practitioners, and policymakers alike. This chapter has mapped the conceptual, ethical, and practical terrain of this transformation, drawing attention to both the profound potential and the serious risks that AI brings to the processes of negotiation, mediation, and arbitration.

This chapter began by examining the conceptual foundations of AI, distinguishing between approaches that view AI as a subject and AI as an intelligent system. These frameworks shape how AI is imagined, evaluated, and implemented in legal contexts. The lens one adopts is not neutral—it affects whether AI is perceived to be a supplement to human judgment, a replacement for professional discretion, or a partner in ethical collaboration.

From there, the chapter turned to concerns about privacy, transparency, and bias, showing that the introduction of AI into ADR reconfigures longstanding commitments to confidentiality, due process, and fairness. These concerns are not peripheral—they go to the heart of ADR's legitimacy. If the promise of dispute resolution lies in its ability to provide respectful, relationally aware forums for conflict, then technologies that obscure, commodify, or distort that process must be treated with deep caution.

At the same time, the practical applications of AI in ADR are increasingly sophisticated and widespread. Tools for legal prediction, document automation, negotiation support, and online triage are reshaping how disputes are framed and resolved. As demonstrated in the case studies and hypotheticals, these tools can bring meaningful benefits—especially in contexts where cost, time, or complexity exclude many people from justice. But they can also undermine essential human values if deployed without reflection.

The future of AI in ADR, as outlined in Sect. 6, will be shaped by choices made now. Will AI tools be allowed to automate and encode historical inequities with little to no human involvement, or will systems that support pluralism, narrative, and human dignity be designed? Will the future settle for efficiency at the expense of empathy, or will tools be demanded that enhance—rather than replace—the capacity to hear, hold, and heal in moments of conflict?

The answer must be rooted in the core commitments outlined in the introduction to this book:

- Relational justice, which reminds us that processes are not just instruments—they are spaces of recognition, repair, and respect.
- Epistemic repair, which insists on addressing whose knowledge counts, and how structural exclusion is perpetuated in seemingly neutral systems.
- Transformative practice, which pushes us to go beyond surface-level efficiency and toward processes that genuinely shift how people relate to one another and to the legal system.

AI, like ADR itself, is not inherently just or unjust. It is a tool—powerful, malleable, and consequential. Whether it contributes to justice depends on how it is imagined, built, operated, and used. As we stand on the threshold of an AI-integrated future, the task ahead is not simply to adopt new technologies, but to shape them according to the ethical, relational, and democratic values we hold most dear.

The work ahead is not merely technical—it is moral, cultural, and institutional. And it will require a new generation of dispute resolution professionals who are not only fluent in technology but committed to justice in all its dimensions.

Questions

1. Imagine two self-represented litigants use an AI-assisted online mediation platform. The AI system suggests that a $15,000 settlement is "fair" based on similar past cases. Both parties feel pressured to accept, even though one believes they deserve far more. To what extent should AI-generated suggestions be treated as legal guidance? Should platforms that influence settlement decisions be subject to the same duties and liabilities as human lawyers or mediators? Where do we draw the line between information, advice, and coercion in digital dispute resolution?

2. A commercial arbitrator uses a predictive analytics tool developed by a private legal tech firm. The parties are unaware of how the tool works, and the arbitrator does not disclose it. After the award is rendered, one party challenges it, alleging algorithmic bias. Should parties have a right to know whether AI tools were used in their dispute resolution process? Does the use of non-transparent, privately owned tools violate principles of natural justice or the duty to give reasons? What disclosure obligations should arbitrators or mediators have when using AI?
3. Many AI systems are trained on Western legal case law and dominant dispute resolution models. This risks marginalizing Indigenous, community-based, or restorative approaches to justice. What would it take to build an AI tool that reflects Indigenous legal traditions or other non-Western conceptions of justice? Should that even be attempted? What risks emerge when machine logic is applied to cultural or relational conflict resolution?
4. Family mediation platforms are being developed that use AI to analyze emotional tone, suggest parenting schedules, and propose child custody arrangements. Should there be legal or ethical limits on the kinds of disputes that can be handled through AI-assisted processes? For example, are custody disputes too emotionally or morally complex to be shaped by algorithmic systems? How should the law respond when AI tools are used in high-stakes, deeply personal contexts?

Glossary

Alternative Dispute Resolution (ADR):	Processes such as negotiation, mediation, and arbitration used to resolve disputes outside of traditional court litigation.
AI as Subject:	A conceptual framework for understanding AI that questions whether machines can think, focusing on intelligence, imitation, and consciousness, as posed by figures like Alan Turing.

AI as System: A conceptual framework viewing AI less philosophically and more as engineered tools designed to simulate or support cognitive tasks, emphasizing functionality over consciousness.

AI Augmentation: The view that AI functions as a "cognitive partner" to humans, enhancing capabilities rather than replacing them.

AI Drift: The subtle shift in process norms under the influence of AI, potentially moving ADR away from dialogue and transformation toward quantification and closure.

Artificial Intelligence (AI): A broad concept encompassing systems designed to simulate or support cognitive tasks or the question of whether machines can think, understood as a constellation of definitions, aspirations, and technical architectures.

Bias (in AI): The risk that AI systems, their training data, assumptions, and social contexts may reflect and perpetuate existing social inequities, such as racism, class stratification, or gendered norms.

Blind Bidding: A negotiation technique, used by platforms like Smartsettle, where parties input preferences and constraints privately, and the system suggests settlements based on overlap, without revealing individual bids.

BC Civil Resolution Tribunal (CRT): A leading example of an online dispute resolution (ODR) platform that uses expert systems to guide users through claim intake, negotiation, and facilitated resolution.

Chinese Room: A thought experiment proposed by John Searle demonstrating that a machine can manipulate symbols according to rules (syntax) without understanding their meaning (semantics), highlighting a limitation of AI imitation.

CoCounsel: A contemporary AI tool mentioned as being used in legal contexts, specifically for legal research by inputting natural language queries to receive curated case law, statute references, or strategic insights.

COMPAS algorithm: An algorithm used in the U.S. criminal justice system that was found to disproportionately flag Black defendants as high risk, serving as a landmark case illustrating the problem of bias in algorithms trained on historical data.

Document Automation: The generation of legal forms, contracts, or agreements using guided software, supported by AI tools, to reduce clerical workload and increase consistency.

Epistemic Repair: A guiding theme emphasizing addressing whose knowledge counts and how structural exclusion is perpetuated in seemingly neutral systems.

Explainable AI (XAI): Techniques such as rule extraction, saliency mapping, or surrogate models advocated to increase transparency and understanding of how AI systems arrive at their conclusions.

Legal Prediction: The use of algorithms to forecast likely outcomes in a dispute based on prior data, useful in ADR for assessing risks and informing settlement decisions.

Online Dispute Resolution (ODR): Platforms and systems that facilitate dispute resolution processes online, increasingly incorporating AI tools for tasks like intake, negotiation, and triage.

Privacy (in AI/ADR): The concern regarding the collection, storage, analysis, and potential reidentification or misuse of sensitive personal data shared within AI-enhanced ADR processes.

Process Substitution: A risk in which AI systems, optimizing for efficiency, consistency, or precedent, reshape the fundamental ethos of ADR, moving away from dialogue and transformation.

Relational Justice: A guiding theme emphasizing that dispute resolution processes are not merely instruments but spaces of recognition, repair, and respect, highlighting the importance of how people are seen, heard, and engaged.

Smartsettle: A Canadian-based AI negotiation platform that facilitates blind bidding and decision optimization, noted for resolving a commercial dispute quickly without human mediator involvement.

Transparency (in AI/ADR): The concern regarding the visibility and understandability of how AI systems function, particularly the opacity of algorithmic decision-making (black boxes) and the implications for procedural fairness and accountability.

Transformative Practice: A guiding theme that pushes beyond surface-level efficiency towards ADR processes that genuinely shift how people relate to one another and the legal system.

Turing Test: A test proposed by Alan Turing suggesting that if a human interlocutor cannot distinguish between a machine and a person through textual conversation, the machine could be considered intelligent, reframing intelligence toward behavioral imitation.

Competing Interests The author has no conflicts of interest to declare that are relevant to the content of this chapter.

References

Alarie, B., Niblett, A., & Yoon, A. H. (2018). How artificial intelligence will affect the practice of law. *University of Toronto Law Journal, 68*(1), 106–124. https://doi.org/10.3138/utlj.2017-0052

Almuslim, I., & Inkpen, D. (2022, March 23). Legal judgment prediction for Canadian appeal cases. *IEEE Xplore*. https://ieeexplore.ieee.org/document/9736341

Dimock, W. C. (2001). Rules of law, laws of science. *Yale Journal of Law & the Humanities, 13*(1), 203–226.

Fricker, M. (2007). *Epistemic injustice: Power and the ethics of knowing*. Oxford University Press.

Gacek, J., & Jochelson, R. (2024). *Justice in the age of Agnosis: Socio-legal explorations of denial, deception, and doubt* (1st ed.). Palgrave Macmillan. https://doi.org/10.1007/978-3-031-54354-8

Hilborne, N. (2019, February 19). Robot mediator settles first-ever court case. *Legal Futures*. https://www.legalfutures.co.uk/latest-news/robot-mediator-settles-first-ever-court-case

Katz, D. M., Bommarito, M. J., & Blackman, J. (2017). A general approach for predicting the behavior of the Supreme Court of the United States. *PloS One, 12*(4). https://doi.org/10.1371/journal.pone.0174698

Larson, J., Mattu, S., Kirchner, L., & Angwin, J. (2016, May 23). How we analyzed the COMPAS recidivism algorithm. *ProPublica*. https://www.propublica.org/article/how-we-analyzed-the-compas-recidivism-algorithm

Llewellyn, J. (2011). Restorative justice: Thinking relationally about justice. In J. Downie & J. Llewellyn (Eds.), *Being relational: Reflections on relational theory and health law* (pp. 89–108). UBC Press.

McCarthy, J., Minsky, M., Rochester, N., & Shannon, C. E. (1955). A proposal for the Dartmouth Summer Research Project on Artificial Intelligence. https://jmc.stanford.edu/articles/dartmouth/dartmouth.pdf

McCorduck, P. (2004). *Machines who think: A personal inquiry into the history and prospects of artificial intelligence* (2nd ed.). CRC Press. https://doi.org/10.1201/9780429258985

Minsky, M. (1968). *Semantic information processing*. MIT Press.

North, D. C. (2005). *Understanding the process of economic change*. Princeton University Press.

Posner, R. A. (2008). Privacy, surveillance, and law. *University of Chicago Law Review, 75*(1), 245–260.

Roskoshnyi, I. (2024). Legal-technological unemployment in the age of artificial intelligence. *Manitoba Law Journal, 47*(3). https://doi.org/10.29173/mlj1428

Searle, J. R. (1980). Minds, brains, and programs. *The Behavioral and Brain Sciences, 3*(3), 417–424. https://doi.org/10.1017/S0140525X00005756

Susskind, R. (2023). *Tomorrow's lawyers: An introduction to your future* (3rd ed.). Oxford University Press.

Thomasen, K. (2023, May 2). Will AI revolutionize the legal profession? The jury is still out. *Peter A. Allard School of Law, UBC.* https://allard.ubc.ca/about-us/news-and-announcements/2023/will-ai-revolutionize-legal-profession-jury-still-out

Toffler, A. (1980). *The third wave.* William Morrow.

Turing, A. M. (1950). Computing machinery and intelligence. *Mind, 59*(236), 433–460. https://doi.org/10.1093/mind/LIX.236.433

Van Hoek, R., & Lacity, M. (2023, November 21). How global companies use AI to prevent supply chain disruptions. *Harvard Business Review.* https://hbr.org/2023/11/how-global-companies-use-ai-to-prevent-supply-chain-disruptions

Zerilli, J., Danaher, J., Maclaurin, J., Gavaghan, C., Knott, A., Liddicoat, J., & Noorman, M. E. (2020). *A citizen's guide to artificial intelligence.* MIT Press.

Conclusion: Cultivating Conflict Transformation in Legal Practice

Laura E. Reimer and Richard Jochelson

Abstract This book explores the integration of conflict transformation principles into legal practice, emphasizing the role of dispute resolution as more than a technical exercise. Centered around three core commitments—relational justice, epistemic repair, and transformative practice—the chapters collectively challenge conventional legal approaches that prioritize procedural efficiency over meaningful engagement. Relational justice reframes legal processes as spaces of recognition, repair, and respect, highlighting the human dimension of conflict. Epistemic repair urges legal practitioners to question whose knowledge is valued in legal settings and to address the structural exclusions embedded in seemingly neutral systems. Transformative practice calls for a deeper reimagining of dispute resolution—not just as problem-solving, but as an opportunity to shift how individuals and institutions relate. Drawing on diverse contexts including Indigenous legal traditions, negotiation pedagogy, technology in ADR, and access to justice, the book equips law students and lawyers

L. E. Reimer (✉) · R. Jochelson
University of Manitoba, Winnipeg, MB, Canada
e-mail: laura.reimer@umanitoba.ca

R. Jochelson
e-mail: richard.jochelson@umanitoba.ca

L. E. Reimer and R. Jochelson (eds.), *The Other Side of the Bar*,
https://doi.org/10.1007/978-981-96-9748-9_13

with tools to respond to conflict with greater empathy, critical insight, and creativity. Rather than viewing law as an endpoint, this collection invites its readers to approach legal practice as an evolving site for relational healing and social transformation. It aims to inspire a generation of practitioners committed to reshaping the justice system from within.

Keywords Relational justice · Epistemic repair · Transformative practice · Dispute resolution · Legal practice · Dignity

Summarizing the Transformation

This book has brought together a diverse and compelling range of voices to illuminate what conflict transformation can look like in legal practice. Across chapters, contributors have offered insights not only into specific tools and methods of dispute resolution—mediation, arbitration, negotiation, restorative justice, and others—but also into the deeper commitments that must guide legal practitioners if they are to approach conflict not just as a problem to be managed, but as a relational and systemic reality to be transformed. The book is a window into "the other side of the bar" and meant to provoke thoughtful, mindful practice.

At the heart of this work lies a commitment to relational justice. The chapters in this collection repeatedly emphasize that legal processes must do more than deliver outcomes; they must honour the dignity of those who participate in them. This commitment to relational justice is especially clear in the chapters on interpersonal conflict and restorative justice, where the emphasis falls on the lived experience of harm and the human capacity for repair. In these contexts, law students and lawyers are reminded that conflict transformation is as much about creating space for people to feel seen and respected as it is about resolving the matter at hand. Even in more formal settings such as arbitration or sports law, the relational dimensions of justice must remain central: how people are treated in the process often shapes their perception of fairness more than the decision itself.

The collection also insists on the importance of epistemic repair—an ethical and political responsibility to interrogate whose voices and knowledges are privileged in legal discourse, and whose are excluded.

Nowhere is this more compellingly argued than in the chapter on Condolence ceremonies and The Great Law of Peace, which introduces the Haudenosaunee tradition of conflict resolution. This chapter reminds readers that Indigenous legal orders are not simply cultural artifacts but are living systems of law with their own norms, procedures, and principles—many of which offer crucial resources for reimagining justice today. Epistemic repair also emerges in chapters such as Access to Justice and Dispute Resolution Skills, and Legal Research as ADR, which call attention to how systemic barriers and professional conventions can obscure alternative ways of knowing and resolving conflict. Future lawyers and legal educators must ask: Whose knowledge do we center when teaching legal practice? What assumptions underlie our sense of what counts as "real" law?

These questions return to the third core commitment that binds this collection together: the pursuit of transformative practice. Across chapters, contributors challenge readers to go beyond mere procedural efficiency and embrace dispute resolution as an opportunity to fundamentally shift how individuals and institutions relate to one another. In Negotiation and The Pedagogical Value of the Canadian National Negotiation Competition, the chapters demonstrate how students can develop not only skills but sensibilities—ways of approaching difference, listening across disagreement, and creatively co-constructing solutions. Likewise, in the chapter on Intelligence Augmentation in ADR, readers are urged to consider how emerging technologies might support, rather than supplant, the capacity for human connection and insight. Here, transformation is not about perfection but about orientation: a willingness to center relationships, to question inherited systems, and to design practices that foster mutual understanding and systemic change.

Taken together, the chapters in this book offer more than a survey of dispute resolution techniques. They offer a pedagogy for legal transformation. They model how law students and practitioners can cultivate habits of critical reflection, humility, and relational engagement—skills as essential to justice as any statute or case law. They also point toward a legal culture that recognizes conflict not simply as breakdown or failure, but as a moment of potential: to listen more deeply, to restore what has been damaged, and to reimagine what justice can be.

This concluding vision builds on themes introduced at the very beginning of this volume, where the fracturing of shared truth, the erosion of institutional trust, and the challenge of navigating cultural and legal pluralism were foregrounded (Reimer & Jochelson, 2025). We live in an age of epistemic fragmentation, where legal professionals are not only interpreters of law but stewards of dialogue and meaning-making. In this context, the relational and epistemic responsibilities of legal practitioners become paramount—not ancillary—to the justice project.

Moreover, this collection reaffirms that alternative dispute resolution is not an "alternative" at the margins of law, but a central site for ethical engagement, civic stewardship, and institutional renewal. As Gacek and Jochelson (2024) have argued, legal practice must confront the structured silences and curated ignorance that permeate systems of power. Dispute resolution, when practiced with integrity, becomes a mechanism of epistemic accountability and cultural recognition—particularly for marginalized voices.

As readers move forward in their studies and professional lives, they are invited to carry these commitments with them—not only into courtrooms and boardrooms, but into classrooms, communities, and conversations. The call to relational justice, epistemic repair, and transformative practice is not a call for perfection, but for presence and participation. It is an invitation to treat every conflict not just as a case to close, but as an opening to justice on the "other side of the bar"—the kind of justice that heals, that includes, and that transforms

Competing Interests The authors have no conflicts of interest to declare in relation to the content of this chapter.

References

Gacek, J., & Jochelson, R. (Eds.). (2024). *Justice in the age of agnosis: Socio-legal explorations of denial, deception, and doubt*. Palgrave Macmillan.

Reimer, L., & Jochelson, R. (Eds.). (2025). *The other side of the bar: Conflict transformation in legal practice*. Palgrave Macmillan.

Index

L. E. Reimer and R. Jochelson (eds.), *The Other Side of the Bar*,
https://doi.org/10.1007/978-981-96-9748-9

J

K

L

Q

R

S

GPSR Compliance

The European Union's (EU) General Product Safety Regulation (GPSR) is a set of rules that requires consumer products to be safe and our obligations to ensure this.

If you have any concerns about our products, you can contact us on ProductSafety@springernature.com

In case Publisher is established outside the EU, the EU authorized representative is:

Springer Nature Customer Service Center GmbH
Europaplatz 3
69115 Heidelberg, Germany

Batch number: 10725849

Printed by Printforce, the Netherlands